Black Earth

First English edition published in 2019 by
HAUS PUBLISHING LTD
4 Cinnamon Row
London SW11 3TW

Originally published under the title *Schwarze Erde*
Copyright © 2016 by Rowohlt Verlag GmbH, Reinbek bei Hamburg

This first paperback edition published in 2022

Translation copyright © 2019 by Eugene H. Hayworth
Preface translation copyright © 2022 by Simon Pare

The moral rights of the authors have been asserted

A CIP catalogue record for this book is available from the British Library

ISBN: 978-1-914982-00-2
eISBN: 978-1-909961-61-6

Typeset in Minion by MacGuru Ltd

Printed in the United Kingdom by Clays Ltd, Elcograf S.p.A.

Black Earth

A Journey through Ukraine

Jens Mühling

Translated from the German by Eugene H. Hayworth

Contents

Will anybody pay for the bloodshed?

No. No one.
The snow will just melt, the green Ukrainian grass
will grow and carpet over the earth, lush crops
will sprout, the air will shimmer with heat above
the fields, and no traces of blood will remain.

Mikhail Bulgakov, *The White Guard*, 1925

Preface

I MET VLADIMIR at the airport of Constanța, a city on the Romanian Black Sea coast not far from the Ukrainian border, in late February 2022. We had taken the same flight from Istanbul. Vladimir was a welder and had spent the past few weeks working on a construction site in Dubai. Two days before our encounter, he had been woken abruptly by a phone call. It was his wife. She was calling from Vladimir's hometown of Mariupol in south-eastern Ukraine. 'Vova,' she cried, 'there are bombs falling.'

Around the same time as I was boarding a plane in Berlin to report on Russia's assault on Ukraine, Vladimir was taking off from Dubai to get home to his wife and three children in Mariupol. We started chatting by chance while waiting for our luggage at Constanța Airport. Vladimir was heading for the Ukrainian border and so was I. This was the only remaining way into the country; all direct flights had been cancelled when the Russian air force had started raids on Ukraine's cities.

I hired a car and offered Vladimir a ride, along with a second Ukrainian returnee whose trip to attend a friend's burial in the Georgian capital Tbilisi had been interrupted by the war. We drove for three hours through the snow-bound Romanian steppe – Vladimir, the welder from Mariupol; Yevgeny, an apple juice producer from Vinnytsia in central Ukraine; and me. My two travelling companions, powerfully built men with rasping voices, were in their forties – prime conscription age – so they knew that this journey led in one direction only.

'A one-way ticket,' Vova muttered. 'Once we're in, they won't let us out again.'

General mobilisation had been decreed on the very first day of the war, meaning that most men were banned from leaving the country. Vladimir and Yevgeny were nevertheless determined to get back to Ukraine: they weren't going to leave their families in the lurch. Yevgeny's journey was relatively simple as Vinnytsia wasn't far from the Moldovan border. Vladimir's, on the other hand, was much more complicated. He had to cross half of Ukraine to reach his hometown of Mariupol, which was being caught in a pincer movement by two advancing Russian troop columns, one from Crimea to the west, the other from the Donbas in the east.

'How the hell are you going to make it there?' Yevgeny asked.

Vladimir gave a shrug. 'I'll get through somehow.'

I said goodbye to them when we arrived at the Danube, which marks the border between Romania and Ukraine. Yevgeny called me the next day from Vinnytsia: he'd got home without any trouble. I had several phone calls with Vladimir too. It took him a few days to reach the embattled eastern part of the country by a combination of train trips and hitch-hiking. He rang me at last from Mariupol with audible joy in his voice. 'I made it!' he cried. 'I'm home!'

I was still beside the Danube at the time, watching a steel pontoon ferry shuttling continuously back and forth between the riverbanks. On its way from the Romanian to the Ukrainian side it was empty; on the way back it was packed with standing refugees. Hundreds of thousands of people fled the country in those early days of the war, the overwhelming majority of them women and children whose husbands and fathers were not allowed to leave due to the mobilisation. With confusion in their eyes, they wheeled their suitcases ashore to be guided through the customs channels by Romanian border officials. Most of those arriving were from Odessa, the Ukrainian port city north of the Romanian border. Haltingly they told me their stories. None of them had expected Russia to attack and almost all had struck out for the border without any particular plan when the first explosions shook Odessa. Hardly anyone knew what lay in store on the far side of customs.

It was another three weeks or so before I heard from Vladimir again. In the meantime I had filed a number of reports about the invasion. I had travelled to Istanbul and Tbilisi to speak to Russian anti-war protestors who had left their country for fear of reprisals. A little later I had crossed the Ukrainian border from Moldova and gone to Odessa to witness the mass exodus of the city's Jewish community.

One evening, when I had just got back to Berlin, my phone rang. It was Vladimir. He still spoke in the same rasping voice, but everything else about him was unrecognisable. I still held in my memory the man I had met that day in the car – Vladimir the welder, vigorous and surprisingly cheerful despite the tense situation, cracking morbid jokes with Yevgeny about the state of the war. Precious little of that man was to be heard on the phone: Vladimir was crying like a child. 'Mariupol is gone,' he kept sobbing. 'Mariupol no longer exists.'

He and his family had sat for two weeks in the cellar of their apartment block while the Russian army encircled the city and shelled it incessantly. 'The ground under our feet shook at every explosion,' Vladimir said. There had been no electricity in Mariupol, no gas, no water, no petrol, no phone reception: the city's supply lines had been severed and it was cut off from the outside world.

Vladimir and his family had only emerged from their cellar when the booming of the artillery barrage intermittently subsided. They and their neighbours then hurriedly collected any firewood they could get their hands on, mostly splintered branches and shattered furniture. They cooked over open fires in the courtyards of gutted residential blocks, gobbled up the food and then hunkered down in their underground hiding places again.

This went on for two weeks until the shelling had attained an unbearable intensity. Vladimir and his family were scared to death of being buried under the concrete ruins of their nine-storey building, so they went for broke. They sprinted out of the cellar, jumped in their car and sped away. The last they saw of their home were the blown-out, soot-stained windows of their top-floor flat.

Vladimir was calling me from Melekine, a coastal village twelve miles west of Mariupol. They hadn't made it any further than that because their tank was dry and there was no petrol anywhere. They were staying in a small guesthouse, trying to rest and recover. They had no idea what to do next. Vladimir's most pressing concern was his eldest daughter, eighteen-year-old Sofia, who was stuck in

Mariupol. 'Dad,' she had said as her family were fleeing from the burning city, 'I'm an adult and I don't want to leave. I'm going to stay with my friends.' Vladimir had heard nothing from her since. There was still no phone reception in Mariupol; he couldn't get through to Sofia.

I was in touch with Vladimir a few more times over the weeks that followed. Once he sent me a few photos without any comment. They showed devastated apartment blocks, concrete ruins with gaping black holes where windows had been, a blurred view of the inside of a flat, a completely burnt-out room with nothing but a scorched bedstead in the middle.

'Horrific,' I wrote back. 'I hope that isn't your neighbourhood?'

Vladimir answered instantaneously. 'That's my building. My flat.'

A friend had sent him the pictures. He had written to Vladimir that the city was now completely destroyed and the streets strewn with corpses that were occasionally collected and tossed into mass graves.

The last time I spoke to Vladimir he and his family had managed to make it a little farther west, away from Mariupol, but they were still in Russian-occupied territory and it had become practically impossible to cross the frontline. He still didn't know where his eldest daughter was.

As I write this preface, the war has been raging for almost four months and there is still no end in sight. It is a difficult time to write about Ukraine, when one is unsure what will be left of it. It isn't just Mariupol that has been virtually flattened by Russian shelling but other besieged cities too. The Russian army has conquered territory in the east and south of the country extending far beyond annexed Crimea and the Russian-controlled separatist areas of the Donbas region, which were seized in 2014. Russia's military is terrorising Ukrainian civilians with horrendous war crimes in the parts of the country it has occupied. I spoke to women whose unarmed husbands had been shot dead for no apparent reason, and my blood froze at every fresh account of executions, torture, pillaging, and rape that came to light.

Russia's attack on Kiev, on the other hand, was a failure. The Kremlin had apparently hoped to seize the Ukrainian capital in a lightning strike and replace the country's government with a puppet regime. However, Russian troops came up against resistance of a ferocity that took many in the West by surprise – most observers had given Ukraine little chance of survival in the early days of the invasion. Since this Ukrainian fightback, Russian military strategists have concentrated on the south and east of the country, where the outcome hangs in the balance.

The journey I describe in this book took place about six years before the invasion began. It is not just the war that has changed the Ukraine I got to know back then, and it is harder to summarise the evolutions not recorded in headlines. The life stories I relate here have continued, and while in some cases I know what has happened since, in most of them I don't. Some people I met have probably had children, others may have died. Some still live where I came across them, while the war has forced many others to flee. Some will have fallen in love, others will have fallen out; some will be happier than before, others won't. I hope, nonetheless, that all the stories of life and grief and love that I made the focus of my book will still give a good insight into Ukraine as a country when reporting has long since moved on to other topics.

I have stayed in touch with a few of the people in my book, or have heard of their fates from other sources. May their stories conclude this foreword.

Ksyusha and Roman, my friends from Kiev, had a second son a few years after my visit. When the first missiles rained down on Kiev, they crammed their children, their dog, two cats, and a few belongings into the car. Along with countless other residents they left their city behind and drove west along hopelessly congested roads, on and on, for days and days. I remember the frenzied phone calls I had with Ksyusha during their escape, the panic in her voice, the fear of being hit by a missile and dying a stupid death merely because a man in the Kremlin was dreaming of lost greatness. When Ksyusha and Roman finally reached the Slovakian border, they were forced to split up. Ksyusha emigrated with their two sons, the dog and the cats, while conscription initially forced her husband to remain in Ukraine. But then Roman got a lucky break. As a civilian pilot, it turned out that he was exempt from frontline combat and could therefore join his family in exile. Ksyusha and Roman found shelter with friends in Zurich, where they and their sons are still living as I write, together with their dog and one of the cats; unfortunately, the other didn't survive the journey. Some seven million refugees have left Ukraine since the start of the war, while another seven million internally displaced citizens have fled from embattled parts of the country to safer regions. Europe has not seen a stream of refugees on this scale since the Second World War.

Valentina Mordvintseva, the Russian archaeologist I got to know in Crimea, had a hard time after we met. Shortly before Russia's annexation of the peninsula in 2014 she had curated an exhibition of Scythian treasures excavated in Crimea for a museum in Amsterdam. The exhibition was ongoing when Russian troops occupied the peninsula and, following a hastily organised referendum, proclaimed it Russian territory. This suddenly made it unclear who legally owned the treasures on display in Amsterdam. The Crimean museums from whose collections Valentina Mordvintseva had assembled the exhibition demanded that the artefacts be returned. Given that these museums were now under Russian control, however, the culture ministry in Kiev objected, arguing that the Scythian gold was Ukrainian property. When I met Valentina in Simferopol in 2015, a Dutch court was busy untangling the ownership claims. This complex process took several years and eventually found in Ukraine's favour. After that, things became increasingly uncomfortable for Valentina in Crimea – not only because some people blamed her, as the exhibition's curator, for the loss of the artefacts, but also because she made it abundantly clear that she rejected the Russian annexation. The last I heard from Valentina after war broke out, she was holed up in a Kiev bomb shelter with her daughter.

Ivan Mamchur, the elderly Second World War veteran in Lviv who had joined an SS battalion as a young man in the mistaken hope that Ukraine might free itself from Stalin's claws with German assistance, died in October 2019 – three-quarters of a century after the Nazi withdrawal from Ukraine and two-and-a-half years before Vladimir

Putin declared that Ukraine had to be liberated from Nazi control.

Vera Yefimovna, the staunch communist from Kiev, must have seen the outbreak of war as a confirmation of her beliefs. For decades she had been living in expectation of the great final class-war showdown between the bourgeoisie and the working class – adversaries embodied by NATO and Russia in her weird worldview. I fear that she may be one of the few Ukrainians who approved of the Russian invasion. When the war started, I rang Vera Yefimovna on her Kiev landline, intrigued to find out what was going through her head. There was a ringtone, but she didn't pick up. Maybe she had already emigrated to Russia, which is what she'd been planning to do when we last met. Maybe she'd died: she was old and had told me about an illness. Maybe she didn't pick up the phone out of precaution, because she knew there were very few people with whom she could now discuss her ideas. In my mind's eye I saw a Soviet apartment on the left bank of the Dnieper with an old telephone ringing shrilly to itself for several minutes before I hung up.

Roman, the young man I got to know in Donetsk, ended up trapped between the frontlines when war broke out. He had just completed a marketing degree in 2014 when Russia incited a separatist guerrilla war in the eastern Donbas region. Despite disapproving of the separatists, Roman had stayed in his hometown of Donetsk to look after his sick grandmother. Eight years later, when the invasion began and the separatists joined in on the Russian side, I sent him a text. He replied that the situation in Donetsk was bleak. He no longer left his home because the separatists were rounding up men in the street and sending them off to the frontline. 'Putin has gone mad,' Roman wrote. 'Now I understand how the Germans felt after the Second World War. I am ashamed of this war.'

Lastly, Yuri, the grocer from the small town of Milove on the Russian border, saw at close quarters how borders shifted in Ukraine. I had met him in 2015 in his small store on Friendship of Peoples Street, a long main road dividing the place in two. The houses on Yuri's side of the road were in Ukraine, those on the other side in Russia. Back then, the inhabitants could cross Friendship of Peoples Street without let or hindrance, even though the friendship between Russia and Ukraine had already cooled. A few years later Yuri wrote to tell me that the Russian border patrols had erected a barbed-wire fence in the middle of the road, splitting Milove along its length. Now people could only drive in one direction on each side. Passing trade thinned out accordingly, and Yuri's shop saw very little footfall. Within a year of the fence's construction, business had deteriorated to such an extent that Yuri had to close his store. Since then he had been working as a guard for a private security firm while continuing to live on Friendship of Peoples Street, and gazing every day at the barbed-wire fence. He wrote that this was what he imagined life in divided Berlin must have been like. A few weeks before the outbreak of hostilities, when Russia had long been massing an invasion force on the other side of the border, I asked Yuri if people in Milove were afraid of war. He replied that absolutely no one in his hometown believed that Russia would attack. When what-no-one-had-believed subsequently came to pass, Milove was the Russian army's first crossing point into Ukraine in the early morning hours of 24 February. I sent another message to Yuri after that but got no answer.

Is there hope for Ukraine? There is, there has to be, but as I write these lines, the country is enduring its darkest hours.

Jens Mühling, Berlin, June 2022
Translated by Simon Pare

1

A Finger on a Map

Przemyśl–Medyka

A QUESTIONING LOOK at the Przemyśl bus station, accompanied by words whose meaning I can only guess, I do not speak Polish.

I reply in Russian, accompanied by gestures pointing east: That way, across the border, to Ukraine.

The man, standing idly beside the bus, nods with a knowing expression, as if he understood more than I have said. He is fat and sweaty and no longer young, his eyes are blurred behind streaky glasses, it is a blazing hot day in late summer. I do not know what he wants from me. At first, I mistook him for the bus driver, but he showed no interest in the ticket I held out for him. Apparently, he just wants to talk, and, paradoxically, the fact that I do not speak his language seems to make me the most qualified listener. The less someone understands, the more there is to explain.

I have stashed my backpack on the bus, which is set to depart for Ukraine in a few minutes. The man fills this brief time span with a monologue in which I can only make out Polish sibilants and historical references: *Franz-Josef... Hitler... Stalin... cossacks... Ukraine... Tsar... Napoleon... Moscow... Kremlin... Lemberg... catholic... orthodox...*

As he speaks, he punctures the air between our faces with his forefinger. He directs my gaze to the old Polish fortress rising in the distance above the roofs of Przemyśl. The next moment he urgently points at church towers and then at things that are hidden from my view, which seem to connect the past in his mind with the present before our eyes. I nod, smile, follow his pointing finger, without understanding much.

When the bus finally departs, the man remains at the station, as idle as before. As I watch his corpulent silhouette fading in the distance, I wonder what force of nature makes some people so obsessed with the past, and whether I attract such people because they sense I am looking for history, looking for stories.

Hardware stores, garden centres, tyre depots and spare-parts dealers slip past the bus windows. Between commercial buildings and parking lots, Poland comes to an end. Further on, not far away now, lies the western part of a country in whose east there is war. A war that is being waged about the past, or so it has seemed to me as I have followed the course of events in recent months. Often the mutual battle cry sounded to my ears like the monologue of the man at the bus station, a history-obsessed crescendo of Slavic sibilants and historical reproaches: *Lenin!... Bandera!... Holodomor!... Holocaust!... Gulag!... Galicia!... Communists!... Fascists!... Imperialists!...*

From the distance, I felt I could not understand much. It was this feeling that has set me on my journey.

I do not remember when I first heard about Ukraine. There must have been a first time, as with any other country, but I have forgotten it, and now, as my bus approaches the border, this gap in my memory suddenly seems significant to me.

As a child, I traced the outlines of the Soviet Union on the world map with my forefinger, fascinated by its monstrous proportions. A sixth of the earth was shaded olive-green; no other country was that large – not even close.

When the Soviet Union disappeared from the map, Russia remained, not substantially smaller than before, still taking up more space on the globe than some continents. The rest of the former Union was eclipsed by the shadow of this Russian giant. As a teenager, I hardly took note of all the other independent states that had suddenly appeared on the map, also because they had not figured in the geography lessons of my childhood, not even as Soviet republics. There were other, much more distant countries that I otherwise knew nothing about, but at least they had stuck in my memory for their capitals' sonorous names, such as Kuala Lumpur, or Ouagadougou. Others had left an impression on me because their flags looked convincing, or botched. With others still, I associated rivers, writers, car marques or just the vague feeling that people had more adventurous lives there.

But I knew nothing of the kind about the new countries on Russia's borders. Strictly speaking, I knew even less than nothing, because after the Soviet breakdown, I had instinctively reorganised my inner map, shifting everything that I had previously placed within the Soviet Union's borders into Russia. Chernobyl, Gogol, Brezhnev, Borscht, Crimea – all Russian, I thought.

All Ukrainian, as I was to learn later.

But even during my first visit to Kiev, a decade before my current trip, I conceived of Ukraine as a sort of Russian suburb, although I quickly realized that its inhabitants did not want to be regarded in that way. From Moscow, where I was working as a journalist at the time, I had crossed the Russian-Ukrainian border. Beyond it, my train travelled past prefabricated concrete buildings that looked just like the prefabricated concrete buildings before the border. The trains were the same, the buses, the kiosks. The men wore the same dark leather jackets, the women's heels were just as high. Even their language seemed the same: everywhere I heard only Russian.

Only five years later did I consciously register my first Ukrainian sentences. This happened at the Darnytsa market, a collection of meat and vegetable stalls in a Kiev suburb comprised of concrete buildings. Around the perimeter of the market grounds, old women flanked the sidewalks, their chequered oilcloth bags full of fruit harvested from the dachas of the surrounding villages and transported to Kiev to sell to the city-dwellers. When I spoke to them in Russian, they usually shifted into Ukrainian after the first two exchanges, apparently without realising it. When I asked questions, because I had understood most, but not all, words of the similar-sounding language, they immediately switched back to Russian, unconsciously slipping back into Ukrainian again after the next two sentences. "Sunshine, it's all the same for us," they said apologetically when I asked questions again.

"They speak *surzhik*," my Kiev friends said of the market women. They turned up their noses at this mixture of Russian and Ukrainian, which you would never hear coming out of the mouths of the city's more educated residents. I, on the other hand, was fascinated by the idea that two languages did not have to be clearly demarcated, that they could blend seamlessly. It was a type of bilingualism I had not come across in any other country.

At that time I spent half a year in Kiev, renting an apartment in one of the concrete blocks near the Darnytsa market. When people asked me what I was doing in Ukraine, I answered truthfully that I was writing a book about Russia, even though I soon realised that my answer did not sit well with the Kievans. Usually, I hastened to add that I was interested in the beginnings of Russian history, in which Kiev, as it were, had played a decisive... At this point in the conversation, I would often be confronted with an irritated rolling of the eyes, which I found understandable, though I did not take it very seriously. Still, the geography of Eastern Europe was shaped in my mind by the contours of the Soviet Union, which as a child I had traced on the map with my forefinger.

But all that changed abruptly in March 2014, when I was sent to the Black Sea on an urgent journalist's mission, to report on a hastily scheduled referendum. Right beneath my feet, a border shifted. Crimea, which had been Ukrainian when I arrived, was Russian when I left.

So suddenly, so unexpectedly had this shift come that it made half the continent dizzy. Politicians seemed perplexed, experts clueless; no one seemed to know any longer where they were standing. Neither did I. By then I had been to Ukraine countless times. But I had not seen anything coming – absolutely none of it.

Less than a year later, I drove through the Donbass, where boundaries had turned into front lines. Somewhere along the way, my driver told me about his passion: the

Black Earth of Ukraine, the most fertile farmland in the world. He was not a farmer, but a coin collector. On weekends, he would plod across the fields with a metal detector, and his heart would beat faster when he discovered coins from times gone by – Austrian, Polish, Russian, Greek, or German coins.

"And Ukrainian ones?" I asked.

He laughed. "Ukrainian coins? But they've only been around for twenty years!"

That was the moment I realised that I had not really understood Ukraine. For a thousand years, people here had tilled their Black Earth without a single Ukrainian coin finding its way into the soil. For a thousand years, foreign coins had passed through their hands, for a thousand years, the Ukrainians had lived between borders which were constantly shifting beneath their feet. And now they were starting to move again.

Back in Berlin, I could not shake off the vague feeling that my internal map did not square with the real world. I started to read whatever I could find about Ukraine, but the feeling remained. A few months later, I packed my backpack and set off. The Polish border was the starting point of my journey, the Russian border my destination. I wanted to find out what lay in between.

"Everything here looks the same to you, doesn't it?"

A young tourist from Warsaw sits next to me on the bus to the Ukrainian border. He is travelling to the Carpathians with his trekking backpack. At first, I do not understand what he means. He taps his forefinger on the window to direct my uncomprehending gaze to the road.

"The same old German cars wherever you look. Poland or Ukraine, you see no difference."

"Of course I do see…"

"But there is one!"

He is a programmer. At home in Warsaw he spends long days staring at his computer screen. In his spare time, he packs up what he needs, crosses the border and goes looking for adventures he cannot find at home.

"Poland has become an office country," he says, making it sound like the saddest fate that can afflict a nation.

"Efficient, but dull, like the rest of Europe."

The weariness in his voice only disappears when he tells me about his trips through the secluded villages of the Carpathians, about encounters with people the likes of whom no longer exist in Poland.

"Ukraine is different." He sighs. "For now."

I nod silently as I think of all the Ukrainians who have told me in the last few years how much they would like to emigrate into the affluent office countries of Western Europe.

Ukraine is different. Russia is different. The East is different. Those people over there, they are so different. How often have I read variations of such sentences since I started to prepare myself for my trip? How many times have I come across attempts at drawing a line across Europe, beyond which one's own world ceases and a stranger, more dangerous one begins?

In the region where our bus is headed, such attempts at delineation have a rather long tradition.

The ancient Greeks used to look toward the northern Black Sea coast with trepidation. Beyond it, in their eyes, the civilised world ended. There, the Steppe was roamed by nomads, who, instead of speaking Greek, uttered croaking noises that sounded like "bar bar", which is why the Greeks called them "barbarians". The barbarians called themselves Scythians, and they were among the first equestrian peoples whose ghostly emergence from the depths of Asia would terrify the sedentary inhabitants of Europe for centuries to come.

The Scythians, who eventually settled down on the Black Sea coast, may in turn have considered the Sarmatians barbarians, as this next nomad tribe ransacked their empire. The game repeated itself as the Sarmatians were followed by Huns, Avars, Pechenegs and Kipchaks.

In the meantime, the Slavs had established their first state in the woodlands north of the Steppe, the principality of Kiev, which was overrun by the Mongols shortly afterwards. To this day, it fills Ukrainians and Russians with a weird kind of martyr's pride that this most powerful of all equestrian peoples did not advance much further into Europe, because from that point onward, the imaginary dividing line being fought over north of the Black Sea no longer separated sedentary Europeans from nomad barbarians, but Christians from pagans.

Still later, it would separate Christians from Christians. In the seventeenth century, under the banner of Orthodoxy, Ukrainian Cossacks rose up against the Polish nobility, because they resented the growing influence of the Catholic Pope. The fact that the Cossacks allied with the Muscovite Tsar in their struggle still upsets many Ukrainians, because it bound the greater part of their homeland to Russia – and thus, a few centuries later again, placed it under the influence of a new faith: Communism. After Lenin's October Revolution, the old Ukrainian dividing line between the Austrian and Russian empires marked the new boundary of the international class struggle.

> Millions are you, and hosts, yea hosts, are we,
> And we shall fight if war you want, take heed.
> Yes, we are Scythians – leafs of the Asian tree,
> Our slanted eyes are bright aglow with greed.

The Russian poet Alexander Blok wrote these lines in 1918, a few months after the Revolution. They were addressed to Europe. Blok warned the languid, effeminate West of the scorching passion of the steppe peoples, for he considered the Slavs to be their spiritual descendants.

Whether Hitler knew the poem is unclear. But most certainly he knew Herodotus' description of that famous battle in which the Scythians lured their enemies, the Persians, deep into their own territory, in order to starve them on scorched earth. Hitler must have thought of the Scythians when his troops froze to death in Ukraine. Perhaps he even suddenly regretted that he had instructed his propaganda artists to portray the inferior Slavs with slanted Asian eyes.

Today, as another war is waged in Ukraine, both sides resort to the old demarcation myths. Russian propagandists claim that the fighting in Donbass is a continuation of the struggle against fascism; the Ukrainian counter-propaganda warns of an eastern despotism that threatens all of Europe. Both sides are united in their assertion that a dividing line running somewhere north of the Black Sea separates two incompatible cultures.

I look out the bus window. Old German cars pass in the opposite lane, interspersed with a few even older ones from the Soviet Union. Tired yellow grass covers the fields, withered in the September heat. I see three workers in blue overalls sitting in the shade of a poplar tree, their backs leaning against the trunk, legs spread out star-shaped, beer bottles in their hands. Nothing in this listless summer landscape looks as if it had the power to separate civilisations.

Does it exist at all, I wonder, this legendary European divide, which has been interpreted so differently over the centuries, so inconsistently, with people always imagining barbarians on the other side, but never on their own? Was it ever more than a legend, designed to facilitate thinking – and, more recently, killing, as it had done before?

I think of my friends and colleagues in Berlin. Some of them find it hard to understand what keeps drawing me to this part of the world.

"Have fun with the Russians," one said as we parted.

"The Ukrainians," I replied.

He rolled his eyes, as one would do with a pedant who corrects grammatical errors in the middle of a friendly conversation.

"Whatever," he said. "Have fun with – those people."

Had I asked him to show me the boundary between Europe and "those people" on a map, he probably would not have looked for it north of the Black Sea, but further west. Most likely, his forefinger would have wandered back and forth undecidedly until it had come across the first viable choice: the European Union's external border.

And just there, my bus ride ends.

2

The Ant Trail

Medyka–Shehyni

IT WAS NOT YET NOON when I got off the bus in the Polish border town of Medyka, but already the slanting September sun had warmed the air to over thirty degrees centigrade. My backpack stirred up a cloud of yellow dust when I dropped it on the tarmac. A seamless blue sky stretched from horizon to horizon, as taut as a fitted sheet, the hills of Galicia slumbering beneath it. The dried-up pastures looked as if they had not seen rain in years.

An old woman came running up to me and waved two packs of cigarettes under my nose, labelled with warnings in Ukrainian. On one I saw the picture of a smoker's lung; on the other, the stylised drawing of a flaccid penis.

"Buy my cigarettes!" the woman said, in Ukrainian.

I fumbled a few złoty coins from my pocket and pointed to the smoker's lung.

"Buy both, so I can go home!"

While I was wondering what that was supposed to mean, four more women surrounded me. All had packs of cigarettes in their hands. Many held a bottle of spirits in the other.

I cast a glance of mock bewilderment around the group. The women giggled. Then they began to explain.

Every morning in the border villages of Ukraine, a procession made up of many women and a few men starts out. Their home towns lie within that thirty-kilometre strip on the Ukrainian side of the border whose inhabitants, under a special agreement, are permitted to visit the thirty-kilometre strip on the Polish side without a visa. With empty handcarts they climb into minibuses that bring them to the Medyka-Shehyni checkpoint, where day after day they buy the same things at the Ukrainian border kiosks: two packs of cigarettes and one bottle of spirits. They push their handcarts through a narrow pedestrian alley lined on both sides by green, man-sized metal fences. After two hundred metres, this corridor passes the first metal container – Ukrainian passport control; after another two hundred metres, there is a second one – Polish customs. In front of both the Ukrainians line up, everyone holding the same things in their hands: two packs of cigarettes and a bottle of spirits. It is the maximum amount people are permitted to carry to the other side per border crossing.

On the Polish side, the Ukrainians line the road connecting the Polish village Medyka with the Ukrainian village Shehyni. They wait for customers. When a Polish car approaches, it is surrounded by Ukrainian merchants. During such encounters, the body language betrays the balance of power between the two sides of the border. The Poles wind down their windows just far enough for the bottles and boxes to be handed through. They turn the goods over critically in their hands and often return them with a silent shake of their heads. The Ukrainians press themselves against the windowpanes, nod gratefully, rummage hastily for change.

When the merchants have managed to sell all their goods, they run back: corridor, container, corridor, container, corridor, kiosk, two packs, one bottle. On bad days, they manage three border crossings; on good days, seven; on very good days, nine. The złoty coins which they collect in their pockets until the evening are rarely worth more than five euros. At the end of the day, still on the Polish side, they tally it all up. Usually they spend their profits in the Polish shops on the border. They buy food and housewares, sometimes textiles, electrical products or building materials, whatever their money can buy. Then they strap their shopping onto their handcarts and head home. This is the end of their working day, which is based on a price differential that one of the women explained to me in the following terms: "In Poland, you pay less for everything you need for living. In Ukraine, you pay less for everything that makes you die faster."

Before I said goodbye to the women, I bought some more of their goods, hoping in this way to shorten their working day: one more smoker's lung, two laryngeal ulcers, one squadron of nicotine-damaged sperm.

They asked where I was going. I pointed east, to the other side of the border. They stared at me in disbelief. What kind of moron, their looks said, would buy cigarettes at Polish prices when he is going to Ukraine?

Around the beginning of the pedestrian corridor merchants squatted in front of spread-out bed sheets piled with used electric drills and grinders, car radios, microwaves, blow dryers and toasters – discarded scraps of prosperity, no longer new in the West, but not yet old in the East. Women rummaged through stacks of worn children's clothes. In between were parked minibuses, loaded to the gunwales with apples, pears and potatoes. On the back of a truck I saw two bare-chested men dozing on a bed of vacuum-packed sausages.

I struck up a conversation with an old Polish parking attendant who was hauling his barrel-shaped belly through the midday heat. His name was Tadyk, and he lived in Medyka. Half in Russian, half in Polish, he told me about the border transactions conducted in his parking lot, the last one before the customs corridor. Medyka, he said, was the starting point of what was known in border jargon as "the ant trail". Polish trucks, whose freight is destined for the other side, unload their goods here to be distributed to the "ants" – Ukrainian cross-border merchants returning from their cigarette and spirits trades. The ants pack the goods onto their handcarts and transport them piece by piece across the border, each one as much as the customs regulations allow for individual use: a refrigerator, three children's jackets, a stack of roof tiles, two kilograms of meat. On the Ukrainian side, other trucks are waiting for them. The ants deliver their load and receive a few złotys in recompense. Little by little the trucks fill up, until the entire freight has changed sides by way of the ant trail.

I let my eyes wander around the parking lot. At the far end two men stood on the back of a pick-up and pitched car tyres to the ground. There was hardly another vehicle in sight.

"Not much going on today?"

Tadyk slid his left hand under his T-shirt and scratched his barrel belly.

"There's not been much going on here for months. There

is war in Ukraine. Nobody works. Nothing moves. Business is dead."

When I turned into the pedestrian corridor, I walked past a large billboard. A smiling worker in blue overalls looked down at the passing ant trail. Beside his face, in Ukrainian, the billboard read: "Looking for work in Poland? Logistics and production, no agency fee."

Under the poster, I walked by two women who were having trouble fitting their purchases onto their handcarts.

"You need a hand?"

They both looked at me with surprise. Then, grinning, one of them pointed to a large cardboard box. It looked heavy. I knelt down and grabbed it. As I lifted it up I almost fell over backwards – the box was as light as a feather. The two women laughed. Perplexed, I looked at the box. From inside came a strange peeping. It wasn't until I saw the air holes in the lid that I realised I was carrying a load of baby chickens.

"Are they cheaper in Poland?"

The women shook their heads. "Better. Grow fatter than ours."

We got through the Polish passport control quickly. In front of the Ukrainian customs checkpoint, we had to wait for a while. Just a metal fence separated us from the merchants in the parallel corridor, who were travelling in the opposite direction. Their queue, which was lined up in front of the Polish customs checkpoint, was significantly longer. While we waited, three men in suits jostled their way through the crowd on the other side. As an old woman protested, the suited men silently waved their Polish EU passports and kept going.

"Are they better than us?" I heard someone in the queue ask in Ukrainian.

"More European," said another.

"Richer."

"Because we spend our money in their stores."

"Have you heard that they sell us only what they don't eat themselves? It's true, I saw it on TV. In the EU you wouldn't even serve such food to animals!"

"Where has anybody seen such meat? Coming apart in the soup before the potatoes are even cooked!"

As the line suddenly began to move, the debate fell silent as abruptly as it had begun. All eyes focused on the customs booth, people anxiously protected their places in the queue, in order to move forward, closer to the fleshpots of Poland.

When we entered the Ukrainian customs container, a uniformed official cast a stern eye over the two women's fully loaded handcart. He pointed to a metal table, where one of his colleagues was rummaging through an old man's suitcase. I put down the chicken box and was about to open my backpack, but the official motioned to me impatiently when he spotted my German passport.

Hesitantly, I looked at the two women.

They laughed. "Go ahead. The chickens aren't that heavy."

At first glance Shehyni, the Ukrainian village on the other side, was hardly any different from Polish Medyka.

On second glance, I noticed that the church crosses here had the Orthodox double crossbeam that the Catholic crosses in Medyka lacked.

On third glance, I saw that there were more vegetables

than flowers growing in the gardens of Shehyni – it had been the opposite in the Polish gardens on the other side.

On fourth glance, I checked my watch. Ukraine was one hour ahead of Poland.

The differences are small, because the border here is so new. The entire region used to be called Galicia before it was divided. Some still speak of Galicia, but it is not a place anymore, only a word that you will look for in vain on maps. For more than four centuries, from 1340 to 1772, Galicia belonged to Poland – until Poland itself became a word no longer to be found on maps. Austria then formally took over the rule of the ethnically mixed region, but in practice the old feudal structure of the Middle Ages was preserved: the land belonged to the Polish nobility and was ploughed by Ukrainian peasants. For the latter, this balance of power proved so precarious that in the three decades leading up to the First World War alone, just under one million Galicians emigrated abroad, fleeing from poverty and hunger. Some descendants of Ukrainian emigrants who now live primarily in Canada and the United States find that the word "Galicia" still brings tears to their eyes.

As a new round of border changes began in Europe after the First World War, fiery speeches were made in the coffee houses of Galicia for the foundation of a separate Ukrainian state. But in the negotiation chambers of the victorious powers there were enough problems even without the Ukrainians. The negotiators pored over their maps, and when they had criss-crossed the continent with fresh borders, there was still no country called Ukraine. Galicia was instead incorporated into the restored Poland.

The new, old rulers did little to make this situation palatable to the disappointed Ukrainians. They replaced Austria's liberal national policy with a strict programme of Polonisation. Ukrainian schools were converted into Polish ones, Orthodox churches destroyed or taken over by Catholics, Ukrainian newspapers abolished or censored, Polish farmers settled in Ukrainian regions.

In the coffee houses of Galicia, the mood soon changed. If a Ukrainian state could not be achieved through political means, argued the patriots, then all that remained was the path of violence. They formed the "Organisation of Ukrainian Nationalists", a terror alliance whose members swore an oath to the "Decalogue of the OUN", a martial ten-point programme which begins with the following principle: "Thou shalt build a Ukrainian state or die fighting for it."

The OUN waged a bloody terror campaign against the Polish authorities that would last nearly twenty years and did not end with the Second World War. In 1939, when the Red Army invaded Galicia, the nationalists opened a second front: from then on, their struggle for independence would be directed against Poles and Russians alike. Temporarily, they even sided with the Nazis, who kindled their hopes for an independent Ukrainian state. Even when Stalin and Hitler drenched the entire region with blood, the internal hostilities did not stop in Galicia.

After the war, the borders shifted once more. Again, no independent Ukraine came of it, which is why the OUN continued their struggle until finally the Soviet Union, which by then had annexed the eastern half of Galicia, and Poland, to whom the western part had fallen, enforced the new demarcation along ethnic lines. Galicia's population was forcibly segregated: Poland drove half a million Ukrainians into the Soviet Union, while the Soviets expelled 850,000 Poles.

Thus, with blood, hatred, and ethnic cleansing, began the history of that artificial dividing line, which sixty years later was to become the external border of the European Union. The fact that here, of all places, Europe is now split into two parts, an internal and an external one, is a nightmarish joke over which Hitler and Stalin would have shed tears of laughter.

From Shehyni I took a bus to Lviv. On the dashboard, there was a small plastic figure of the Virgin Mary. It wore the same pain-enduring expression on its face as the statues of the Virgin Mary that periodically passed by outside the windows. They stood in front of every village church, and every time we travelled past one, half the people on the bus crossed themselves. I had the feeling I was still in Poland, not in Ukraine, where instead of the Virgin Mary the buses usually have icons on their dashboards.

I've come to the wrong place, I suddenly thought – it was a mistake to begin my trip in this atypical corner of the country that is so unlike the rest of Ukraine, where even the Orthodox faith has Catholic traits. Then I remembered that any other starting point along the country's borders would have been just as atypical – and that it is precisely this lack of uniformity that makes up Ukraine.

It was dusk when I reached Lviv, the former Austrian city of Lemberg, capital and heart of Galicia. From the bus station, I took a tram to the city centre. In the semi-darkness,

I saw a monument roll past the windows to the left of the tracks, the larger-than-life statue of a man.

I recognised Stepan Bandera, the assassinated leader of the Ukrainian Nationalists.

3

The Love Story of Inge and Bohdan

Munich, 1959

ON THE OUTSKIRTS OF EAST BERLIN, in a remote stretch of forest near Lake Müggelsee, a strange scene takes place on a late summer day in the year 1957. Three inconspicuously dressed men enter the forest. A leashed dog runs alongside them, a small mongrel. When the group has reached the deepest part of the forest, one of the men ties the dog to a tree. The second pulls a small metal tube out of his pocket, about as thick as a thumb and twenty centimetres long, with a handle at the bottom. The dog sniffs the implement with curiosity as the third man holds it in front of his nose. A short hissing sound can be heard. Immediately the dog's legs give way; silently it collapses on the forest floor. For about two to three minutes, spasmodic convulsions pass through its body, then it stops moving. With a satisfied nod, the men put away the metal tube and go their separate ways. They leave the dead dog behind.

Because no one has observed this scene, no one associates it with the corpse that is discovered about a month later, in October 1957, on the other side of the Iron Curtain, in the stairwell of an apartment building in Munich. The deceased is a man named Lev Rebet, a Ukrainian in his late

forties who was an exiled member of the resistance movement OUN. In the course of the autopsy, the Bavarian coroners find no sign of an unnatural death; all they can detect
is a blocked coronary vessel. Their diagnosis: myocardial
infarction, in layman's terms a heart attack.

Two years later, in October 1959, another body is found
in the hallway of a residential building in Munich. Again,
all evidence points towards a heart attack. But as this dead
man also was a member of the exiled Ukrainian resistance
movement, and a prominent one at that, the prosecutor
looks more closely. During the autopsy, cyanide poisoning
is detected. The coroners speculate about suicide, but they
are at a loss to explain the tiny glass fragments discovered
in the dead man's face.

The body is buried at Munich's Waldfriedhof cemetery,
where to this day the grave serves as a pilgrimage site for
nationalist Ukrainians. The light grey gravestone displays
the deceased's name both in Cyrillic and Latin letters:
Stepan Bandera, 1 January 1909 – 15 October 1959.

The relatives and companions who gather at Bandera's
funeral in 1959 don't care much for the Bavarian prosecu-
tors' diagnosis. There is more anger than sorrow in their
eulogies. They are convinced that Stepan Bandera, the
famous resistance fighter and notorious Nazi collaborator,
was murdered.

Only two years later do they learn that they were right.

In August 1961, a young man, not tall, but athletically
built, walks into the police headquarters on Tempelhofer
Damm in West Berlin. He says that his name is Bohdan
Stashynsky, that he was born in the Ukrainian part of the
Soviet Union, and that he has a confession to make. When

the police realise what it is about, they immediately notify U.S. military intelligence.

Stashynsky is questioned for several days. He describes in detail to his interrogators two murders that he claims to have committed in Munich. He talks about his recruitment by Soviet intelligence, about his KGB training in Kiev, about the false papers he has been equipped with to spy on the Ukrainian expatriate community in West Germany. Stashynsky describes the murder weapon he was given by two KGB officers in East Berlin: a tube-shaped revolver that sprays gaseous cyanide into the victim's respiratory tracts when the trigger is pulled. He talks about antidote capsules filled with sodium thiosulfate and amyl nitrite, which he had to take before and after triggering the gun to protect himself from the murderous gas. Stashynsky also mentions the little dog on which he was made to test the weapon.

The investigators are sceptical. KGB murders, wonder weapons, test animals, antidote capsules – the story sounds fantastic, made-up, contrived. An interrogation with reversed roles ensues: the murderer tries to prove his crimes to the investigators. But the longer Stashynsky speaks, the more credible his story seems. At no point does the Ukrainian contradict himself, he knows details that only the killer could know, and he presents documents that confirm his story, among them copies of the coded telegrams that he sent to his commanding officers in East Berlin after the murder: "In a city familiar to me, I met with the subject familiar to me and greeted him. I'm sure the greeting has turned out well." Stashynsky also shows the investigators the KGB certificate that highlights his "involvement in handling an important problem" – meaning the murder of

Bandera, for which he was awarded the "Order of the Red Banner", one of the highest Soviet military decorations.

One detail, however, remains a mystery to the investigators until the very end. Stashynsky has committed murders which would have never been identified as murders without his confession. He did not leave any tracks, and no one was suspecting him. So why did he turn himself in?

The murderer's answer is simple: he is in love.

The young woman Stashynsky met in April 1957, at a dance in East Berlin's Friedrichstadtpalast, is called Inge Pohl. She is twenty, five years younger than the KGB agent, and she works as a hairdresser in the western part of the city. When the Ukrainian approached her, he introduced himself under his alias, Joseph Lehmann – it is the pseudonym that the Secret Service gave him for his mission in Berlin, where Stashynsky poses as a Polish interpreter with German family roots. He keeps his true identity a secret from Inge, but not his communist beliefs. The young woman makes fun of him because of that – she herself does not think much of the New World that the Soviet rulers promise to create in the eastern part of the city. The two are too much in love to be bothered by their ideological differences. In April 1959, two years after meeting at the Friedrichstadtpalast, Inge and Bohdan get engaged.

At this point, Stashynsky has already committed his first contract killing. And slowly, so he tells the investigators, his double life begins to take its toll on him. He paints a broader picture of his background now, talking about his childhood, his native village in western Ukraine, and his school days, when the language of instruction changed constantly – first from Ukrainian to Polish, later from Polish to Russian,

shortly thereafter to German, then back to Russian, following the tides of conquests in Galicia. As a child, Stashynsky
says, he had witnessed how Ukrainians and Poles went for
each other's throats in his native village, how later the Jews
were murdered, finally how German and Soviet troops massacred each other. Amid the war chaos, part of his family had
joined the Ukrainian nationalists to fight against the Red
Army. Stashynsky himself believed more in a Soviet future
for Ukraine. Communism, which promised a violence-free
world without class or country borders, seemed closer to his
viewpoint than the old nationalist thinking that had brought
so much suffering to Galicia. When after the war he met a
KGB officer who wanted to recruit him as a "Scout for Peace",
Stashynsky agreed. The linguistically gifted young man still
believed himself to be on the right side when he was sent
to Western Germany to spy on the Ukrainian nationalist
movement. He only began to doubt his mission when he was
asked to shed blood in the name of peace. But his moral scru-
ples were not strong enough to keep him from killing. Only
the encounter with Inge – so Stashynsky will later maintain
at his trial – brought about a genuine change of heart.

When his superiors in East Berlin learn about the engage-
ment, they lean on Stashynsky to end the relationship. A
KGB agent, they argue, cannot possibly get involved with
a foreigner, certainly not a with class enemy from Berlin's
Western sectors – and incidentally, adds one of the officers with a wink, there is no lack of beautiful girls in the
Soviet Union. Growing more and more desperate, Stashynsky begins to lie: at root, he claims, Inge is committed to the
communist cause, and she could ultimately make a model
Soviet citizen.

"My soul was at stake," Stashynsky will say in court. "I already detested what I had done, and I was standing at a crossroads. If I gave up on marrying my fiancée, I might have become loyal to the party line again and turned into a die-hard KGB man."

Only after his conversation with the officer does Stashynsky force himself to make a confession to his fiancée. When he tells Inge who he really is, he expects the worst. But the improbable happens: not only does his lover forgive him, she even promises to save him. The twenty-two-year-old hairdresser Inge Pohl, who has just learned that her fiancé is not some quaint weekend communist, but a professional KGB killer, agrees to embark on a highly risky mission: along with Stashynsky, she travels to Moscow to mislead the intelligence service about her loyalty to the party and receive permission to marry.

During the two-month stay in Moscow, Stashynsky becomes increasingly estranged from his employers. On the surface, he and Inge feign enthusiasm, while inwardly they think only of escape. When they find that their room in a Moscow dormitory is bugged, their private conversations become a charade – they can only exchange their true feelings in writing or on walks. Nevertheless, they achieve their goal: when Inge leaves after two months, the secret service agrees to the wedding.

After that, things happen very fast. A few months after Inge's departure, Stashynsky, who is still in Moscow, learns that his fiancée is expecting a child in Germany. When he reports this news, his officer insists on an abortion – the baby, he argues, comes at an inconvenient time, Stashynsky is not needed as a father, but as an agent. Should he not agree to an abortion, the child will have to be placed in a Soviet orphanage.

On March 31, 1961, a boy named Peter is born in Berlin. While his parents are still thinking about how they can protect their child from the KGB, the newborn dies of pneumonia. Stashynsky implores his superiors to let him attend the funeral in Germany, which they grant only after he raises the question of his wife's nervous condition – he must calm Inge down, he says, so she does not divulge any secrets.

Upon his arrival in East Berlin, Stashynsky is welcomed by two Stasi agents who end up sticking to him like glue – the KGB seems to have lost confidence in their agent. Accompanied by his guards, Stashynsky travels to the East Berlin suburb of Dallgow, where Inge is staying for the time being with her parents. The funeral is supposed to take place there the following day. The Stasi watchdogs park their car opposite the front door. When Inge and Bohdan realise that they will not be left unsupervised, they decide to escape before the funeral. They sneak into the garden through a back door and head for the nearest town, Falkensee, from where they take a taxi to central East Berlin. At Friedrichstraße station they board the S-Bahn and travel to the western part of the city, where, on the afternoon of August 12, 1961, Stashynsky turns himself in to the police.

Not until the following day do Inge and Bohdan realise that they literally got away by the skin of their teeth. A few hours after their escape, the entire S-Bahn service between East and West Berlin was shut down, and early the next morning, the socialist GDR government rolled out the barbed wire. It was the day the building of the Berlin Wall began.

On 19 October 1962, Bohdan Stashynsky is sentenced to eight years' imprisonment, not for murder, but for aiding and abetting. The lenient sentence is politically motivated. The shock of Berlin's partition is fresh, the Cold War has reached its climax, and West Germany's federal supreme court wishes to emphasise that the real culprits in the Munich murders are hiding in Moscow.

Before he has served his full sentence, Stashynsky is released from custody for good conduct. Thereafter, he disappears without trace. Rumour has it that he and Inge started a new life in South Africa, under false names, far away from their homelands. Some claim that after the collapse of the Soviet Union the couple moved to independent Ukraine, where Bohdan and Inge are said to have died peacefully a few years later; it is not known who predeceased whom. Indeed, no one knows whether any of this is true.

On a rainy day in August, a few weeks before I left for Ukraine, I had searched for Stepan Bandera's grave at Munich's Waldfriedhof cemetery.

It was a Sunday, so the cemetery office was closed. There was no porter on duty, there wasn't even a gardener in sight. Of the cemetery's many prominent dead, the site map at the main entrance noted only one: Kurt Huber, a member of the White Rose resistance movement, grave number 21-W-22. Wrong side of the barricades, I thought instinctively: the man I was looking for had not fought against the Nazis, but alongside them.

When I finally discovered the grave under a group of tall pine trees on the northern edge of the cemetery, it was just as deserted as the rest of the rainy forest cemetery. Slugs crawled over the grey stone cross on whose pedestal two Ukrainian flags lay spread out, blue and yellow and soggy. A few votive candles burned at the foot of the cross. In amongst them lay withered poppies and, for some reason, a handful of cellophane-wrapped sweets.

There are many reasons to object to the reverence in which Bandera is held in parts of Ukraine today – not only his collaboration with the Nazis, but also the pogroms against Poles, Jews and communists which his guerrilla army was involved in. Another factor that counts against him is his failure. Bandera fought for an independent Ukraine, but it was a struggle that failed utterly to achieve its aim.

In the late 1930s, after the Red Army had invaded Galicia, Bandera joined forces with the Nazis, who played a rather obvious game with the Ukrainian nationalists from the very outset. In league with the Wehrmacht, his partisan troops set about fighting the Soviets. This marriage of convenience did not last long. When the Germans pushed the Red Army out of Galicia in 1941, Bandera thought that Ukraine's hour had come – he immediately proclaimed an independent republic. Less than a week later, he found himself in a Gestapo prison cell in Kraków, from which he was later transferred to Sachsenhausen concentration camp. Hitler had other plans for Ukraine, which Bandera might have realised if only he had read *Mein Kampf* more carefully.

Two of his brothers were murdered in Auschwitz. The Germans spared Bandera, presumably because they considered him a trump card that they might pull out of their sleeve on a suitable occasion. When the tide of war turned against the Nazis, they released Bandera from the concentration camp, presumably hoping this might draw the Ukrainian nationalists to their side again. But it was too late; the defeat of the Third Reich was imminent.

Bandera spent the short rest of his life as an exile in Munich, far away from Ukraine, whose liberation he had not advanced by as much as a single step. He did not die with a gun in his hand, as he had sworn during his OUN inauguration, but with a bag of tomatoes in his arms. His killer got him on the way back from a shopping trip.

A few tram stops from the Waldfriedhof cemetery there is a small Ukrainian Orthodox church, which Bandera visited often until his death.

When I got there and entered the community centre, I burst into a Sunday meeting of exiled Ukrainians and their offspring. Children in embroidered folksy shirts chased one another from room to room. Their parents stood around in groups beneath a grey-brown tapestry whose pattern revealed a likeness of the walrus-bearded Ukrainian national poet Taras Shevchenko.

A microphone crackled. "And now, dear guests, let us listen to the music of a young kobzar, who has come to us from far-off Donetsk…"

The kobzar sat on a chair in the middle of the room, his bandura on his lap. The instrument looked like the illegitimate offspring of a mandolin and a zither. It had the bulbous shape and long neck of the mother, and the father's innumerable strings.

The kobzar played and sang. His Ukrainian was highly mannered, which is why I could only make out that the lyrics were about war. I assumed he was singing a Cossack song, as kobzars usually do, but when I asked the old man standing next to me, he shook his head. "It's about a UPA fighter who says goodbye to his mother before going to war. You know what the UPA is?"

"Bandera's army," I said, nodding.

Silently, we continued listening. Out of the corner of my eye, I studied the small, bald man beside me, whose facial expression reminded me of a curious bird. He was so old that a thought suddenly went through my head.

"Did you know Bandera?"

He turned to me.

"I'm his son-in-law!"

Andriy Kutsan, whose voice seemed too high for his eighty years, had met his prominent father-in-law only one time in his life. In the 1950s, after graduating from high school, he had visited Bandera at his apartment, as many young exiles in Munich did at the time, when they wanted to put their lives at the service of the Ukrainian cause. "Foreign languages!" Bandera had replied when Kutsan asked him for guidance about his future life. The young man followed the advice and went to study in Spain. When, shortly afterwards, he heard about the murder of the nationalist leader, Kutsan had no inkling that a few years later he would marry Bandera's orphaned daughter.

Natalya Stepanivna had died early, and when I met Kutsan in Munich there was a new woman at his side. Together, the two looked after Bandera's grave at the Wald-friedhof, which had not been an easy task latterly. The stone cross had been overturned repeatedly since the beginning of Russian-Ukrainian hostilities. Kutsan suspected that Russian propagandists were behind the attacks, even though the gravestone had been smeared with hate messages in English and Polish.

"The Polish version was full of spelling errors," said Kutsan's wife. "That couldn't have been Poles."

I could think of a few other ethnic groups with good reason to hate Bandera, but I decided to hold my peace. Kutsan was an amiable man, and you couldn't blame him for tending his father-in-law's grave.

Before we left, I asked whether there were any surviving veterans of the Bandera movement in Ukraine today.

"Try Lviv," he said. "The Lontsky prison."

4

The Love Story of SC-108 and SD-214

Lviv

LVIV LOOKED LIKE the illegitimate child Salzburg might have given birth to after a fling with Kraków. From the mother it had inherited its old-world atmosphere, the coffee houses, the cobblestones, and the students with the drawing folders and instrument cases. From the father it had countless baroque churches – and the Lontsky prison.

The prison, when it was still a prison, had been located on Lontsky Street, hence its name. Now that it was a museum, it was located on the renamed Stepan Bandera Street, near the Bandera monument, which I had seen from the tram the evening before.

I bought a ticket and was assigned a museum guide.

The guide made a slight curtsy. "Pani Kristina. Very nice to meet you."

I made a small bow. "Pan Jens. The pleasure is all mine."

"You speak Ukrainian?" she asked in Ukrainian.

"I understand most of it," I replied in Russian.

Pani Kristina grimaced. "Russian – no! I will speak English."

All the quirks of Galicia seemed to be included in this small exchange: the Austrian stiffness of manners, the Polish address by first name (for which I was ridiculed when I tried it later in other parts of the country), and the reservation about anything that smells like Russia.

Even though she was the first and only Ukrainian who forced me to converse in English during my trip, I took an immediate liking to Pani Kristina. As she led me through the narrow prison corridors, past display panels full of yellowed case files and execution orders, the horror of her surroundings was reflected in her eyes, as if she was only just becoming aware of what she was seeing. Her eyes seemed to say more than her words.

The prison had been built immediately after the First World War, when Poland took command of Galicia and the former Austrian police station on Lontsky Street was complemented by a new building for political prisoners. Soon, the first Ukrainian underground fighters ended up in the cells. Bandera was also detained here, when he stood in court in 1936, after his terrorist forces had murdered the Polish director of a high school in Lviv.

In 1939, after the invasion of the Red Army, the prison was taken over by the Soviets, who added new inmates to the well-established ones: anti-communists, priests, aristocrats and other counterrevolutionaries who stood in the way of Galicia's socialist future.

Two years later, when the Wehrmacht was advancing on Lviv and it became clear that the city would fall into German hands, Moscow cabled a fatal order to the prison authorities. All the cells were empty when the Gestapo took over the institution in June 1941. It was easy to guess what had happened to the prisoners: the ground in the prison yard had recently been turned over.

It was a propaganda gift for the Nazis. The Gestapo rounded up a few dozen Jews from the city's newly established ghetto. In the prison yard, shovels were thrown at their feet. The Jews dug until nearly a thousand corpses were lined up at the foot of the prison wall. Then the Nazis summoned the inhabitants of Lviv to identify their dead.

Pani Kristina led me into one of the cells. On the rear wall a monochrome film was being projected which showed grainy images of the murdered prisoners in an endless loop. Mourning relatives, friends, and lovers knelt between the dead, their faces twisted in pain. The images were German propaganda shots, filmed to remind the Ukrainian people of the crimes of the Soviets – and to distract from the murders the Nazis themselves were committing in Ukraine at the same time.

We stared at the flickering wall of the cell silently for two or three minutes. When Pani Kristina looked at me, her eyes reflected more indignation than terror.

"In Soviet times, they showed us these films at school," she said. "But at the time our teachers claimed the prisoners were murdered not by the Russians, but by Germans."

In the one and a half years of the German occupation, the cells on Lontsky Street quickly filled up with new inmates. Some of them were released when the Red Army reconquered the city in 1943. Again, underground fighters of the nationalist movement were now imprisoned. Even long after the war, up until the last years of the Soviet era, Ukrainian dissidents had sat behind the bars of Lontsky Prison.

"There are still a few old interrogation cells in the basement," said Pani Kristina. "That is where prisoners ended up when the secret service tried to force confessions out of them. We usually do not show them to visitors, the cellar is not in very good condition. But maybe you want…?"

I did want.

As we walked down the staircase, Pani Kristina asked what city I came from.

"Berlin? I've only been in your country once. In Saarbrücken. So many Muslims! Do they integrate into German society? You know, the Russians here in Ukraine don't integrate at all – everywhere they speak their Russian, they refuse to learn Ukrainian…"

The basement was damp and dark. Pani Kristina unlocked a barred cell door and led me into the narrow space. With her right shoe she drew a horizontal line across the wall, about ten centimetres above the stone floor.

"The water was this high here at the time. It was a form of sleep deprivation, because the prisoners couldn't lie down on the floor."

She stared at the invisible water line on the wall.

"A former prisoner told me that at night he put his shoes under his head, so his mouth remained above water and he could sleep for at least a few minutes."

When she turned to me, her horrified look seemed to ask: Can you imagine that?

"Why was the man here?" I asked.

"Pan Ivan? He fought on the wrong side in the war. Or on the right side, depending on your point of view. He was in the OUN."

I asked her if Pan Ivan was still alive.

"You want to talk to him?"

I nodded.

Pani Kristina thought for a moment. Then she led me back to the first floor, to her office, where she introduced me to a second Pani Kristina – the young woman looked amazingly similar to her.

"Pani Severina. My daughter. It will be a pleasure for her to accompany you to see Pan Ivan."

"Mama…"

"A pleasure, Severinka!"

On the way to the tram stop I apologised verbosely to Severina, but she interrupted me with a smile.

"It's okay. I have time."

Inside the crowded tramcar, the passengers were fanning the air with folded newspapers. Still, the unusual September heat continued. Severina, who studied music, had repeatedly fumbled on a violin exam the previous day because her sweaty hands had slipped from the fingerboard.

"When I was a child, my mum hounded me into the music school," she said. "As a teenager I hated it. I was so tired of practising that I wanted to pack it in. When I told Mum, she gave me a startled look like I'd driven a knife into her belly."

I could literally see Pani Kristina's offended look before me.

"But all she said was: 'Fine, stop. You will never play again.' That sounded so final that I changed my mind. And today I'm happy."

I asked her if she had thanked her mother for it.

Severina laughed. "For what? For being manipulative?"

Still laughing, she added: "Yes, I have. She's a good mother."

Ivan Mamchur lived on the ground floor of a concrete building on the southern edge of the city. On the wall of his living room hung an old Soviet radio, an Elektronika 203 model. It was broadcasting a parliamentary debate that quietly accompanied our conversation. I could not follow the rapid ebb and flow of the Ukrainian speeches. I recognised only a single recurring word that accompanied Mamchur's narrative in all its grammatical variations: *Ukrayina... Ukrayiny... Ukrayinska... Ukrayinskoho... Ukryintsy...*

Mamchur did not mind speaking Russian with me. He had spent enough time in the labour camps of the Soviet Union to acquire the language.

"Kompot?"

He placed a jar of homemade fruit syrup and two glasses on the table. With an apologetic gesture, he asked me to pour. He was a wiry, supple man, but on bad days his trembling hands did not obey him anymore. Mamchur's ninetieth birthday was not far behind him. He spent most of his pension on medication, and it was only towards the end of our long conversation that I realised he could barely see me, though his dark eyes seemed alert. He was blind in one; the other was weak.

But his mind was clear, and his memories, which he navigated with a librarian's sense of order, compensated for the books he could no longer read. He had been born in 1925, in Rokytne, a village near Lviv. His parents were farmers, but they realised early on that their son had not been born into the world to plough. When the village schoolteacher advised them to let the gifted boy continue learning, they listened to his advice. Thereafter, Ivan attended the Ukrainian Gymnasium of Lviv, one of the few schools that had not changed the language of instruction after Galicia was returned to Poland.

He was fifteen when the Red Army marched into Lviv. A few older classmates and teachers of the school were active in the nationalist movement. Mamchur watched them disappear, one after the other. They reappeared only after the German invasion, when their bodies were excavated in the courtyard of Lontsky Prison.

The nationalist movement split into two parts at this time. Bandera led the more radical wing, whose guerrilla army fought underground against the Red Army. The Germans offered the more conservative wing the opportunity to set up a Ukrainian division in the ranks of the SS.

Mamchur, who felt he was old enough to fight but did not know who he should join, asked the director of his school for advice.

You do not have any combat experience, the director said. You will not last long in the woods. Register with the Germans. They will train you before you go to war.

Mamchur was eighteen when he joined the SS Division "Galicia", along with thirteen thousand other Ukrainians.

"*Un-ter-fuh-rer-schu-le.*"

"I beg your pardon?"

"*Un-ter-fuh-rer-schu-le.*" Mamchur repeated the German word. "That's where I was trained. In Berlin."

Mamchur was still in officer training when the war ended. Along with the older fighters of his division, who had been deployed on the eastern front, he found himself in a British prisoner of war camp after Germany's defeat, along with Nazi collaborators from other parts of the Soviet Union. Most of them were returned to their home regions immediately after the war, where Stalin had them executed or sent to the camps.

The Galician Ukrainians were more fortunate, because the English regarded them as Polish citizens. Thus, they escaped extradition to the Soviet Union. After being released from the POW camp, almost all members of the Galician SS division emigrated to the west, to England, Canada, or the United States.

Not so Mamchur.

"I had taken the OUN oath," he said.

When I realised what he meant, I looked at him incredulously. "Thou shalt build a Ukrainian state...?"

"... or die fighting for it," he added, nodding.

He returned to Lviv. As a stowaway aboard freight trains, he made his way across war-torn Europe to his home region.

When he arrived in Galicia, which had meanwhile been annexed by the Soviet Union with the blessing of the victorious powers, he did not know what had become of the nationalist movement, where its members were hiding, or how to contact them. Without identification papers, he lived undercover in Lviv. His parents secretly provided him with food.

After a few months, he met a man in a park by chance, and after long, tentative conversations recognised him as a kindred spirit. The man put him in contact with the surviving part of the OUN. Mamchur was recruited as a member of the propaganda branch. He secretly wandered the streets at night and pasted the walls of Soviet Lviv with agitation posters.

Against Stalin!
Against Soviet power!
Don't believe their lies!
Remember the terror, the shootings, the hunger!
The OUN is active, it is alive!
For a free Ukraine!

He fly-posted his last poster on August 22, 1946. There was still glue on his hands when two NKVD agents cuffed them the next day. Under duress, a recently arrested OUN member had put the Soviet secret service on his trail.

For four months Mamchur sat in the interrogation cell of Lontsky Prison. At night he slept with his shoes under his head, to keep his mouth above water. Soon he could tell the rats apart by the pattern of their fur.

He was sentenced to ten years in the camps. First, they sent him to the north, to the Arctic Ocean, where a canal was being excavated. Mamchur pushed carts full of frozen earth across the frozen earth for two long years.

Later, he was sent southeast, to Kazakhstan, where a new city, Kengir, was being built. For six years, Mamchur rolled wheelbarrows filled with bricks through the sun-scorched steppe.

There were about twenty thousand political prisoners in the Kengir camp. Many of them were convicted for reasons similar to Mamchur's. Most came from Ukraine; others had taken part in the partisan fight against the Soviet Union in the Baltics; still others were nationally minded Poles, Belarusians, and Moldovans.

"But we did not know that at the time," Mamchur said. "In prison, no one talked about his history. We no longer had a nationality; we didn't even have names. There was only a number on our uniforms. I was known as SC-108."

On his work shifts in the steppe, SC-108 one day noticed a girl named SD-214. She was imprisoned in the adjacent women's section of the camp. SD-214 had long, dark hair. She was beautiful, in a way that seemed familiar to SC-108. When he succeeded in speaking to the young woman during an unobserved moment, it confirmed what he had suspected: she came from Galicia, and she was in the camp because she had joined the nationalists in the war.

SC-108 gathered up his courage. "What's your name?" he asked.

SD-214 blushed. "Olga," she whispered.

Whenever the two saw each other after that, they exchanged glances. Sometimes they managed to smuggle letters from one section of the camp to the other. But they could not talk to each other for a long time after their first meeting. Their paths rarely crossed, and when they did, there were always guards nearby.

They would only meet each other again when the uprising broke out.

In 1954, a year after Stalin's death, there were rumblings in the camp. News from the outside world got around. There was talk of change, change for the better: the butcher had died; his most willing executioners had been dismissed; people were breathing a sigh of relief. But in the camp, everything had stayed the same. The watery soup hadn't become any thicker; the working days no shorter; the guards no more human.

One night in May, when most of the prisoners were already back in their barracks, a commotion broke out in the yard of the men's section. In retrospect, nobody could say how it had started. Everyone rushed into the open air. When the guards arrived in the yard, they fired blindly into the crowd. Thirteen prisoners died on the spot. Others bled to death in the hospital, where fifty severely injured people screamed all night long.

The next morning, when the sun rose over the steppe, the prisoners refused to go to their work assignments. The guards shouted; the guards begged; the guards threatened; the guards made promises. When they realised that the prisoners were serious, they were so frightened that they fled from the camp.

The Kengir uprising lasted forty days. It was by far the longest and most severe revolt in the history of the gulag. The inmates barricaded themselves in the camp, tore down the walls that divided the prisoners' sections, and joined forces. They chose representatives and made demands: No more barred windows! No latches on the barracks! No restrictions on correspondence! No convict numbers on the uniforms! Eight-hour workdays! Amnesties! Punishment for the murderers of Kengir prison! Free passage between the women's and men's division!

The last demand was the most important to some of the prisoners, because many of the women and men had grown closer during the days of revolt. For the first time now, it turned out that the Soviet persecution of religious believers also had its good sides: there were imprisoned priests of all faiths in the camp, who gave their blessing to all couples desiring to get married.

SC-108 and SD-214, who had in the meantime ripped their numbers off their uniforms, also saw each other again during the uprising. They talked about their hopes, about the time after the camp, about a common future, about Ukraine. Olga and Ivan were happy in those days, for the first time in a very long time. Simultaneously, they had the feeling that at any moment their happiness could end.

In the early morning hours of June 26, a dark rumbling woke the prisoners. Four tanks simultaneously broke through the prison barriers. There was nothing the inmates could do to oppose them. When the tanks turned away after half an hour, at least five hundred people were dead. Some say the number was twice that high.

The leaders of the rebellion were executed. More than a thousand prisoners – the young, the strong, the unbiddable – were banished to other, even more remote islands of the Gulag Archipelago. The rest were left to rebuild the devastated camp. Weeping, they walled themselves in.

Mamchur was among those who had been chosen for relocation. He was sure he would die if he had to return to the north. In the last days of the uprising he had developed a fever, his head throbbed, and he could hardly stand upright.

Hepatitis, the camp doctor said. He struck the number SC-108 from the deportation list. Next to it he wrote, "Not able to travel."

Mamchur was released from the camp the same year, his sentence served. He stayed in Kengir until 1956, to wait for Olga. Together, they returned to Ukraine.

I looked at the framed photo that was standing between us on the dining table. Olga was young in the picture, young and so strikingly beautiful that my eyes had kept wandering in her direction while Mamchur had been telling his story.

"She is...?"

He nodded. "Thirty years ago."

We were silent for a few moments. The tinny voices on the radio suddenly seemed louder; I had almost stopped noticing them towards the end of the story.

I cleared my throat. "You knew about the Jews?" I asked.

"Of course. Everyone in Lviv knew the ghetto."

"But nonetheless you wanted to fight for the Nazis?"

"Not for them. With them. The OUN leaders had insisted that our SS division would only be used to fight against the Bolsheviks."

"And you believed that?"

"I did not know then that Hitler wanted to make Ukraine a German colony. I had not read *Mein Kampf*. But we had nothing to do with the pogroms. That was another part of the SS."

"But it was the SS."

For a few seconds Mamchur stared silently at the tabletop. Then his weak eyes searched mine.

"Do you know," he asked, "what was strange about the Jews in the ghetto?"

I looked at him expectantly.

"They did what the Germans told them," he continued. "They did not resist. They even sang songs while they were marched to their deaths. It looked as if they had accepted the fate that their God had burdened them with. Of course, I was sorry. They were people; they wanted to live. But when I saw them, I knew that I did not want to end that way. I wanted to fight for my freedom."

Again, we fell silent. Answers and questions went through my head, questions and answers, but I did not know how to formulate them. Unconsciously, I had been waiting, I only now realised, for an admission of guilt. I understood immediately how presumptuous that was: to me, a German, of all people, Mamchur was supposed to confess mistakes that he had committed more than seventy years ago? He had made his decisions. He had paid dearly for them. If he was waiting for a judge, it certainly wasn't me.

Most of Mamchur's former SS comrades from the Galician division had got off a lot more lightly. They had not returned to Ukraine after the end of the war, but emigrated to the west. Mamchur had run into some of them again in the 1990s at commemorative events in Lviv, which attracted SS veterans from around the world. The men Mamchur had talked to had fat American bellies and fat American wallets. In tears, one of them had complained to him about the poor Ukrainian his children spoke. Ivan, he lamented, my comrade, tell me, what was the use of raising them as patriots?

Mamchur only told me this story when I visited him again two days later, to ask a few questions I had not thought of the first time around. Our conversation was more random at this meeting, less chronological, jumping from memory to memory.

For a time Mamchur was lost in a story he had experienced in the first two years of his imprisonment, at the Arctic Ocean, during the construction of the canal. His mother, he said, was allowed to send him letters from time to time, and sometimes she hid a few rouble notes between the pages, and when the guards did not steal this money from inside the letters, he used it to buy berries, which the inhabitants from the surrounding villages offered to the prisoners through the camp fence, until one day a fellow prisoner told the guards about the money in the letters, and they confronted Mamchur and ordered him to undress, because they were looking for the fifteen roubles he had hidden in his underpants, and when he had stripped down to those pants and was freezing and the money still had not appeared, he ran away, and the guards ran after him, and he ran across the frozen earth in his underpants, and he ran for his life, because he knew he would die if he could not buy any berries, because his body would not hold out without the vitamins, it was barely holding out as it was, he lived in constant expectation of death, and as he ran past a fellow prisoner, he pressed his fifteen roubles into the man's hand and ran on, and then then they caught up with him and beat him until he lost consciousness, and as he came to...

Abruptly Mamchur stopped.

"Sorry..."

"Sorry?"

I only now realised there were tears running down his cheeks.

"These memories... sometimes... sorry..."

He stared at the bag of fruit I had brought him, for his kompot.

"Sometimes," he said when he had composed himself, "I still can't believe that it is now so easy to buy fruit."

In the evening I went to a bar called "Bunker" that Ukrainian friends had mentioned to me. The entrance was hidden inside the staircase of a residential building; without directions, you could not find the place. When I knocked, a soldier pushed the door open from the inside – he wore the old field uniform of the Bandera troops and held an assault rifle under his right arm.

I did not understand the Ukrainian command that he bellowed. My friends had instructed me that upon entry I would be asked for a password: the old nationalist salutation. Uncertainly, I looked at the soldier and said, "Glory to the heroes."

He shook his head. With the exasperated expression of a teacher who is correcting the same mistake for the thousandth time, he pointed the barrel of his assault rifle at me: "Glory to Ukraine!" Then he turned the muzzle on himself: "Glory to the heroes!"

"Oh," I said. I wanted to add: "I got it the wrong way round, I'm sorry", but I did not dare to speak Russian in the presence of an armed nationalist, so I just pointed in turns to him and to myself, grinning idiotically.

He grabbed my arm and pulled me into the bar, letting the door slam shut.

Inside, steep stairs plunged down to the basement, where bunker-like rooms were criss-crossed with rough supporting beams. All the walls were densely packed with military memorabilia – historical uniform items, medals, binoculars, maps, battle plans, radios, portraits of Ukrainian nationalist leaders.

The bar was busy. Groups of cheerful drinkers moved from wall to wall and examined the exhibits. At an air rifle stand, two men fired at targets with the likenesses of Lenin, Stalin and Putin. In the next room there were Second World War vintage weapons spread across the floor. In the middle of the arsenal sat a little boy in diapers. Under the amused eyes of his father, he was playing with a rusty grenade launcher that was twice his size.

I downed a pitcher of beer and felt like a killjoy. The encounter with Ivan Mamchur was still going through my head, I could not form a clear opinion about it. What I had experienced as a tragedy in the afternoon struck me now in the Bunker bar as a farce, and even though I did not begrudge the other guests their fun, I could not bring myself to feel comfortable with this carnival version of wartime woes.

I paid and left the basement bar.

On the way to the ground floor a fire escape branched off; its zigzag course ran along the side wall of the building, up to a terrace. There were a few tables and chairs on the flat roof, but they were empty, the unlit porch was abandoned in the moonlight.

I stepped to the handrail and looked out into the night. It was still so warm that none of the passers-by far below me on the street were wearing a jacket. In the house opposite, a woman was washing dishes, her shadow jerking back and forth behind the kitchen curtains as she scrubbed. On the roofs of Lviv, pigeons slept.

Behind me was a huge anti-aircraft gun from the Second World War. The gunner's seat was mounted on a pedestal, the barrel pointed into the darkness. Shortly after me, two men came out onto the veranda. One of them swung himself into the flak seat and fired invisible volleys on the Town Hall tower.

"E-e-e-e-e! E-e-e-e-e!"

I wondered if that was how the war would sound that was waiting for me in the east of the country.

The old Galicia, the multi-national empire of the Austrian era, was lost in the turmoil of the twentieth century. Few parts of today's Lviv still betray the fact that Poles, Ukrainians, Jews, Germans, Austrians, and other nationalities had once lived here together more or less peacefully; that the city, when it was called Lemberg, must have been an odd mixture of languages, beliefs, cuisines, costumes, and worldviews.

But I discovered one place where the old, dead Galicia was as present as if it had only just been buried: the Lychakivsky cemetery.

For an entire morning I wandered aimlessly through the hilly cemetery grounds in the east of the city centre. In the shade of ancient trees, cats were sleeping on gravestones adorned with Cyrillic and Latin inscriptions, decorated with Orthodox or Catholic-Protestant crosses, Ukrainian tridents and old Austrian imperial coats of arms, commemorative words and Bible verses in all the languages of the Austrian Empire.

Even the names of the dead, which I filled several pages of my notebook with, conveyed an idea of the former atmosphere of Galicia.

IGNACY GRELINGER-GRELINSKI
2. SIERPNIA 1824–16. KWIETNIA 1869

FERDINAND SCHRIMPF

STANISŁAW JULIUSZ ZBOROWSKI
10. KWIET. 1842–4. SIERP. 1870

НАДЕЖДА МИРОНОВНА КЛИМОВСКАЯ
(NADEZHDA MIRONOVNA KLIMOVSKAYA)
24.IV.1900–30.XI.1981

МОИСЕЙ ЗИНОВЬЕВИЧ ГИНЗБУРГ
(MOISEY ZINOVEVICH GINSBURG)
10.III.1924–1.I.1992

Even more intriguing were the family graves, in whose inscriptions the nationalities of Galicia often mixed and combined to form multilingual compositions of surnames, maiden names, children's names, and professional titles.

ANTONI SCHUBERT
1808–1888
ROZALIA ZBR. KAPRI SCHUBERTOWA
1815–1899
DR. ROMUALD SCHUBERT
1842–1905

DR. RUDOLF HERMAN GÜNSBERG
JOANNA Z. SIMONOW GÜNSBERGOWA
ALFRED SIMON
HELENA Z. GÜNSBERGOW SIMONOWA

EMIL GABERLE
EM. PREZYDENT DYREKCJI POCZL I TELEGRAFOW
14.VI.1852–3.III.1930
WILHELMINA GABERLE
1861–11.XI.1947
EUSTACHY GABERLE

1891–9.III.1947
ZOFIA GABERLE
1902–1989
KAZIMIERZ GABERLE
1896–1970

Even the downfall of Galicia had left its mark on the cemetery. At its southeastern edge, there was a field of honour for fighters of the nationalist movement. About one hundred stone crosses stood in rank and file. Under the names of most of the dead, I read the abbreviations "OUN" and "UPA"; a few others had the inscription "Galician Division".

The day before, I had asked Ivan Mamchur where he wanted to be buried.

In Rokytne, he had answered. In my village, beside Olga. My name is already on our gravestone.

Immediately next to the field of honour, I came across a few dozen new graves. They were covered all over with fresh flowers and wreaths. As I got closer, I realised that these resting places were war graves too. Thirty-eight wooden crosses marked the graves of fighters from Lviv who in the past year and a half had fallen in the Donbass.

On the way back from the cemetery to the city centre, I noticed a large poster on the facade of a building. It showed the outlines of Europe, coloured in blue, framed by a circle of yellow EU stars. Underneath, in big letters, it said: "Ukraine is the geographical centre of Europe."

Perplexed, I stopped. The Ukrainian borders were highlighted on the poster. South of them, the map ended abruptly; half of the Black Sea coast and the whole of Turkey had been ripped off. From my perspective, Ukraine was not in the middle of this crippled continent, but at its southeastern edge.

Seeking help, I looked around. The entrance of the building was open.

In the stairwell, I first noticed the photograph of a young man, resting in a window niche between memorial candles and plastic flowers. Pasted beneath it there was a note, framed in black: "Igor Kostenko, 31. 12. 1991 – 20. 02. 2014, student of Geography at the University of Lviv, died a hero's death in front of the Kiev October Palace. Eternal remembrance."

At that moment, a raucous group of students rushed into the corridor from the upper floor. They fell silent when I asked them about the photo.

"He was shot at Independence Square," a boy said softly. "By a sniper."

The other four avoided my eyes sheepishly.

I changed the subject. "Is this the geography department?"

Their eyes lit up. "Yes!"

"Are you studying here?"

"Yes!"

I asked about the meaning of the poster on the building's facade, about the centre of Europe.

"Geographically, we are right in the middle!"

"It depends on how you measure it."

"Whether you count Iceland as Europe or not."

"And Kazakhstan."

"And how you draw the border in the Caucasus."

"But if you do everything right, we are the centre of Europe!"

"The exact centre is somewhere in the Carpathians."

"Not just anywhere! The name of the place is Dilove."

5

In the Middle of Whatever

Dilove–Rakhiv

ON THE MAP, I discovered Dilove on the southern edge of the Carpathians, that sickle-shaped mountain range whose rocky blade stretches from Romania to Slovakia, and mid-way between them cuts off the southwestern tip of Ukraine from the rest of the country.

My train left Lviv behind as the September sun reached its zenith. The dacha landscape at the edge of the city was a chequerboard of golden light and sharp-edged shadows. A warm headwind blew in through the train window. White synthetic curtains were snatched out into the open, fluttered back into the train coach, smacked passengers in the face, were knotted around window handles with curses, and broke free again.

Parts of the Galician countryside that I crossed that day appeared to have fallen out of time. Among rolling hills there were simple, low stone houses surrounded by vegetable plots, haystacks, and fruit trees. Chickens pecked in the dust of the dirt roads; tethered goats grazed in front of fences; sometimes women in flower-patterned headscarves prodded solitary cows on ahead of them. I rarely saw tractors, silos, barns, or stables. Hardly anyone here seemed to be producing surplus stock for the market, hardly any piece of land seemed to feed more than a single family. It looked as if Galicia was returning to pre-industrial times.

Just before the sun went down, the figure of a woman appeared for a fraction of a second on the railway embankment outside. She wore a grey raincoat and was kneeling, motionless in the grass, with her hands clasped in her lap and her eyes fixed on the passing train. For several days, I could not get the picture out of my mind, because it had looked to me as if a Galician Anna Karenina was waiting for the train that would end her suffering. But maybe she was just collecting mushrooms.

Behind Ivano-Frankivsk the hills gave out. The land turned completely flat, as if working up momentum for the Carpathians. An hour later, I saw the first foothills of the mountains passing by the windows in the twilight. It was dark when I arrived in Rakhiv.

My hotel room was at the back of the building. Directly behind the window, a steep slope rose up. I had to lean out to see the mountain ridge, which stood out faintly against the black sky. A choir of dogs howled in the darkness. The air smelt like rain, and it was much cooler than in Lviv.

During the night I dreamt of the woman in the raincoat. She stopped the train with a gesture of her hand. When I got off, she had become a child, the raincoat had disappeared. The child asked me questions in a language I did not understand. Then the train went on, along with my backpack. I ran along the rails and heard the woman in the raincoat laughing behind me.

Ukrainians call the southwestern tip of their country

"Transcarpathia", because from Kiev's point of view it lies behind the mountains. Hungarians and Czechs call it "Subcarpathia", because from their perspective it lies at the foot of the mountains. For almost a millennium the area belonged to Hungary, until it was incorporated into Czechoslovakia after the First World War. In the chaotic early days of the next war the inhabitants of the region, mostly Ukrainians, declared their own Carpathian republic, which existed for just one day – on the evening of March 15, 1939, the Hungarians invaded again, closely followed by the Czechs, who took back command in 1944. The Soviet Union, which meanwhile had extended its borders all the way to the mountain crests, incorporated the Transcarpathian tip shortly after the war – and kept it until 1991, when the region, together with the rest of Ukraine, became independent.

"My grandmother still spoke Czech in school!"

The taxi driver who drove me the few kilometres that separated Rakhiv from the centre of Europe had thick black hair that seemed to cover his entire body. He lifted a hairy hand from the steering wheel, and on its big fingers counted the nationalities of his home region.

"Ukrainians!" – one finger – "Romanians!" – two – "Slovaks!" – three – "Czechs" – four – "Hungarians" – five. His hand clenched to form a black hairball and started all over again. "Moldovans! Russians! Germans! Poles! Lithuanians! Belarusians! I could go on forever!"

His Ukrainian sounded different from the Ukrainian in Lviv.

"We have our own *surzhik* here," he explained. "We mix Ukrainian with Hungarian. You are here for the Hutsul festival?"

"For what?"

"The festival. On Sunday, the Hutsuls descend into the valley."

"Who are the Hutsuls?"

He made a circular motion with his index finger.

"Us. Me. Everyone here. The mountain people."

I asked him which mountain he lived on.

He laughed. "That was earlier. The Hutsuls have not lived in the mountains for a long time."

"But on Sunday they descend into the valley?"

"Yes! So you are here for the festival after all?"

The centre of Europe is located next to a windy parking lot. Mountain slopes rise up to the left and right of the winding country road that connects Transcarpathia and Romania; the border is less than five kilometres to the south. Parallel to the road flows the Tisa, a tributary of the Danube, which now, in late summer, was more stone bed than stream. Its dry banks seemed to be waiting eagerly for the next thaw. A café and a small natural history museum flanked the car park, where a few traders sat in front of their booths waiting. They sold carved wooden spoons, sheepskins, drinking horns, embroidered folk shirts – Hutsul souvenirs.

Right beside the road stood a small stone obelisk, painted in blue and white and about as high as my chest. A few Ukrainian tourists photographed each other next to the monument, the men standing with legs wide apart and grinning, the women in sultry poses. Their tour guide's commentary was half lost among the giggles of those being photographed.

"... Here you can see the geographical centre of Europe, discovered in the nineteenth century by Austrian engineers during the construction of the Transcarpathian railway line. Anyone who walks around the base three times and then touches the metal rod under the inscription..."

In turn, the tourists circled the pedestal. I had only understood half the Ukrainian commentary and asked one of the men about the meaning of the ritual.

"It's supposed to bring you wealth."

His wife shook her head vigorously.

"Luck, not wealth!"

On the base of the monument was an inscription painted in gold:

LOCUS PERENNIS
DILICENTISSIME CUM LIBELLA LIB
RATIONIS QUAE EST IN AUSTRIA
ET HUNGARIA CONFECTA CUM MEN
SURA GRADUM MERIDIONALIUM ET
PARALLELOUMIERUM EUROPEUM
MDCCCLXXXVII

My Latin from my school days was pretty rusty. But it was still just good enough to get the gist that the inscription referred to surveys in Austria-Hungary, to latitudes and longitudes, and to a point that had been determined in 1887.

It was also good enough to make me doubt that the inscription said anything about the centre of Europe.

When I asked about it at the Natural History Museum beside the parking lot, the woman at the counter shook her head uncertainly.

"I don't know anything about that. But we have very interesting stuffed birds here!"

She advised me to try the Rakhiv Biosphere Reserve, whose administration was responsible for the preservation of the monument. I stood on the side of the road with my thumb out and found a driver who took me back to the city.

Fedir Gamor, the director of the nature park, was a friendly man in his sixties. Smiling, he listened to my question about the centre of Europe.

"I'm glad that you are visiting us," he said. "Did you know that our reserve is about ninety percent forest, most of it primeval, which scarcely exists in Europe anymore? Naturalists from Germany with a special interest in our old beech trees often come and visit us…"

After a few minutes, I repeated my question.

"I'm very pleased by your interest. As for the fauna, we are home to sixty-four species of mammals, one hundred and seventy-three types of birds, nine reptiles and thirteen amphibians respectively, twenty-three species of fish, more than ten thousand invertebrates…"

"… and the centre of…?"

"… Incidentally, we cooperate closely with biosphere reserves in Poland, Romania, Slovakia, Hungary, the Czech Republic, Switzerland, Austria…"

"… Austria, isn't that where these engineers came from in the nineteenth century, who…"

"… May I perhaps give you a copy of our quarterly magazine, *Green Carpathians*?"

I liked Gamor. When I realised that he preferred to steer clear of the centre of Europe, I settled on a conversation about the Carpathians.

He drew the outline of the mountain range on the surface of his desk with his index finger.

"Here we are. Here is Kiev. It was only last year that a direct train connection was reinstated from the capital to Rakhiv – that's what we've been fighting for, for a long time."

His index finger slipped further south, deeper into the truncated area of the country beyond the mountains.

"But unfortunately, the train service doesn't run beyond Rakhiv," he said regretfully.

He slid his finger down to the southwestern borders.

"Romania, Hungary, Slovakia – they are all very close. But the Iron Curtain cut Transcarpathia off from Europe. I dream of being able to take the train to Budapest, to Prague, to Vienna, but there are no railway lines."

He paused briefly and looked at me as if he was thinking about something. Then his fingers moved back a little.

"Here is Dilove."

I pricked up my ears.

"Have you seen the museum? The car park, the cafe, the merchants, the tourists?"

I nodded.

"Twenty years ago none of that existed. There was nothing but this old monument. We developed all of that. Today the tourists come to Dilove even from neighbouring countries; they drive by car across the border to see the centre of Europe."

He lifted his finger from the invisible desk map and leaned back, smiling.

"You know, I'm a biologist, not a geographer. I do not know how this survey point was calculated. It just so happened that our reserve is responsible for the monument, and we make the most of it."

He was silent for a moment. Then, suddenly, something seemed to occur to him. He yanked open a desk drawer and rummaged around.

"A few years ago there was a research group from Switzerland here. They wrote an article about us, in German. Where did I put it?"

His head disappeared beneath the desk.

"They were also interested in the centre of Europe. They wanted to take a look at the Austrian archives, to see if there were any documents on the subject."

Triumphantly, Gamor reemerged clutching a brochure.

"Here! I don't even know what they finally ended up writing."

I scanned the article and quickly found the paragraph which mentioned the Austrian obelisk.

… the monument probably embodies the secret hope of this almost forgotten border region that the economic and cultural exchange with Western Europe will be revived and the nearby town of Rakhiv will flourish again as the 'Paris of the Hutsuls'…

Gamor looked at me intently. "So?"

Sheepishly, I put the booklet aside. I didn't have the heart to translate the sentence to him.

"Very interesting," I said. "By the way, I wanted to ask you about those beech forests you mentioned…"

On the way back from the biosphere reserve to the city centre, I passed a small cemetery, which ran from the road to the foot of a mountain slope. I glanced over the fence. The gravestones were not inscribed in Cyrillic, but Latin.

Carefully I opened the entrance gate. I expected to find an ethnic mix similar to that in the Lychakivsky cemetery in Lviv, but when I looked closely at the graves, I saw neither Polish nor Ukrainian names. The cemetery was Hungarian.

MEDVE FERENC
1933–2001

BRÁNDISZ ATTILIO
1914–1999
EMLÉKED SZIVÜNKBEN ÖRÖKKÉ ÉLNI FOGSZ

BEDNARCSEK
ERZSEBET
1920–1987
IMRE
1915–1981

WEINRAUCH
SANDORNÉ
1914–1987
SÁNDOR
1918–1982

Near the entrance there was a small memorial stone which listed thirty-six Hungarian names, apparently victims of Stalinist persecution during the war years.

A SZTALINISMUS 1944–45 BEN ELHURCOLT RAHOI
ALDOZATAINAK AZ EMLEKERE

Not far away, a high wooden cross towered over the graves. Below the pierced feet of a shining golden Messiah was a plaque with a weathered, bilingual inscription. I did not understand the Hungarian version, and only half of the archaic German.

DURCH FREIES ERBIETEN DER
RAHOER CONVENTIONIRTEN FORSTARBEITER
AUS DEM BRUDERLADS VERMÖGEN
IM JAHRE 1873 ERHOBEN.

But as in Lviv, the old diversity of the Transcarpathian border region seemed to have survived almost only in cemeteries. In the three days that I spent in Rakhiv, I rarely heard anything other than Ukrainian in the streets, mixed occasionally with Russian curses.

Personally I could still barely formulate a straight sentence in Ukrainian, but my listening comprehension had rapidly improved within the first week of being in the western parts of the country. Nor did I have any other choice, for even though most of the people here did not mind that I spoke Russian to them, they usually answered my questions in Ukrainian. Paradoxically, I felt that these bilingual conversations slowly altered my view of the country. Much more than during my earlier visits to Kiev, where Russian questions were usually answered in Russian, I now had the feeling of travelling through a foreign country, rather than a less familiar part of Russia. It was absurd: as my ability to communicate had grown poorer, I took Ukraine more seriously.

While I was waiting for the day of the Hutsul festival, I met a man who I could hardly understand at all. It happened in the middle of a forest. I had been aimlessly following one of Rakhiv's back streets in order to see the mountains up close. Before long the little wooden houses on the roadside became less frequent, and when the last one gave out after a bend, I climbed uphill among dense trees for an hour and a half without meeting a single human being.

I followed the course of a mountain stream whose babbling drowned out all the other sounds of the forest. Thus I did not hear that someone was approaching; I only saw the man when he was practically on top of me. He seemed to be a bit younger than me, but his appearance was so strangely timeless that I was not sure. A shapeless sack dangled from a stick over his shoulder. He wore rubber boots and an antiquated rain cape, from beneath whose hood shone a wheat-yellow mop of hair. His blue eyes sparkled, his smile was broad, and his facial expressions slow. He looked like the good-natured hero from a Slavic fairy tale – a Hutsul, descending into the valley.

At first I did not understand his request for a cigarette – he spoke in a strange, drawling dialect. I fumbled one of the contraband Ukrainian packs out of my pocket, which had crossed the Polish border with me. We stood together smoking in the forest.

I asked him where he was going.

He pointed to the sack, which he had dropped on the forest floor, and said something about shopping.

I asked him where he came from.

With a vague gesture, he pointed to the mountains.

Although I could not imagine it, I asked if he lived up there.

He nodded.

Somewhere deep in the woods, as I understood from what he told me, was his house. He mentioned goats, sheep, and a dog. Incredulous, I looked in the direction he had pointed. Thick, dark forest surrounded us; only a narrow, stony footpath meandered along the edge of the streambed. It was hard to imagine anyone living in such isolation.

"Hutsul?" I asked.

"Hutsul," he said, smiling.

Then he shouldered his sack and went on his way.

I walked on uphill. The road became steeper, narrower, and more difficult. After a while, I was not sure if I was even following a path. The old Hutsul legends that I had read the night before in my hotel room went through my mind – of green-eyed forest nymphs who posed riddles to wayfarers and tickled to death anyone who could not solve them; of mountain witches who threw their long, pendulous breasts backwards over their shoulders when they were not using them as wings for flying; of felt-bearded, fiery-eyed robbers who hunted for treasure deep in the woods, giving to the poor what they took from the rich.

The sky above the treetops had gradually clouded over, and in the distance I soon heard the first rumble of thunder. I would have turned around if I had not had one goal in mind: the Hutsul's house, which had to be here somewhere, far away from any road. If he took that route regularly, how could I give up? I walked on, even long after I had admitted to myself I was no longer following a path, but only the bed of a stream in whose mud I had not seen any footprints for a long time.

I gave up when my boots got stuck in ankle-deep mud

and the undergrowth was so dense that I would have needed a Hutsul's axe to clear it. Somewhere, I must have missed a turn.

Shortly after I turned back, a sudden wind ripped through the trees. Seconds later the rain began. Sopping wet, I reached Rakhiv with the disappointing feeling that I would never be a Hutsul.

When the day of the festival came, the Hutsuls gathered together on the main street of Rakhiv in orderly procession groups. The women wore scarlet skirts and floral wreaths in their hair, the men embroidered vests and narrow-brimmed, Tyrolean hats. Many of them dragged wooden *trebitas* through the rain – long, slim Carpathian trumpets that were often twice the height of those who were carrying them. It looked like there was a pole-vaulting team marching through Rakhiv.

When the parade began, it was accompanied by a squawking loudspeaker voice that seemed to come from the mouth of a Soviet bronze soldier. On the concrete grandstand of the Second World War memorial, the worthies of Rakhiv stood lined up under umbrellas. One by one they stepped to the microphone to announce the parade participants, who were marching past holding banners spelling out their places of origin.

"… We can now see the folklore collective from the urban-type settlement Velyky Bychkiv, ten thousand inhabitants, one of the oldest places in our beautiful Hutsul region, first mentioned in a document written in 1358, known for its sulphuric acid plant and its salt refinery – applause for Velyky Bychkiv! Coming up next is the folklore collective from the village of Dilove, two and a half thousand inhabitants, known worldwide as the geographical centre of Europe..."

The parade thrust its way across the city to a large open-air stage at the foot of the mountains, where the stream of participants and spectators dispersed among kebab stalls, souvenir stands, and beer tents. Folklore ensembles and local pop stars appeared on stage, interrupted by speeches from grey-suited officials. Both were tiring. I was more attracted to the improvised tent stands where the villages of the Hutsul region were showcasing themselves. Every village had brought a few musicians, who attempted to drown out the musicians from the next tent with their fiddles, flutes, zithers, and accordions. It sounded like a great Hutsul folk symphony whose movements were not played consecutively, but simultaneously.

Petro Ferents, the mayor of a place called Bohdan with a population of three thousand, was dead drunk, although you couldn't tell. His village's speciality was home-distilled vodka made from violets. He had clinked glasses with the governor and with all of the governor's deputies; he had clinked glasses with the mayors from all the neighbouring villages and with all the musicians from Bohdan; he had clinked glasses with each visiting member of the Czech and Hungarian delegations; and he toasted more than once with the German journalist who unexpectedly appeared in front of his tent.

"I only do this when I'm on duty," Ferents confided to me. "Usually I don't drink a drop."

He had a beautiful, melancholy face, long and narrow, with prominent cheekbones. As he spoke, I stared, endlessly fascinated, at the dark spot in the middle of his blue-shadowed chin – the dimple seemed to be so deep that he could not shave it.

I realised after a few sentences that Ferents was overqualified for the post of village mayor. When I asked who the Hutsuls were, he answered my question with a long, erudite monologue.

"A sub-ethnos of Ukrainians," he said. "Like the Lombards in Italy or the Bavarians in Germany."

He told me about the old traditions of craftsmanship that had once made the Hutsuls sought-after specialists in Europe, about the clearing and rafting techniques used to transport wood from the most remote corners of the mountains, and about the sawmills and woodcarving skills for which they were envied.

When I asked if there was anything left of all that, he shook his head.

"It was all over and done with once the Soviet era began. The Russians have systematically destroyed all the national traditions here."

"… How true. How *eminently* true."

A drunk teenager from Ferents's home village had planted himself beside us with his legs spread akimbo. What the mayor was saying clearly went over his head, but because he wanted to join in the discussion, he kept interjecting phrases that he seemed to have picked up from television debates. I had to get a grip on myself to stop myself from laughing at his dead-serious expression. Ferents just ignored him.

"… You might even say, *profoundly* true!"

With his forefinger, Ferents directed my eyes to the large festival stage where a dance ensemble in brightly coloured Hutsul blouses were currently twirling.

"That is all that is left of our traditions. Folklore."

"… Otherwise there is nothing left *whatsoever*!"

Ferents continued to talk about the Soviet era, the repression and the terror.

"Imagine a field with the top fifty centimetres of soil removed. What will grow there?"

I assumed that he would answer his rhetorical question himself, but he waited for my response.

"Not much?"

"Correct."

"… That is even *more than* correct!"

Ferents looked into my eyes. "Ukraine is this field. The Soviets destroyed the upper layers of our society, deported them, expelled them. That left drinkers, bandits, people without any initiative. We are still suffering the consequences today. Ukraine is a sick nation."

"… A *thoroughly* sick nation!"

I asked him what the inhabitants of his village lived on.

"Some of them are paid by the state – bureaucrats, school and kindergarten teachers, the village doctor. Others live by doing odd jobs in the EU, on the other side of the border. And the rest…"

Ferents paused; it seemed he did not know how to end the sentence. The drunk teenager chipped in.

"… The rest are smugglers!"

I looked at Ferents, expecting that he would contradict him. Instead, he nodded sheepishly. "Cigarettes, liquor, whatever sells in the EU."

Shortly after that a few officials in suits appeared. Ferents groaned – one of his colleagues was already busy filling the next round of plastic cups with violet vodka.

He asked me to wait. "Eat something in the meantime. It won't take long."

It did take long. I sat down at a table and tried some homemade smoked sausages from Bohdan. Across from me sat a determined drinker. I watched him in admiration. He focused on holding himself upright, one eye closed, the other at half-mast. In one hand he held a shot glass, in the other a piece of bread. Fifteen minutes later, he lay snoring on the tabletop. Another quarter of an hour later he was sitting upright again, the cup still in one hand, the piece of bread in the other.

I watched Ferents. Laughing, he chatted with the officials. It looked as if he enjoyed his work, and he was certainly a good mayor. But I could not imagine his life in Bohdan. His education, his eloquence – what could he do with those skills in this smugglers' den?

"Are there people in your village you can talk to?" I asked him when he sat down beside me again.

"My wife," he said thoughtfully. "My children."

He stared at the tabletop. "Practically no one."

Then he suddenly looked me in the eye. "You know, it was a mistake. After my studies I could have made a career in the county capital, in Uzhhorod. Back then I decided against it. Now I know that I'd have been better off there. It was a mistake…"

I tried to cheer him up, but he shook his head absent-mindedly. The last cup of violet vodka seemed to have tipped him over the edge.

"… A mistake."

When we shook hands in farewell, the drunk man across from us slowly slipped under the table, as if in slow motion.

A few months later, after I had returned from Ukraine to Berlin, I spoke to a colleague who knew Latin about the monument of Dilove. He confirmed what I had suspected: the inscription said nothing about the centre of Europe.

As luck would have it, this colleague was interested not only in classical philology, but also in geographical curiosities. A few years before, he told me, he had tried to prove that the midpoint of the European Union had to be located almost exactly inside Helmut Kohl's body – or, in other words: near the former German Chancellor's residence in his home town, Oggersheim. He had gathered almost all the evidence to achieve his goal when an EU expansion intervened, shifting the centre of the Union to the east.

The colleague could vaguely remember that he had come across Dilove during his research. With the clues he gave me, I found out that the Ukrainian Obelisk was one of seven identical marker stones that Austrian geographers had erected in Central Europe at the end of the nineteenth century, as fixed points to be used for surveying the Habsburg Empire. Each one had the same inscription as the one in Dilove. None of them had anything to do with the centre of Europe.

I never found out how the legend of Dilove had come about. At some point during the Soviet period someone must have stumbled over the forgotten marker stone and misinterpreted it, either from a lack of knowledge of Latin, or from patriotic pride. Presumably, he had passed his enthusiasm on to the local authorities, who did not understand the weathered inscription on the stone, but had immediately refurbished it with gold paint. The small spelling errors they had incorporated into it in the process amused my colleague, but in Dilove they had apparently never bothered anyone.

Imperial feelings may have also played a role in the story – the gratification of being able to locate the centre of Europe in the Soviet Union, if only at its outermost edge. I was more sympathetic to the philosophical, down-to-earth approach to the monument taken by Fedir Gamor, the park director. Europe's history had relegated Transcarpathia to the geographical margins. Wasn't it reasonable compensation that this place should emerge as the centre of Europe now?

In addition to Dilove, I encountered a dozen or more other European cities during my research that were vying to be the geographical centre of the continent, on more or less dubious grounds. It did not surprise me. The question about where Europe begins and where it ends is as old as it is unanswerable, and as long as the borders are disputed, the centre also remains a question of personal preference.

For me personally, the heart of the continent will always be in Dilove, beside a windy Transcarpathian parking lot, in the deadest corner of Europe.

The evening before my departure to Chernivtsi, a wedding party was celebrating in the restaurant of my hotel. All the tables were pushed together to form one large one, covered from end to end with cold cuts and vodka bottles. Most of the wedding guests sat listlessly in front of their plates, absorbed in dull, digestive meditation. A speaker was pumping Russian disco-pop into the room, but no one seemed to be in the mood for dancing. At the head of the table sat the wedding couple. The groom stared glassy-eyed into space; he seemed to be wrestling with his equilibrium. The bride shot him anxious sidelong glances.

Hungry, I looked at the waitress. She found a small table for me, half-hidden behind the bar.

I was still leafing through the menu when a man with a beer mug in his hand appeared in front of me. Questioningly, he pointed to the chair opposite. I nodded.

He did not seem to belong to the wedding party. His expression was tired and depressed; he must have been around fifty, I guessed. I had expected him to start a conversation, but he drank his beer in silence.

"Visiting the Hutsul festival?" I finally asked.

His eyes grew more animated. "For the fifteenth time. Each year I come here from Lviv."

"Because you're Hutsul?"

"Boyko."

"Boyko?"

He pointed vaguely to a point of the compass somewhere behind my back.

"Sort of like the Hutsuls, but from another part of the Carpathians. And you?"

"I'm from Germany."

He raised his eyebrows in interest.

"Germany…"

He put his beer mug down on the table and leaned toward me.

"We should exchange addresses. You could come to Lviv sometime, and I might even come to Germany. When the waitress comes, we'll ask her to bring us something to write with."

"First we should ask her to bring us something to eat," I

joked. There was something strange about his sudden interest, and I wanted to buy some time.

"My father spoke German," the man suddenly announced. "He had learned it in the Austrian period. And during the war he was in Germany. In that other Germany."

He twisted his mouth into a conspiratorial smile.

"Hitler's Germany."

I asked what his father had done there. To myself, I pegged him as an SS veteran – the conversation with Ivan Mamchur was still fresh in my mind.

"He worked in a mine. Later he was in prison. When the Germans released him, he went back to Lviv."

I nodded, without understanding.

"Back then there was this kind of programme. Young Ukrainians were transported to Germany, to work."

Finally I understood. "Your father was a forced labourer?"

He nodded. "Exactly. That's what they called them."

While I was searching for a response, he inclined his upper body a little further in my direction.

"You know, I have to tell you one thing."

I looked at him expectantly.

"I am convinced that the world would be a better place if there were no Jews in it."

It took me a few moments to digest this sentence – to process the idea that the presumed son of an SS veteran had transformed into the anti-Semitic son of a Nazi victim right before my eyes.

"Then you have chosen the wrong person to talk to," I said once I'd got a grip on myself.

He looked at me in surprise. "You're a Jew?"

I could feel the anger rising inside me.

"No. One doesn't have to be a Jew to disagree with your opinion."

For a few seconds, he stared silently into his beer mug. When he raised his head, his face was as expressionless as it had been at the very beginning.

"You know, it's strange, somehow there are always problems, when the Jews…"

"You won't convince me."

"Whenever the Jews…"

"You're talking to the wrong person."

He looked at me in silence. Then he pushed his chair back abruptly, picked up his half-full beer mug and left.

6

Dr. Stumpp Celebrates
a Sad Christmas

Berdychiv, 1941

BETWEEN 1941 AND 1943, a man who is no longer young, but not yet old, travels through the Ukrainian Soviet Republic. In his luggage, the German researcher carries racial registration forms – his so-called *Sippenkarten*. He travels from village to village, looking for ethnic German inhabitants, to whom he presents his questionnaires.

Along the way, in a spare hour, the researcher indulges in the small pleasure of filling out one of the cards himself.

Family name: Stumpp, Dr.
First name: Karl
Date of birth: May 12, 1896
Place of birth: Alexanderhilf
Height: 1.82 metres
Hair colour: dark blond
Eye colour: grey
Race: "nordisch-westisch"

At the end of the form, Dr. Karl Stumpp modestly places

himself in the *Rassenwertungsklasse* 2, the second-highest category in his scheme of racial valuation. The fact that he had once suffered a bout of tuberculosis, which he does not conceal on the form, must be why he does not place himself in the top class.

Stumpp's trip to Ukraine is in some ways a homecoming. Alexanderhilf, the village where he grew up, is located near Odessa. The researcher is a Ukrainian German; his ancestors were among those immigrants who in the eighteenth century streamed into the Russian Empire, at the invitation of Catherine the Great. In order to populate her newly conquered lands on the Volga, the western shore of the Dnieper, and the Black Sea, the Empress recruited settlers from Western Europe. Tens of thousands of land-seeking German farmers had answered her call, including Stumpp's ancestors.

By the time he returns there, the explorer has not seen his Ukrainian homeland for over twenty years. Along with the retreating German troops, Stumpp had left the Black Sea coast behind him during the First World War, fleeing from the Soviet army. He ended up in Tübingen, where he studied geography and received his doctorate for his work on the German settlements in the Black Sea region. For the next ten years he taught at a girls' school in Romania, where he also found the time to publish academic studies about the history of the Germans in Bessarabia, thus laying the foundation for his future academic career.

Stumpp's big moment came when the National Socialists seized power. Leaving Romania behind, he returned *Heim ins Reich* in 1933, where he quickly became the leading expert on German culture abroad. He knew about the National Socialists' desire to push east, those dreams of German expansion that Hitler had harboured since the twenties. Earlier than most, Stumpp must have guessed that his ethnic German compatriots in Ukraine would play a pioneering role in the Nazis' plans for conquest. Did his heart beat faster when he read what Hitler wrote in *Mein Kampf*? "But when we speak of new territory in Europe today," the party leader had typed on the keys of a typewriter in his Bavarian prison cell in 1924, "we must principally think of Russia and the border states subject to her."

Throughout the thirties Stumpp campaigned tirelessly for the cause of the Ukrainian and Russian Germans. Based in Stuttgart, where he worked for the *Deutsches Ausland-Institut*, he built up a card index of genealogical data, with the aim of cataloguing the German settlements in Eastern Europe.

Now that Germany's desire to push east has become a reality, Stumpp returns to Ukraine in the wake of the Wehrmacht. He is accompanied by an eighty-member research unit, the *Sonderkommando Dr. Stumpp*, whose members criss-cross occupied Ukraine over the next two years, going from village to village and door to door, looking for ethnic German residents, to whom Stumpp and his team present their racial profiling cards.

Their expedition is part of the *Generalplan Ost*, whose implementation in Ukraine is personally being supervised by the head of the SS, Heinrich Himmler, who is quartered in a bunker near Zhytomyr. While the Wehrmacht advances eastward, deeper into the Soviet Union, the plans that Hitler had outlined in *Mein Kampf* are already being implemented west of the front: Ukraine is being converted into the new German *Lebensraum*. Stumpp's unit is part of a whole army of German scientists who move through the conquered eastern territories beginning in 1941, to lay the foundation of the Reich. In the near future, they hope, the black earth of Ukraine will be ploughed by German settlers.

Until that happens, ethnic German Ukrainians are expected to till the soil. The freshly arrived academic battalion builds schools for them, hospitals, newspapers, youth organisations, and women's groups. South of Zhytomyr, near Himmler's bunker, an entire German city springs up, the model settlement Hegewald, where more than forty thousand *Volksdeutsche* are relocated, about one-tenth of the ethnic German population living in Soviet Ukraine at the time of occupation.

Stumpp's assignment is to locate the Germans. His unit is supposed to unravel the demographic tangle of Ukraine, to reorganise villages, classify people, separate the Germans from the non-Germans. Stumpp soon realises this is no easy task. The Ukraine which he re-encounters in 1941 is no longer the Ukraine which he left behind in the First World War. Two decades of Soviet rule have turned the region upside-down, and the profound changes have not failed to leave their mark on the ethnic German population. Many have learned to adapt to the new regime. Communist banners adorn their peasant huts, and not everyone enthusiastically exchanges their wall decorations for the portraits of the Führer that Stumpp's assistants distribute around the villages.

Many of the German settlements do not correspond to the ideal image that Stumpp has propagated in Germany during the thirties. Himmler's SS troops, who Stumpp's unit reports to, expected to find village communities in Ukraine whose orderliness and love of work would set them apart, at first sight, from their "sub-human" Slavic neighbours; villages inhabited only by Germans, who speak German, celebrate German holidays, and sing German songs. In actual fact, the SS is often confronted with poor, dilapidated huts, whose inhabitants are the offspring of mixed marriages, or live in such relationships themselves. In their veins, German blood mingles with Ukrainian, Polish, and Jewish, and when questioned in German, they can often only respond haltingly in their "native" tongue.

"We don't think much of your ethnic Germans," an SS officer tells one of Stumpp's team shortly after the start of the Ukraine mission. Parts of the leadership in Berlin seem to share this scepticism, which becomes apparent to Stumpp when Hermann Göring publicly suggests shooting the male population of Ukraine indiscriminately and letting "the stallions of the SS" loose on the remaining women, in order to father German offspring. Even in the ranks of his own unit, Stumpp sometimes senses doubts about the value of their mission – in some villages the German inhabitants and their Slavic neighbours are so similar that the scientists have to rely on speculations about the shape of eyelids and chin lines in order to be able to fill in their racial profiling cards.

Even Stumpp himself occasionally seems to despair of his work. He experiences his personal low point on December 24 in the war year of 1941. In the Central Ukrainian city of Berdychiv, he celebrates Christmas as the guest of an ethnic German family. The break does not turn out well for the researcher. In a disappointed letter to Germany, Stumpp writes that nowhere in Berdychiv was there any sugar or flour to be found, meaning he could not enjoy his beloved German *Lebkuchen* gingerbread at the party. Nor did his host family bother to decorate the Christmas tree, be it out of poverty or cultural negligence. "I found it very depressing," Stumpp complains. But the worst was yet to come: "The children stood around the tree and sang Ukrainian songs."

Stumpp confesses such weak moments only in his private correspondence; outwardly he unwaveringly champions the cause of the ethnic Germans. To the doubters in the SS, he objects, not unreasonably, that it was the persecution by the Soviet regime that brought the German minority to its lamentable state – German schools, churches, and newspapers have been closed and abolished, while almost every family was mourning executed, deported, or otherwise liquidated relatives; many survivors had to lie about their German roots in order to save their lives.

Does Stumpp make the case for the ethnic Germans because he worries about his academic reputation? Or because he fears for his compatriots? He knows that during the war years his racial profile cards have an immediate bearing on people's fates. His unit grades Ukrainian Germans into four different categories on a descending scale – depending on their racial purity, entire village populations are declared either suitable *Übermensch* material, or re-educable problem cases, or ethnically contaminated rejects who must share the fate of the Slavic population: expulsion, enslavement, extermination.

Stumpp's standards differ from those of the SS. As long as he can detect even just one drop of German blood, Germans remain Germans for him, even if they have forgotten the songs of their homeland and no longer know how to bake German Christmas treats. Stumpp's work, some people claim with hindsight about the war years, therefore saved lives.

But only select lives. At the expense of others.

The Ukrainian city of Berdychiv, where Stumpp celebrated his sad Christmas of 1941, had almost seventy thousand inhabitants before the war. According to Stumpp's lists, there were only twenty-six ethnic German families among them. The far larger part of the population, a little more than half, were Jewish. Of these Jews, twenty thousand were already missing when Stumpp visited the city in December. The SS had shot them just before his arrival. In his letter lamenting the lack of *Lebkuchen*, the German researcher did not say a word about these executions, or about the ghetto in which Berdychiv's remaining Jews were starving during the Christmas celebrations.

Nor did Stumpp comment on the murder of the Ukrainian Jews anywhere else, even though it took place right in front of his eyes – and even though his lists meticulously recorded it. He and his staff worked in Ukraine for a good year and a half, from late 1941 to early 1943. They visited many villages more than once during this period, in order to document changes in the population structure. In addition to the ethnic Germans, their lists also included the other ethnic groups of Ukraine, among them the Jews. In the town of Sume, for example, Stumpp's staff had found 4,818 Jews in 1941; a year later, there were only five of them left. Of Horodnitsa's 3,795 Jews, eleven were left, and nine of Slovechno's 5,600. In Radomishl, where 5,840 Jews had once lived, and in Malin, where the number had been 8,745, Stumpp's staff did not register a single one in 1942.

The Jews disappeared from Stumpp's lists without trace. Where were they? Why were their houses empty, and how could their furniture, their clothes, all of their possessions be distributed to the ethnic Germans by Stumpp's unit? How far was Stumpp aware of what had happened to the Jews? Did he see them dying? Did he take part in the killings himself, as an American intelligence official later claimed? Or did Stumpp simply look away, glad that he did not have to lend a hand himself in the "liberation of Europe from the Bolshevik Jewish plague", which he wrote about in a diary entry?

When the war ended, Ukraine was no longer the region it had been before the war. Gone was the ethnic jumble of its villages, gone the Polish-Yiddish-German-Czech-Romanian-Hungarian babel of voices.

Gone too was the total incomprehension that many farmers had displayed as late as the turn of the century when asked what ethnic group they belonged to, for even though they could name their language, their faith, and their home village, they had no idea what the townspeople meant by "nationality".

It was only after Lenin's October Revolution, when the first Soviet planners passed through the Ukrainian villages, that a drawn-out, disastrous process of ethnic disentangling and human sorting began, which would be perverted by the Nazis during the war and was to find its tragic conclusion after Stalin's victory.

The beginnings of this process seemed quite promising.

In the twenties the Soviets, still giddy with the future-embracing fever of the early Lenin years, granted Ukraine the principle of national self-government, in order to end the repressive social order of the Tsarist era – never again should Polish landowners rule over Ukrainian farmers; henceforth classless Ukrainians, Poles, Germans, Romanians, and Czechs would govern their own Soviet administrative districts.

When sorting the rural population of Ukraine into their various ethnicities, the Soviet planners encountered problems very similar to those that would later bother Dr. Stumpp and his research unit: many families were ethnically mixed, a farmer could hardly tell what nationality he belonged to, and the boundaries between peoples were not clearly drawn. But as the newly established administrative units were equipped with schools, hospitals, newspapers, and cultural institutions for their respective minorities, people soon began to assign themselves voluntarily to one or another ethnic group. This gave rise to that "perfect and almost exaggerated national autonomy" which international observers such as the writer Joseph Roth found so inspiring in the twenties.

But once the frenzy of the early Soviet years had died down, the planners became fearful of their own work. The revolution had failed to spread to the rest of the world, as Lenin had predicted it would. On the contrary, increasingly reactionary regimes had formed on the western borders of the Soviet Union, which declared Communism their mortal enemy. In the late twenties Stalin began, with characteristic paranoia, to perceive the nationally administered districts of Ukraine as a gateway for foreign powers: what if agents of fascist Berlin infiltrated the ethnic German raions of Ukraine? What if Polish, Romanian, and Czech nationalists gave their Ukrainian compatriots the wrong ideas? Stalin answered these questions in his own mind with deportations and repressions. Tens of thousands of members of Ukraine's minorities were forcibly relocated to other parts of the Soviet Union; their schools, their newspapers, and their cultural institutions were shut down. Systematically the rulers in Moscow now fought the nationalities that only a decade earlier they themselves had, in a sense, called into being.

When the Nazis invaded, the second phase of the Ukrainian purges began, seamlessly picking up where the first had stopped. The demographic statistics which the Soviet planners had used to sort the nationalities of Ukraine twenty years earlier now helped Stumpp's unit in their search for ethnic Germans – and the SS in their search for Jews. When the Germans withdrew two years later, a large part of the Jewish population had disappeared from Ukraine. Approximately one and a half million had been killed; half a million had fled.

Those ethnic Germans who had not already been deported to Siberia and Central Asia were expelled from the Soviet Union collectively at the end of the war. At the same time Stalin, with the consent of the other victorious powers, reorganised Europe's borders. Poland shifted to the left on the map; it gained the eastern part of the German Reich and lost the western part of Ukraine. Then Stalin used the ongoing hostilities between Poles and Ukrainians as a welcome opportunity to usher in the last phase of the Ukrainian purges. After the war he forcibly expelled eight hundred and fifty thousand Poles from the Ukrainian Soviet republic into Polish territory, while half a million Ukrainians were driven out of Poland into the Soviet Union.

After that, the multilingual, multiethnic region that Ukraine had been in the pre-war years was finally and irretrievably gone. Its minorities were dead or scattered to the winds, its languages forgotten, its national districts disbanded. For the first time in their history, the Ukrainians now occupied their part of the earth mostly on their own. However, they were now citizens of a state that would never again engage in experiments with national self-government.

Gone, also, was that Ukraine in whose western part Joseph Roth, the writer from Galicia, had been raised. "Only against one's better judgment," Roth had written about his home in 1928, could a person "force oneself to accept that naive view that the nations of Europe live in neatly separated geographical areas, like on a chessboard." It would only take two decades for Roth's "naive view" to become a European reality.

Dr. Karl Stumpp, whose role in the Ukrainian chess match had been small, but not insignificant, lived in Stuttgart after the war, undisturbed. With some academic success, he continued his research into the history of the ethnic Germans abroad, for which the data that he had been able to gather in Ukraine during the war proved very valuable. In addition, Stumpp ran the *Landsmannschaft* of Russian Germans, under whose umbrella all those who had been expelled from the Soviet Union rallied after the war. The researcher also found the time to establish two ethnic German societies in Nebraska and North Dakota, where to this day those of German descent can still make use of his registration lists from the war to reconstruct their family histories.

In 1966, Stumpp was awarded the First Class Order of Merit, Germany's highest state decoration, for his service to Germans abroad. The Institute for Foreign Relations and the German division of the Red Cross later honoured him with further accolades. When Dr. Karl Stumpp died peacefully in Stuttgart in 1982, the world regarded him as an honourable man.

Stumpp's former employer, the *Deutsches Ausland-Institut*, also continued its work after the war, under a new name and with a change of focus, but in the same building in Stuttgart.

Outside the main entrance of the baroque building there is a flight of thirteen steps which, in the summer of 2003, twenty years after Stumpp's death, a young man in an ill-fitting suit ascended. He entered the premises of the Institute for Foreign Relations, as the organisation now calls itself, in a state of high anxiety. He was about to undergo a job interview.

He was hired. The organisation sent him to Moscow, where he worked for two years as editor of a German newspaper. It was the first stop on a professional journey that would take the young man all over Eastern Europe.

The young man had never heard of Dr. Karl Stumpp when he climbed the thirteen front steps of the building that summer day in 2003. Equally alien to him was the history of the Institute, which frankly did not interest him very much; he just wanted to go to Moscow. The fact that his interview took place in the same building, maybe even in the same room where Karl Stumpp had begun his racial studies of the Ukrainian Germans seventy years earlier; that both of them, Stumpp and he, had followed an inner urge to go east, driven of course by different motives, but perhaps by a similar ambition; that institutions outlast ideologies and that people are prone to forget this – all of this became clear to the young man only twelve years later, when he journeyed across Ukraine in Stumpp's footsteps.

That young man was me.

7

Scrape Your Strings Darker

Chernivtsi

IN THE OLD JEWISH CEMETERY of Chernivtsi, the September sun had warmed the stones. They were overgrown with brambles, in whose shadows lurked millions of red bugs. When I pushed some of the spiny stems aside to read an inscription, the bugs dispersed frantically, and teeming columns of red dots began crawling over the Hebrew, Latin, and Cyrillic letters on the gravestones.

HIER RUHT IRO MORCHE FRÖHLICH
3. XII. 1882–13. II. 1919
(Here rests Iro Morche Fröhlich)

HIER RUHT PEPI BERGMANN GEB. TRICHTER
GEST. 5. NOVEMBER 1925 IM 38. LEBENSJAHR
(Here rests Pepi Bergmann, née Trichter, died November 5, 1925, at the age of 38)

HIER RUHT CHAJE BIRNBAUM AUS SNJATYN
GEST. 29.11.1924 IM 58. LEBENSJAHR
(Here rests Chaje Birnbaum from Snjatyn, died November 29, 1924, at the age of 58)

HIER RUHT DAVID TITTINGER
KAISERLICHER RATH, REICHSRATHS- UND
LANDTAGSABGEORDNETER,
PRÄSIDENT DER CZERNOWITZER FRUCHT- UND
PRODUKTENBÖRSE,
VIZEPRÄSIDENT DER BUKOWINER HANDELS-
UND GEWERBEKAMMER,
MITGLIED DES GEMEINDERATHES DER
LANDESHAUPTSTADT CZERNOWITZ
UND DES VORSTANDES DER ISRAELITISCHEN
CULTUSGEMEINDE
GEBOREN IN SUCZAWA AM 3. FEBRUAR 1839
GESTORBEN IN CZERNOWITZ AM 29. MAI 1900
*(Here rests David Tittinger, Councillor to the Kaiser,
Deputy of the Imperial and State Parliaments, President
of the Czernowitz Fruit and Groceries Exchange, Vice-
President of the Bukovinian Chamber of Commerce and
Industry, Member of the Town Council of Czernowitz
and Chairman of the Israelite Religious Community, born
in Suczawa on February 3, 1839, died in Czernowitz on
May 29, 1900)*

ANTOINETTE ONITZKANSKI GEB. TITTINGER
1. IV. 1850–19. III. 1926
(Antoinette Onitzkanski, née Tittinger)

OBERBEZIRKSRAT DR. HERMANN TITTINGER
RITTER D. FRANZ JOSEF ORDENS U. BES. D.
GOLD. VERDIENSTKREUZES M.D.K.
11. XI. 1851–21. VI. 1932
(Senior District Councilman Dr. Hermann Tittinger,

Knight of the Franz Josef Order and Bearer of the Golden
Merit Cross with a Crown)

REGINA METSCH
DIE AM 23. SEPT. 1931 EINEM RUCHLOSEN
MORDE ZUM OPFER FIEL
(Regina Metsch, who fell victim to a heinous murder on
September 23, 1931)

The cemetery is large. On a hill above the town, there are rows and rows of headstones, stretching so far and so wide that from any given point you cannot see where the cemetery ends. It would take hours and days to walk along all the horizontal and vertical rows, and only at the end would you begin to have an idea of how Jewish the old Chernivtsi was.

But even more numerous are the graves that are missing. For a long time I searched for inscriptions from the war years, until I realised how foolish that was. The murdered Jews of the German-Romanian occupation era could have filled a second, a third, a tenth cemetery, but they had not been laid to rest in Chernivtsi, or anywhere else. Their bodies remained unburied, like those of the married couple Leo and Friederike Antschel, to whose death no stone bears witness, only a poem, written in the language of their murderers.

Paul Antschel was born in Romanian Cernăuți in 1920. Before he died, he would change his surname twice and his nationality once. In the same period, the name of his birthplace changed three times, and then once more after Antschel had taken his own life.

The city had just made the first change when Leo Antschel and his wife Friederike announced the birth of their first – and only – child in 1920. The couple had fallen in love while Cernăuți was called Czernowitz and belonged to the more remote parts of the Habsburg Empire. Technically, the Austrians were in charge, but in the entanglement of Jewish-Ukrainian-German-Romanian-Polish-Armenian nationalities in the Bukovina, where every cobbler's son had mastered three languages and five dialects, that was something hardly anyone noticed.

Paul Antschel spoke German at home, which his literature-loving mother had enforced against the will of his father, who had pleaded unsuccessfully for Hebrew, in a dispute most likely conducted in Yiddish. The son spoke Hebrew in elementary school, before moving on to a Romanian grammar school, only to graduate from a Ukrainian one later.

He grew up among those "flute-blowing mountain shepherds, perfumed and garlic-chewing operetta officers, Chagallian Hasidim with long sidelocks under their black hats, spur-jingling Romanian soldiers and industrious German burghers", whom Gregor von Rezzori, born six years before Antschel, a writer whose Sicilian ancestors had arrived in the eclectic world of the Bukovina via Vienna, recalled in his Chernivtsi memoirs. The Romanians' rise to power after the First World War, von Rezzori wrote, had not been taken very seriously by anyone in Czernowitz – it was attributed about the same importance as a set change in the local operetta theatre.

When Hitler and Stalin carved up Central Europe between themselves twenty years later in their pact of

1939, the Soviet Union took command in Cernăuţi, and its inhabitants had to get used to the Russian name Chernovtsy. Initially some Czernowitzers may have thought this changing of the guard was nothing but another new operetta setting. But very soon the spectator stands started to empty eerily.

The first who had to go were around twenty-five thousand Germans and Austrians, about one-sixth of the city's population at the time, whose removal Hitler and Stalin had agreed upon. Gregor von Rezzori's family too was among those who were resettled behind the German front under the slogan *Heim ins Reich*. About the same time, a few thousand "class enemies", most of them Jews, left Chernovtsy in an easterly direction, packed by NKVD officers into freight cars that did not stop again until Siberia. Afraid of landing up there as well, parts of the Romanian upper class fled to Bucharest.

Paul Antschel, who had recently started his studies in Romance languages, remained in the city with his parents for the time being. He would regret this decision for the rest of his life. Chernovtsy became Cernăuţi again in July 1941, when Romania, which in the meantime had allied itself with Nazi Germany, reconquered the city. More than half the population was Jewish at that time. The Antschel family ended up in the ghetto together, but they would leave separately. The occupying forces transferred the son to a Romanian labour camp and his parents to a Transnistrian concentration camp, where his father died of typhoid fever and his mother was shot.

Freed from the camp by Soviet troops shortly before the end of the war, Paul Antschel returned in 1944 to his hometown, which now bore the Russian name Chernovtsy again. In conversations with friends he re-encountered at university he talked about his agonising self-blame – he could not shake the feeling he had abandoned his parents. Antschel was working on a poem at that time, a poem whose German verses he would later refer to as the tombstone that had been denied to his murdered parents.

> ... scrape your strings darker you'll rise then in smoke to the sky
> you'll have a grave in the clouds there you won't lie too cramped...

"Antschel" became "Ancel" when the poet moved to Bucharest in 1945 to continue his studies. A few years later he fled to Paris, where he inverted the syllables of the Romanian version of his surname to form his pen-name.

Today, the former town of Czernowitz lies on the southern edge of the Ukrainian Bukovina and is called Chernivtsi. Paul Antschel lies in the Cimetière de Thiais in Paris, and his gravestone bears the name Paul Celan.

When the drowned author of the poem *Todesfuge* ("Death Fugue") was recovered from a fishing net in the Seine on May 1, 1970, hardly anyone in Soviet Chernovtsy got the news. He was the city's most famous son, but the city knew nothing about him. Celan had become renowned in a foreign country, under an assumed name, on the other side of the Iron Curtain, which was about as far away from the Soviet Union as the moon. German-speaking exiled poets seldom appeared in the party newspapers, and in Celan's hometown few were left who could remember the student Paul Antschel.

Almost half a century passed before the house where Celan had been born was decorated with a memorial plaque, and the small bust of the poet, which I passed by on Vulitsa Golovna, the former Main Street, had only existed for a few years.

I walked through Ukrainian Chernivtsi with the irritating feeling that I was visiting a prop warehouse where, for whatever reason, the sets of a play that was no longer performed were being stored. Everything was still there, everything was well maintained and in working order – the baroque churches, the vine-covered town houses with the Habsburg coat of arms on their pediments, the winding cobbled streets, the old hotels, the coffee houses. But all these architectural elements looked like the legacies of a strange, submerged culture which, beyond their obvious beauty, had no discernible significance for today's Chernivtsi. Unlike Lviv, whose inhabitants had proudly appropriated the historical heritage of their city, there seemed to be an unbridgeable gap here between the past and present.

"The whole city has left."

Bronislav Tutelman counted the emigrants on the fingers of his left hand.

"My brother – in Israel. My wife – in America, together with our son. Our second son – Israel. My cousins – America, Israel, Europe..."

Tutelman was one of the few Jews who had not left Chernivtsi. By his estimate, less than fifteen hundred of them remained.

We sat in the smoky conservatory of his apartment. A

mutual friend from Berlin had brought us together. Tutelman was in his mid-sixties, a tiny man with a snow-white stubble. He wore a tracksuit which had seen better days, and although the sunlight only dimly penetrated the smoke of his contraband Moldovan cigarettes, his photochromic glasses never brightened up completely.

His apartment had to have been a palace once. The parquet creaked under our shoes as Tutelman showed me the four huge rooms where he had lived alone since the departure of his family. Opulent, ornately tiled stoves ended just below the stuccoed ceilings, which were so high that they made the short Tutelman look like a white-haired child. The rooms had retained the splendid atmosphere of the Austrian Empire; not even the Soviet furniture had been able to dispel it.

There were pictures hanging and lying around all over the place. Throughout his entire life, Tutelman had painted and photographed. He had been an artist even in the Soviet era, a member of Chernivtsi's tiny dissident scene. I saw colourful street scenes reminiscent of Chagall, interspersed with more abstract, monochrome drawings and collage-like conceptual art. Even more than the paintings, it was the photos that I found myself drawn to. For decades, Tutelman had roamed with his camera through the old Jewish cemetery, details of whose weathered tombstones decorated his apartment in their hundreds. He must have known the cemetery grounds better than anyone else in Chernivtsi, although he told me that even he still came across overgrown corners he had never seen before.

What kept him in Chernivtsi was difficult to put into words. His parents, who had been born here about the same time as Paul Celan and Gregor von Rezzori, had survived the Holocaust because they fled to Central Asia during the war. When they returned to the Bukovina, many of their Jewish neighbours were just packing their bags – shortly after the war, departure from the Soviet Union was still possible, and many doubted whether life under Stalin would really be any better than under Hitler. It was the first of three waves of emigration, during which Chernivtsi lost the surviving part of its Jewish population in the postwar period.

When Tutelman was born in 1950, his parents were already living in the apartment whose conservatory we were sitting in. The bourgeois quarters had been converted into a communal apartment occupied by several families, each of which shared a room. At that time, Tutelman estimated, about two-thirds of the inhabitants in the house had been Jews.

"As a child I would stand on the balcony for hours and listen to the neighbours, who talked in Yiddish from balustrade to balustrade," he recalled. "You still heard Yiddish everywhere in the city, and my parents spoke it among themselves. Only Hebrew was taboo – that was the language of the Zionists, so you could get into trouble speaking it."

A second wave of emigrants began to move in the seventies, when international pressure eased the travel restrictions for Jews in the Soviet Union. Tutelman had then seen entire streets disappear toward Israel. The majority of those remaining, including his family, finally left Chernivtsi during the chaotic years after the collapse of the Soviet Union.

Tutelman lit a fresh cigarette. The smoke drifted towards the window, where diagonal sunbeams cut it into sharp-edged white patterns.

"Nowadays, I am the only Jew in the whole house," he said. "When I walk through the streets, at every turn I think: somebody used to live over there; there's another one missing back there; here, everybody is gone."

Had I said goodbye to Tutelman at this point, he would have remained in my mind just a lonely old man. But nothing was further from the truth, which I understood shortly afterwards when we left the apartment together. Just a few steps from the house, we turned into a pedestrian zone, the old Vulitsa Panska, which had been called Herrengasse in Austrian times. We had barely swung our way into the stream of pedestrians when it started. Every few metres someone came dashing up to us. Tutelman was welcomed boisterously, forced to shake hands, exchange kisses on the cheek, dispense compliments, receive news, transmit greetings, offer wedding congratulations, formulate condolences, gaze in wonder at newborns. He seemed to know half the town.

"But that's nothing!" he protested when I asked him about it. "You should have seen how it used to be, before everyone left. Back then it took me three hours to walk to the end of the street!"

Later in the afternoon we sat at an outdoor cafe. We had ordered vodka and drank it while eating *salo* – white lard cut in thin slices, the national dish of Ukraine. Even the more religious among the Ukrainian Jews, Tutelman said grinning, would forget about their kosher diet when you put *salo* in front of them.

"The emigrants in Israel have their relatives bring suitcases full of the stuff from Ukraine."

After his third vodka he started to talk about his dissident days, about the time when two flights daily had departed from Chernovtsy via Kiev to Moscow, and a ticket had cost little more than a decent drinking spree. Back then he had constantly sat in the Moscow kitchens of like-minded artists, some of whom he was still in contact with, although they rarely saw each other now that the flight connections had become irregular and more expensive.

Tutelman had never learned Ukrainian. His world had been the Russian-speaking dissident scene. Nevertheless, in the conflict with Russia he was vehemently on the side of the Ukrainians, because he considered Moscow's new chauvinism to be a continuation of the old Soviet imperialism which he had hated all his life.

"We are stopping Moscow's advance on the West with Ukrainian blood," he said.

After his fifth vodka he found his way back to his sentimental views about the city. Chernivtsi was growing more and more provincial, he complained. The old people had left, and the ones who had replaced them had no connection to the city. He cursed the newcomers from the Ukrainian countryside, who yanked everything out of the old apartments that was beautiful about them – the tiled stoves, the stucco, the parquet. He complained about narrow-minded Ukrainian intellectuals, who had no use for the Jewish-Austrian culture of the old Czernowitz, who were not interested in writers like Paul Celan and Gregor von Rezzori because they were not Ukrainian, because they had not written in Ukrainian.

"The whole city has emigrated," he repeated. "The Chernivtsi I knew exists now only in my apartment."

As I listened to him, I could not help thinking about a

series of photos that he had shown me a few hours earlier. Over the years, Tutelman had photographed his small, overgrown balcony from an unvarying perspective. The seasons changed, the vines were sometimes snow-covered, sometimes bright green, sometimes tinged with autumn colours, but always it was the same old balcony that hung above the same old town.

When I recalled the images, I sensed that I suddenly understood what bound Bronislav Tutelman to his home town. The old Czernowitz had shrunk to the size of four rooms. He was the last occupant, and deep in his heart he seemed to have decided to take the city with him to his grave.

"To where? Germany?"

The woman behind the post-office counter looked at me with a startled expression. I had asked for stamps.

She stood up and cupped her hands around her mouth. Her shout rang out through the emptiness of the old post office hall.

"Iriiiiiiina!"

Irina was young and blonde and experienced in matters of international shipping. She took the unwritten postcards from my hands and led me to a sales counter that was completely covered with sheets of stamps.

"But you will have to send the cards today. You hear me?"

I looked at her, uncomprehending.

"The exchange rate! I can sell you the appropriate stamps today, but no one knows whether the international postage will be the same tomorrow."

I understood. News about the faltering national currency had accompanied my journey.

With the tips of her long fingernails, Irina tapped a few numbers on her calculator. It took a quarter of an hour for her to piece together the appropriate values, separate the stamps from the sheets, and allocate seven to each postcard respectively. By the end, the cards were very colourful and almost completely pasted over.

Irina beamed.

"There you go! The address will still fit."

I left Chernivtsi by train for Vinnytsia.

Half an hour after my departure, my phone began to buzz. Three consecutive text messages welcomed me first to Moldova, then to Ukraine, and then again to Moldova.

The conductor answered my question with a meandering gesture. The tracks, he told me, ran partly north, partly south of the border. On two short sections the train travelled through Moldovan territory.

"When the route was constructed here, there was no Moldova," he said, smiling. "And no Ukraine."

Shortly after that, the fourth text message arrived. Welcome to Ukraine, I read. Welcome to a country, I thought, whose railway lines are older than its borders.

8

The Miracle of Kalynivka

Vinnytsia–Kalynivka

YOU COULD TELL how much time had passed by looking at the trees. Pines and birches had taken root between the concrete rubble, and in the knee-high grass the fruit from an apple tree was rotting. Almost exactly seventy years ago the seeds of these trees must have sprouted, shortly after three powerful explosions had churned up the forest floor.

The old bunker area was surrounded by taller, older pines, which had already been there when the Germans arrived in November, 1941, and had ordered a clearing to be made in the forest. North of the city of Vinnytsia, a few hundred Ukrainian forced labourers lowered three concrete shelters into the ground: one for the soldiers, one for the officers, one for the Führer.

A sign at the entrance to the site read "Hauptquartier Werwolf". It had been converted into an open-air museum a few years earlier. I was the only visitor. The needle-covered forest floor swallowed the sound of my footsteps. Nothing could be heard in the silence except the songs of birds. Each time I bit into the apple I had picked while passing one of the trees, I was startled by the eerily loud crunching sound it made.

Three times Hitler had spent the night in his Werewolf's lair. Of all the headquarters which he used during the war years, this was the easternmost one. During his first visit, in the high summer months of 1942, such an oppressive heat had built up in the underground chambers that the Werewolf caught a viral infection and had to direct his troop movements with a fever of almost forty degrees. Hitler made sure to arrange his two visits in the following year during the cooler seasons.

When the Red Army was advancing on Vinnytsia in March, 1944, the Germans destroyed the entire complex. The wooden structures above ground were burned, the bunkers blown up. Today, only concrete fragments and bent metal rods protrude from the rough forest floor.

The swimming pool alone remains intact. I was on my way to the exit when I discovered it. The rectangular concrete basin was set into the forest floor under the open sky, growing slightly deeper towards the front end. It looked remarkably well-preserved, as if the water had been drained out only yesterday.

For several minutes I stood at the concrete edge and stared into the empty basin where seventy-three years earlier, who knows, Adolf Hitler may have cooled his pale, feverish Führer's body.

The train from Chernivtsi to Vinnytsia had taken me to that part of Ukraine which, unlike the regions I had seen so far, had been under Russian influence since way before the Second World War. Central Ukraine had become part of the Soviet Union a generation and a World War earlier than the Western part of the country, and prior to that, before

Lenin's revolution, it had not belonged to the Habsburg Empire, but to the realm of the Muscovite Tsars.

I was having a hard time trying to square these different historical backgrounds with the everyday reality in both parts of the country. The differences in architecture were reasonably easy to recognise – the Austrian influences were missing in Central Ukraine. But were there also differences to be noted in the people? I got the impression that in Vinnytsia, more Russian was spoken in the street, but I wasn't sure. When travelling by bus, I imagined there was less Ukrainian music played on the radio, but I could have been mistaken. It seemed to me that the coffee had become worse, but maybe I was just drinking it in the wrong places.

The first unambiguous difference caught my eye in the Town Hall square of Kalynivka, a small town north of Vinnytsia. In front of the concrete administration building there was the pedestal of a monument. The monument itself, however, was missing. I had seen enough Soviet town squares in my life to know who should have been standing on the pedestal: Lenin.

The revolutionary leader seemed to have disappeared not very long ago; apparently the statue had been toppled after the clashes on Maidan Square in Kiev. On the front side of the orphaned pedestal, someone had painted the figure of a shot-down demonstrator, with large white angel wings. On the back, facing the Town Hall, were the words: "Power is not eternal!", and underneath, painted in the national colours of blue and yellow, an old slogan of the Bandera Movement: "Ukraine above all!"

In the further course of my journey, empty pedestals like the one in Kalynivka would become a familiar sight.

Hundreds of Lenin monuments had been toppled in the past months. But only in retrospect did I notice that I had not seen any such vacant pedestals in Western Ukraine. Not because there had not been any Lenin statues – after the war, with the advance of Soviet power, every town hall square between Lviv and Chernivtsi had been duly decorated with likenesses of the communist leader. But people in Western Ukraine had dismantled these monuments in the nineties, immediately after the Soviet demise, along with their pedestals. The part of the country where Lenin had arrived last had been the first to drive him out again.

Kalynivka was small, and I quickly found what I was looking for: the cross.

Even from the street I could see it, inside a chapel with a roof that rested on glass walls. The cross rose to just below the ceiling. It was painted blue and had to be five, perhaps six metres tall. A Christ figure was painted on the wooden surface – the body stretched along the main beam, arms across the crossbeam, the pierced feet terminating where the slanting third beam of the Orthodox cross began. Painted blood streamed from a wound between Christ's ribs.

Once, so the legend went, real blood had sprung from this wooden wound.

In front of the chapel stood a covered well. Beside it, an old woman was fussing with flower pots. Her headscarf had slipped down her neck; she had frizzy, red-dyed hair with grey roots. When I addressed her, I wasn't sure whether she could see me or not – her eyes were milky and curiously unfocused.

"The cross? You don't know anything about the cross? God has brought us together! I'll tell you everything!"

When she said "everything", she meant "everything". She talked to me for a good half-hour, while I could only nod silently.

"Where should I begin? I worked in Italy. Then the cross called out to me! Great temptations had come over my children as a punishment for my sins. When I came to Kalynivka, I begged Father Volodymyr to let me stay. I wanted to work for him, as a cleaner, or a gardener, anything – I just wanted to be near the cross. I had to pray for my children; the cross would save them! Father Volodymyr did not want it. He thought I was possessed by the evil spirit, but I stayed anyway. Please do not tell Father Volodymyr that I have spoken to you, it is better not to mention that we met..."

Her narrative kept circling erratically around the same recurring motifs: her children, temptations, prayers. Inwardly, I had already given up hope of learning about the history of the cross from her, but eventually she started to talk about it.

"... It is old, our cross. It was already standing here before the infidels came. A man put it up because he was childless. He asked God: What must I do to avoid having lived in this world in vain? God told him to dig a well, so people would drink and pray for him. Beside it, he put up the cross. When he died, godless soldiers came. One shot at the Saviour, but the bullets fell to the ground, only the last one hit the target, and the Saviour's blood started to flow from the wound! From everywhere, people came to pray. The blind could see again, the dumb began to speak, the lame no longer needed their crutches. Scientists were sent. They examined the cross and found that the true blood of our Lord Jesus Christ flowed out of the wound, but you could not talk about it, it was forbidden..."

As she spoke, she moved closer and closer to me, until I could feel her rapid breath on my face.

"... Soon our cross will reveal its full power. I sense that it will happen soon, very soon! From all over the world people will flock to Kalynivka, there will be as many pilgrims as there are in Jerusalem, I know it. We are living in the last chapter of the gospel. Everything is a consequence of our sins, even the war in our country. We shout 'Glory to Ukraine' when we should be shouting 'Glory to God!' We think we have our lives in hand, but we are mistaken, because everything comes from God, including the temptations he sends my children as a punishment for my sins..."

I tentatively enquired what temptations she meant, but she wasn't about to desist from her monologue. In my mind I saw her children ending up on the wrong path, taking drugs, converting to Buddhism, discovering gay inclinations. But whatever actual or imagined temptations distressed their mother so, I never found out. Maybe she did not exactly know herself.

Before I took my leave of her, I asked where I could find Father Volodymyr. She gave me a long-winded explanation of how to get to the church.

"... But don't tell him I've talked to you. Don't mention me! Are you a believer? Baptized? You must get baptised as an Orthodox Christian, you understand? Only Orthodox, nothing else..."

For a while I listened as she kept talking, be it to herself or to me, as I set off along the dusty road.

"… Only Orthodox!"

There were two Orthodox churches in Kalynivka. One belonged to the Moscow Patriarchate, the other to the Kievan Patriarchate. Unfortunately, the old woman had not told me which of the two was the one where Father Volodymyr preached – and in which I should get baptised. It wasn't an easy choice. The two church hierarchies were not well disposed towards each other, and the war between Russia and Ukraine had not improved their relationship.

I found the Kievan Patriarchate Church first. It was closed, but there was a note with phone numbers on the front door. After a few attempts, I got the priest on the line.

"Father Volodymyr?"

"No. This is the other church."

"Forgive me. I am interested in the miracle of Kalynivka. Perhaps you would allow me to ask a few questions…?"

"The other church."

"I see. That's… you mean that your church doesn't recognise the miracle?"

For a moment, there was silence on the other end of the line.

"I did not say that," the priest replied coolly. "It is just that the cross is taken care of by the other church. Things just turned out that way."

The Church of the Moscow Patriarchate was at least three times larger than that of the Kievan Patriarchate. Father Volodymyr's voice filled it effortlessly. His booming, good humoured bass seemed to come from the depths of the colossal belly bulging beneath his cassock. A snow-white Santa Claus beard hung down to his chest; above it his plump red cheeks glowed. He looked like he'd stepped straight out of a Bolshevik propaganda poster – the laughing priest who fills his stomach at the expense of his starving flock.

"… Only a few small disagreements, nothing serious. Actually, here in Kalynivka we all get along very well!"

I had asked him about the church dispute. According to the Moscow Patriarchate, to which he belonged, the Orthodox Church in Ukraine was traditionally just a regional offshoot of Russian Orthodoxy. Resistance to this subordination had first arisen in the period between the world wars, when Ukrainian clerics had tried to establish a national church. Only much later, in the nineties, had this been half-successful – after the country's independence, a small proportion of the Ukrainian communities had renounced the Moscow Patriarchate and installed their own church leader.

"But no church in the world recognises the Kievan Patriarch," Father Volodymyr said, laughing. "Of course, that sometimes annoys my dear colleague here in Kalynivka a bit, which I completely understand! But that is how things are."

As I listened to him, I watched his monumental beard rise and fall before my eyes, and I had a hard time resisting the childish desire to reach out and touch the soft white hair.

"Of course he'd like it if more believers came to his church. That's what every priest wants, after all. But his church is new. Many people here have grown accustomed to ours. And as long as they are praying at all, it's not that important which church they do it in, is it? Glory to Ukraine, for all I care, but in worship, we glorify God!"

I asked him about the small memorial stone I had walked past in the churchyard. It paid tribute to the victims of the Holodomor, that artificially generated famine that Stalin had used in the thirties to murder millions of Ukrainian peasants. It was the kind of memorial you would more likely encounter next to churches of the Kievan Patriarchate.

"Actually, it was supposed to be placed beside City Hall," Father Volodymyr said. "But who would notice it there? Who would stop and pray for the dead? I spoke to the people in charge, and we agreed to place the stone next to the church. During our services, we pray for the Holodomor victims anyway, so it's better off here."

I liked Father Volodymyr. But I could see how the other priest must have hated him. In his affable way, he had monopolised the city. It wasn't just the miraculous cross that belonged to him – he had also hijacked the Holodomor commemoration.

He came from the Carpathians. In the western Ukrainian regions, which had only become part of the Soviet Union after the war, the religious persecution had not been as bad as in the rest of the country, he explained.

"There were monasteries. There were churches. There were services. One of my great-uncles was a priest. I grew up with the faith, and when I got older, I decided to become a priest myself."

He had gone to Moscow during the Soviet era, to study at an Orthodox seminary. After his ordination to the priesthood, he had directed a church in Omsk, Siberia, before being transferred back to Ukraine in the 1980s.

"Shortly after I arrived in Kalynivka, the story with the cross began."

Suddenly, the air was filled with the sound of an Orthodox choir singing. It grew louder as Father Volodymyr drew his phone out of his cassock. The choir was his ringtone.

"Vasyl? Yes, we are waiting for you…"

The phone disappeared into his cassock. "My son. He can tell you more about the cross."

His son was also a priest. He also wore a black cassock, but there the similarities between Vasyl and Volodymyr Rosman ended. The son was the exact opposite of his father – gaunt, quiet, serious.

In a side room off the choir loft, Father Vasyl told me what he had found out about the cross. He showed me documents that he had dug up in the Soviet city archives during his studies for the priesthood. In addition, he had questioned the older inhabitants of Kalynivka. Father Vasyl remembered a conversation with an old woman.

"I had brought my daughter to the meeting, who was still little then. The old woman chatted with the child for a few minutes, then she asked me how she could help me. When I mentioned the cross, she gave me a startled look. She shook her head and said: Sonny, I can't hear you, my ears are old! She suddenly pretended to be deaf, even though she had just spoken to my daughter. Nearly ninety years had passed, but some people were still afraid to talk about the cross."

Father Vasyl could not figure out exactly when the cross had been put up, or by whom. Some claimed that it was a burial cross for three murdered merchants who had been interred beside a well, the place where they had died. From others, Father Vasyl heard the version that the old woman had told me at the chapel: a childless man had dug the well at God's command and erected a cross next to it.

"The version about the murdered merchants sounds unlikely," Father Vasyl said. "Only suicides were buried outside the cemeteries, and who would get the idea to bury corpses next to a drinking well? The truth is probably a mixture of the two versions: a man who had lost his children as the result of a crime, placed a cross next to a well in their honour."

There is convincing evidence that a six-metre-high wooden cross was already standing beside the road between Vinnytsia and Kalynivka when Lenin's Bolsheviks seized power in St. Petersburg and, after a bloody civil war, brought the Ukrainian part of the Tsarist empire under their control.

On Saturday July 7, 1923, three Red Army soldiers were walking along the road. When they reached the well, they stopped to refresh themselves – their throats were burning, they had been drinking along the way. Fuelled by alcohol, one of the Red Army soldiers began firing at the cross. He aimed at a large icon that was attached to the wooden beams, depicting Christ at his crucifixion. Twenty-four shots missed their target.

In a letter written shortly after the incident, which Father Vasyl had found in the archives, it says: "Every bullet fell to the ground in front of the cross, and it wasn't until he shot for the twenty-fifth time that he hit Jesus Christ in the right shoulder, and the blood began to flow."

Word quickly spread that a miracle had happened in Kalynivka. The first believers who prayed in front of the cross until their throats were hoarse came from the surrounding villages, but soon the news reached more distant regions. Processions set off, priests and their congregations crowded the roads, people flocked to Kalynivka from all over to see the miracle with their own eyes.

The local party bosses did not know how to react. There was no God, that much had been drummed into them, and if He did exist after all, He certainly did not smear icons with blood, and if He did, then certainly not in Kalynivka. But how could they explain this to the people who by now were encamped around the cross in their thousands? A party letter from the time warns against ill-considered reactions. "It would be all too easy," it advises, "to make mistakes in this matter and even get your neck broken."

The party bosses decided to call in more senior party bosses. As a precaution, they posted a twelve-man guard next to the cross, who were to maintain order until a decision had been made higher up the ladder.

The next highest party committee convened a commission of inquiry. On August 2, two doctors, three priests, two local community representatives and several party officials arrived at the cross, where by then more than fifteen thousand people had gathered to pray. On that day alone, eighty new processions had arrived in Kalynivka.

The commissioners leant a ladder against the wooden cross. They inspected the bullet-pierced icon extensively. With a cotton swab they took a sample of the red liquid which appeared to have seeped out of the image. They silently ignored the questions that were yelled at them from a thousand voices in the crowd.

When the commission presented its report a little later, it quoted, among other things, a laboratory analysis. "The reddish liquid examined contains no blood," it said, "neither human nor the blood of any animal." Instead, traces of iron had been found. The icon's metal fittings, the Commissioners wrote, were heavily rusted in several places, especially on the back side. The rain, which in recent weeks had fallen heavily, had dissolved the rust and washed it through the bullet hole to the front side, where it had run down the icon in trickles. This, the report concluded, "might give the impression of a stream of blood."

The old people who had spoken to Father Vasyl, however, were certain that there had been a drought that summer. No rain had fallen for weeks, they said, either before or after the miracle.

Meanwhile, the stream of pilgrims did not stop. The crowd grew bigger and bigger. Incense clouded the road. All day and all night the ecstatic prayers of believers could be heard, mixed with the Orthodox liturgies of the priests, who begged for God's mercy around the clock: *Gooooospooooo-diiiii pooooo-miiiii-luuuuuy…*

After the crowd around the cross had grown to more than twenty-five thousand people in September, the party bosses decided to act. They sent in agitators who circulated rumours: the blood, they told the faithful, came not from Christ, but from a rabbit. Fake priests had smeared it on the icon to mislead the working masses.

Meanwhile, the real priests were done away with. Clergymen who had led processions to the cross were arrested and banished on party command, along with other "unreliable, anti-Soviet elements" from the vicinity of Kalynivka. "On the night of September 23," a report states, "an eviction operation was conducted, directed against those who provoked and agitated for the 'Miracle of Kalynivka'. Forty people were arrested."

But pilgrims continued to flock to the cross, even after party members removed the bullet-pierced icon on the night of October 1. Finally, in early November, the cross was completely demolished. The well was covered up, the ground was ploughed, and the adjacent cornfield was extended to the edge of the road to conceal the location of the cross.

None of these measures helped. When spring came, the people in Kalynivka started whispering that mysterious ears of corn had sprung up in the field, ears which interlaced with each other to form the shape of a cross. Others said that Lenin, who had died in January from the effects of a stroke, had fallen victim to God's wrath because he had desecrated the cross of Kalynivka.

"Particularly in March and April," the party reported, "it was noted that the pilgrimages had resumed and new crosses had been erected. The instigators were tracked down and the crosses destroyed."

But scarcely had one cross been removed than a new one appeared on the road. The party promptly took each one down. It went on like that for years: the crosses appeared, disappeared, appeared once more, were taken down again. Over time, the rhythm of this cat-and-mouse game slowed down, but in the party reports Father Vasyl had found in the city archives, new crosses were still being documented after the war, and occasional ones even way into the eighties.

"You've seen the rest," Father Vasyl said. "When the Soviet era ended, there was an old man here in Kalynivka who could still remember the miracle. He told my father about it, and in 1993 we put up a new cross. The well came a few years later, and after that the chapel."

Father Vasyl leaned back. His story was finished. A moment of silence ensued, which ended abruptly when Father Volodymyr flung the door open.

"Have you told him about the miracles?"

I felt my concentration ebbing away as I listened to the long enumeration of miracles, and in my notebook I later found only halfhearted notes about discarded crutches, sudden pregnancies, recovered children. It seemed to me that I had already heard the real miracle story: the one of the sudden return to faith that had occurred in the nineties, not only here in Kalynivka, but in half of the Soviet Union. According to Father Volodymyr, more than twenty-five thousand people now regularly participated in the processions that took place on every anniversary of the blood miracle – the pilgrims were again as numerous as they had been at the very beginning of the story.

At the very front of the annual processions, Father Volodymyr often saw the old party leaders march along, some of whom might have been personally responsible for ordering the demolition of crosses back in the Soviet era. Father Volodymyr did not resent them. He was a Christian, resentment had never been his thing, and new sheep in the flock were always welcome – whatever pastures they might have grazed on before.

On my way back from the church to the bus station, I passed the Town Hall Square again. For a few minutes I stood in front of the empty monument pedestal and tried to imagine which one of the canonical variations of Lenin had once stood there. Had it been the brooding Lenin, with his head down and his fists buried in his pockets? The signposting Lenin, one arm outstretched, his finger pointing the way to the socialist future? Or the campaigning Lenin, hands raised in the gesture of an orator, lips half-open?

He had lost the crusade against the crosses. It was Lenin who had ushered it in, even if the bloodiest battles had been waged only after his death. Would he have laughed or cried if he had been told that Stalin would one day replace all the crosses with monuments of Lenin?

My eyes fell on the naive drawing of the assassinated Maidan demonstrator which graced the empty pedestal. I suddenly spotted a detail I hadn't noticed before. More specifically, I could have sworn that it hadn't been there when I had seen the image for the first time. Above the demonstrator's head hung a small, golden halo.

9

At Rabbi Nachman's Grave

Uman

I LEFT THE WONDROUS Kalynivka behind me and took a bus to the city of Uman, 100 kilometres to the east. The bus took a circuitous route through the villages, and soon it was jammed full of sacks of potatoes, baskets of apples, onion bags and the attendant dacha gardeners who stood crowded together in the centre aisle.

Next to me sat an elderly woman with a giant pumpkin on her lap.

"I've never spoken to a foreigner," she said. "Never. This is the first time."

After this solemn confession, she fell silent. There seemed to be no topic of conversation that would have been appropriate for the seriousness of our encounter, and when I started asking questions myself, I got only shy, mono-syllabic answers. Had the harvest been good this year? "Normal." Was her garden large? "Medium." Were her pumpkins always so magnificent? "Partly."

Suddenly, a man who had overheard our attempts at conversation leaned down to me from the aisle. He wore a black peaked cap, and he must have been about fifty. An ironic smile played around the corners of his mouth.

"Here's a question! When did the war start?"

"Which one?"

"The big one. "

"Uh… 1939?"

"Ha!"

He thwacked his right fist into his left palm.

"Germans are honest!"

I looked at him uncomprehendingly.

He grinned. "Don't tell me you haven't seen the Soviet war memorials? Our whole country is full of them! And all of them say: The Great Patriotic War, 1941–1945! The Russians want us to believe that the war did not begin until that evil man Hitler attacked our beloved Stalin. But in 1939, our beloved Stalin joined forces with that evil man Hitler to seize Western Ukraine. That's something the Russians would rather not talk about!"

As his lecture gathered momentum, he repeatedly laughed a short, bleating goat's laugh.

"Most of all they lie to themselves. They believe that they are called Russians, although they have always been called Muscovites. Peter the Great made up that nonsense about the Russians, because he didn't like the fact that his empire had no history. He simply claimed that the Muscovites were descendants of the Kievan Rus, although that, of course, is what *we* are – the Ukrainians. He stole our name and our history! Did you know that?"

I tried to nod vaguely, but it came out more like a shake of the head. "I've heard that theory…"

"It is not a theory, it is the truth! I am a tractor mechanic, and if even someone like me knows it, then it must be true!"

Then he asked me what brought a German to the

Ukrainian province. I told him what had attracted me to Kalynivka. The man knew the story of the miraculous cross. The woman with the pumpkin had never heard it, though.

"Of course you have not heard it," the man said. "They didn't tell us such stories at school. The same goes for the story of the War. All these years they have lied to us! They never talked about the Holodomor either. They wanted to starve the Ukrainians, to destroy us!"

The woman with the pumpkin nodded. "We Ukrainians were always in the way," she said seriously. "Everyone wanted to get rid of us."

The man leaned down even further toward our seat, smiling conspiratorially.

"Even our own government is trying to get rid of us. Do you think it is a coincidence that everything is getting more expensive? We survived the Holodomor, so now they are trying out something new – raising gas prices until we all freeze to death!"

Again, he laughed his bleating laugh. The blacker his stories were, the more they seemed to amuse him. The woman in the neighbouring seat, on the other hand, stared more and more unhappily at her pumpkin.

"What do you expect in a country like Ukraine," the man said. "The good people have all been killed or expelled. The only ones left are the bad ones!"

I felt a strong urge to cheer up the woman with the pumpkin.

"Don't listen to him," I said, smiling. "I know a lot of good people in Ukraine. You too, right?"

Uncertain, she returned my foreigner's gaze.

"Partly."

It was the 18th of the month of Tishrei, 5571, when word got around in Uman that Rabbi Nachman of Bratslav was dying. His inconsolable students gathered around the *tzadik*'s deathbed, their sidelocks trembling in rhythm with their sighs. Smiling, the Rabbi let his eyes wander round the circle. He had always smiled, and he had always urged his students to smile, and before he departed this world with a smile, he left behind a big promise: he, Rabbi Nachman of Bratslav, vowed to save any believer who came to pray at his grave on the day of Rosh Hashanah by personally pulling them out of hell by their sidelocks.

When I arrived in Uman, it had been 204 years since Nachman's death and 5,775 years since the creation of the world. According to the Jewish calendar, the New Year was just around the corner, and thirty thousand Hasidim from around the world were heeding the call of the Rabbi.

I had seen the Rosh Hashanah celebrations in photos, but no image could prepare me for the sight of Pushkin Street. In the middle of an ordinary Ukrainian provincial town, another world suddenly opened up. The pilgrims were streaming down the street shoulder to shoulder, almost everyone the spitting image of his neighbour – the same sidelocks and beards, the same black frock coats and white shirts, the same stiff felt hats and fur caps, the same gold-embroidered prayer cloaks. The boys were scaled-down copies of their fathers, and there were no women to be seen on Pushkin Street, not a single one.

Year after year the pilgrims brought back into Ukraine a world of faith that had almost completely vanished from it in the twentieth century – even though it had once conquered half the continent from here. In the early eighteenth century, Hasidism spread like a divine wildfire through the shtetls of Eastern Europe. Its founder, Israel ben Eliezer, known as the *Baal Shem Tov* (the "Master of the Good Name"), was a rabbi from what is now western Ukraine. What he preached was unheard of: God, his students learned, was present in everything, and anyone who loved God had to learn to recognise His agency in things both good and evil. Basically, this was not even difficult, the *Baal Shem Tov* revealed to his baffled students, for evil was not evil in its divine origin, it only became evil when it was associated with humanity. To admire the beauty of a woman is not evil, because it comes from God; it only becomes evil when humans covet it. But if your neighbour lusts after your wife, do not be angry with him, because his desire comes from God too.

Accordingly, students of the *Baal Shem Tov* learned to confront the evil in the world with cheerfulness, and after the death of their master, they cheerfully splintered off into ever newer, ever more cheerful movements, gathering in each case around a *tzadik*, the charismatic Rabbi of a Hasidic community. In the late eighteenth century, a great-grandson of the *Baal Shem Tov* founded the most cheerful one of all. Rabbi Nachman of Bratslav recommended that his students talk to God as if they were talking to a friend, freed from internal deliberations and doubts, following only their own emotions as directly and as uninhibitedly as possible. One of the ecstatic prayer techniques he developed was the method of the "inner scream" – feel, the rabbi taught, how a scream builds in your head; hear it slowly swell, ever increasing, until the scream is so loud in your head that you can barely stand it.

Conservative Jews wondered whether the screaming, smiling Rabbi of Bratslav might even consider himself the Messiah, although his followers always denied this. For a long time, Nachman was regarded as not completely kosher by the more scriptural branches of Judaism. Nevertheless, Bratslav Hasidism spread rapidly, and when Rabbi Nachman, not yet forty years old, died of tuberculosis in 1810, word spread quickly about where the most cheerful Jews should celebrate their New Year's festival in the future.

More than half a century separates today's pilgrims from those Hasidim who visited the grave of their *tzadik* after Rabbi Nachman's death. The centres of the Bratslav movement are located in other parts of the world today, especially in New York and Jerusalem. It was only in the final years of the Soviet era that the first cautious pilgrims returned to Uman. Year after year there were more, and today around Rosh Hashanah the city has a good one-third more inhabitants than usual.

Throughout Uman as a whole, not much of this was in evidence. The stream of pilgrims was concentrated almost exclusively on Pushkin Street, at whose edges the same nine-storey prefabricated buildings are strung together like they are all over the former Soviet Union, from Kaliningrad to Kamchatka. When I looked up, I saw groups of Hasidic pilgrims, to whom the Ukrainian residents rent their apartments during the New Year festival, standing on every one of the concrete balconies.

I did not know exactly where the grave was, but it was not hard to find. The pilgrims led me in the right direction. At the lower end of Pushkin Street, a small side arm branched off and ended, after another bend, in front of a single-storey house. Even a long way from the building, the crowd was so dense that I could only move forward by tagging along behind the most pushy visitors. Everywhere I could see praying Hasidim rocking the upper part of their bodies back and forth in rhythm, staring straight ahead at the open books in their hands, muttering or shouting Hebrew incantations. Their sidelocks swung in time to the beat of their movements, back and forth, back and forth. Their prayers were deafening.

It was only once I'd got closer that I realised a make-shift pavilion had been constructed immediately adjacent to the single-storey house, into which the stream of pilgrims was pushing. Inside, the noise of the prayers multiplied into something unreal. I had never heard anything like it. A piercing wail filled the air, punctuated by crashes of thunder, which only made sense to me when I noticed individual pilgrims leaping up and down in ecstatic prayer. In doing so, many of them hurled themselves against the pavilion walls, time and again. The room was filled to bursting, and because the path was now almost blocked around the narrow entrance, some pilgrims had started to clamber inside through the side windows. I even saw two teenagers crawl through a gap in the roof, upside down, their side-locks dangling. They shimmied down into the crowd on scaffolding poles.

All faces were turned to the narrow end of the room, where the open pavilion structure abutted the external wall of the small neighbouring house. Set in the wall of the house, I could see Rabbi Nachman's memorial slab. Without really wanting to, I was caught up in the line that had formed in front of the shrine. I abandoned all attempts at resistance and let myself be propelled forward. As I drew closer, several men waved to me from the crowd, smiling and pointing to the back of their heads. A Hasid who was standing beside me inclined his mouth to my ear. "They are asking you to cover your head!" he shouted in English.

With a gesture of apology I raised my hands – I had nothing suitable to put on. As I started to wriggle out of the line the man who had shouted in my ear held me back by the arm. With his left hand he took off his black fedora and gave me the kippah he was wearing underneath.

"Thank you!" I yelled.

"Tuvia!" he shouted.

It took a moment for me to realise that "Tuvia" was his name.

Two policemen in Israeli uniforms protected the barred passageway in front of the gravestone, letting the pilgrims through one at a time. Praying, sighing, groaning Hasidim pressed their cheeks to the stone slab before being pushed along by the security guards. It all happened so fast that in retrospect, I only remember the sharp odour of masculine perspiration wafting over Rabbi Nachman's grave.

At the far end of the barred passageway, I tried to give Tuvia his kippah back, but he shook his head.

"Who knows? You may still need it."

In a quieter corner we talked. It was difficult to estimate Tuvia's age. Silvery streaks flecked his beard and his side-locks, and the traditional black Hasidic clothing gave his gaunt features a patriarchal severity. But his eyes and his clear voice seemed to be those of a much younger person. He looked like a man in his mid-thirties, disguised as someone from the Old Testament.

Tuvia had grown up in a Hasidic community in the United States, but he had lived in Jerusalem for a long time. It was his fifteenth visit to the Rabbi's grave, he said. He had made the pilgrimage to Uman every year since 2001.

"That's a long time," I said appreciatively.

He nodded. "But there are people here who were travelling to Uman back when the city was still Soviet." He pointed to the prayer hall. "None of that existed back then. At first, people didn't even know where the grave was."

The first pilgrims had discovered the unmarked resting place in the backyard of the one-storey house that is now adjoined by the pavilion.

"In those days, an old Ukrainian woman still lived there," Tuvia said. "She let the Hasidim pray secretly in her courtyard. In the early years, only a few dozen people dared to come to Uman. Then more and more started arriving every year. When I first came here, there weren't even half as many pilgrims as there are now. And there have never been as many here as this year."

"Even though there is a war going on in Ukraine?" I asked.

He smiled. "We are further away from the front here than in Jerusalem."

I asked him if his ancestors had lived in Ukraine.

Tuvia shook his head. "In Lithuania."

Actually, he explained to me, he came from an old rabbinic dynasty that had rejected Bratslav Hasidism when it emerged in the eighteenth century. "My ancestors were traditional scribes who had no time for Nachman."

But, he continued, these were ancient disputes that had been settled long ago. "The Hasidim here in Uman come from everywhere. They differ in their customs, but not in their dogmas."

What they had in common, he explained, was the belief that everything happens for a reason. "Trouble with your girlfriend? There is a reason. A guy bumps into you? Had to happen. Your encounter with me? No coincidence. God has His hand in the game, no matter what happens. Anyone who has internalised that will go through life happier."

"Now I understand why you all smile like that," I said, smiling.

Tuvia nodded. "I don't know what religion you belong to, and I don't want to spoil your day, but I can tell you that in our faith there is more happiness than in any other."

Over the following days, I often thought back to Tuvia's words when I saw the radiant faces of the Hasidim. There were times when the ecstatic happiness in the prayer hall intensified so incredibly that every miracle seemed conceivable. At such moments, I think I might have accepted it without much surprise if Rabbi Nachman had suddenly pushed aside his stone slab in order to grab the assembled worshippers by their sidelocks and lead them to heaven.

It was not until the second or third day that the Hasidic smiles suddenly put me in mind of Ivan Mamchur, the OUN veteran I had met in Lviv. I remembered what he had told me about the resignation he had noticed during the war among the Jews in the ghetto – how in his eyes they had sheepishly awaited their murder, singing and without resistance, as if it were the will of God. Although I was not sure whether Mamchur might have fabricated his observations after the fact to justify his own decisions, his account suddenly struck a jarring note. It sounded like the dark flip side of the Hasidic credo Tuvia had revealed to me.

During the four days I spent in Uman, I gradually realised how different the pilgrims actually were from one another, although at first sight they had seemed like an army of clones. I spoke with estate agents from London and rabbis from New York, with Parisian kiosk vendors and – in awkward sign language – with poor Israeli villagers. All were dressed almost identically, but their different origins were apparent in the details. Some wore well-cut suits under their frock coats, others threadbare, greasy synthetic trousers. But, a Hasidic computer programmer from Canada told me, I'd still only understood the half of it. "There are a few extremely influential businessmen going around here, though you'd never guess how rich they are from their clothes," he said. Other pilgrims were destitute, he continued; they saved for years to finance the trip to Uman.

When I asked why there were no women in Uman, I was given a variety of answers. "There is barely any room even for the men here," said one. Prayer, others claimed, was for men. Women, said others again, distracted the men from praying.

Hardly any of the pilgrims had seen much of Ukraine. Most of the Hasidim took charter flights from Israel to Kiev, where they boarded buses that travelled directly to Pushkin Street in Uman without stopping. During the New Year's celebrations, as many as ten to twelve pilgrims shared tiny rooms in apartment blocks, for which they paid absurd prices. In my hotel, which was half-empty, one night cost less than ten euros, but it was a half an hour's walk from Pushkin Street. "Much too far," a businessman from

Jerusalem explained. "We have to stay as close as possible to the grave."

For the Ukrainian residents, hosting the pilgrims was like winning the lottery. An old woman calculated her rental income for me: twelve Hasidim had stayed in her one-room apartment during the New Year celebration, and each paid her four hundred dollars. "In a week I can earn five times my annual pension." She stayed with friends during the holidays. The only annoying thing, she added, was the garbage. "The Jews are not permitted to clear up after themselves on their holidays. At the end of the week the apartment looks like a pigsty."

Outside on the street, too, the rubbish started piling up by the second day. The Hasidim dropped it where they stood, because disposing of it would constitute work, and thus a sin. The mountains of trash were generally limited to Pushkin Street. Only to the south did the garbage trail lead a little further, to a small lake, which I only discovered on the second day of my stay. It was about a hundred metres long and half as wide. Around the shore, faces turned to the surface of the water, stood a densely packed ring of praying Hasidim. The air was filled with the babel of a thousand voices that swelled and howled at irregular intervals and then ebbed to a murmur. It was a New Year's ritual, Tuvia had explained to me, a kind of symbolic rite that had to take place on the shore of a natural body of water.

When I walked around the lake for the first time, I only watched the enraptured faces of the worshippers. I noticed the cross only the next day, even though it was hard to miss. Next to the lake there rose a chain of low, rocky bluffs. Exactly at their centre, a few metres above the heads of the praying Hasidim, hung a life-size, crucified likeness of the Messiah.

Because I could not believe that this strange contrast had occurred by chance, I walked around the lake and climbed the bluffs. As I got closer, I met two Ukrainian policemen keeping watch beside the cross. The figure of Christ, they explained to me, had suddenly appeared here two or three years ago. They did not know who had put it there.

"We make sure it stays there," said one of the policemen. He pointed to the praying Hasidim at the foot of the rocky slope. "There are a few radicals among the Jews who would like to throw the cross into the lake. From time to time they try, and we hold them back."

Generally speaking, he added, the festival was running peacefully this year. "No brawling, which is rare. We're not surprised when there's trouble. I've heard that most of the Jews here have been in gaol. That's why they make the pilgrimage to the Rabbi's grave. So he will pull them out of Hell."

Just then I noticed that his colleague had grown nervous.

"Here comes one," he hissed.

Across the bluffs a Hasid was approaching us, with energetic steps and bouncing, reddish sidelocks.

"I know that one," said the policeman I had been talking to. "He's harmless."

The Hasid reached the cross. Without stopping, he spat on the ground in front of the Christ figure, loudly and demonstratively.

The police observed the man in silence as he walked past us without looking up. I also watched him silently, too surprised to say anything.

"Does that happen often?" I asked after he had disappeared around the next bend.

The policemen nodded gloomily. "All day."

I felt sorry for them. Whoever had placed the cross here seemed to have done so in order to make life difficult for them.

"Good evening, young man!"

At the entrance to my hotel I was approached by an elderly lady who, I quickly realised, liked to be regarded as a lady, but was loath to be thought of as elderly. Her orange-dyed hair was piled high in a voluminous bun, and although dusk was falling, she was sporting huge sunglasses.

"I've had my eye on you, young man," she said. "Your appearance is, how shall I put it... unusual. In the best sense. Am I right in assuming that you're not from around here?"

Reacting to her mannered tone, I lifted my eyebrows in surprise. "How did you guess?"

In fact, it was not hard to guess – we were standing outside the entrance to a hotel after all.

"Call it a woman's intuition." She giggled coquettishly. "Young man, have you seen our park?"

I shook my head. The park was right next to the hotel, but I had not yet got around to visiting it. All I knew was that it must be huge – its perimeter encompassed a large part of the city centre on the map.

The lady clapped her hands together theatrically. "Young man, you *must* see it! Allow me to invite you on a poetic promenade. Only the two of us, tomorrow morning at eight."

"I'm not sure if tomorrow…"

"You won't find a better guide, young man. Nobody knows our park as well as I do. You cannot refuse a lady's invitation! Haven't you noticed that I am putting my charms to the test? If you'll be waiting for me tomorrow morning, I'll know that my charm still works…"

The next morning I paid for a single ticket at the park's ticket booth. My companion had dressed up. A brown, clingy summer dress emphasised her slim figure, and her bun seemed even more voluminous than the previous day.

It was a radiant day. The morning sun was just rising behind the trees, bathing the park in its golden light. Galina grasped my arm.

"Just look at this beauty," she whispered in rapture. "You will not forget our promenade for a long time, young man."

Unfortunately, she proved to be right.

Galina was from Eastern Ukraine. She was Russian. She had ended up in Uman during her Soviet youth, apparently because of a man, whom she only alluded to in recounting her life story. Nine years ago he had disappeared from her life, by whatever means. She was left with a dog, a cat, and an unfulfilled need for male affection.

Although she had spent most of her life in Central Ukraine, in her heart she was still a child of the Donbass, the border industrial region where war had been raging for the last eighteen months.

"My heart breaks when I think of the people in my home region," she said. "They are at the mercy of the Ukrainian fascists. These monsters do not even spare women and young children, they kill anyone who dares to speak

Russian. They have turned Ukraine into a concentration camp!"

I had to laugh. Rarely had I heard the propaganda myths from Russian television in a more concentrated form.

"You don't believe me? It's true! The President had to flee to Russia because the fascists were trying to kill him. If Putin had not intervened, there wouldn't be anybody left alive in the Donbass today. It's all an American conspiracy..."

Discreetly, I tried to steer the conversation back to the subject of the park. Galina was happy to answer my questions, because they concerned her favourite topic: love.

"This park owes its origins to a woman." Her voice was ceremonial and solemn, as if she were reciting a poem. "Ask yourself, young man, aren't women the cause of *everything*? Would the works of men be conceivable without the charms of women?"

The woman she was talking about was a legendary beauty from the late eighteenth century. Zofia Potocka was reputed to have been Greek, but her origin was as bound up in myth as her later life. It was said that when she was seventeen years old, her impoverished mother put her on offer as a courtesan in the diplomatic quarter of Istanbul, but Galina presented this version to me as a malicious rumour started by a jealous rival.

After her first, unsuccessful marriage, Zofia had met the man whose name she would later bear: Count Stanisław Potocki, a Polish magnate whose wealthy family ruled over the parts of Central Ukraine governed by Poland at that time. In Uman, where he possessed extensive lands, the Count presented his newly wedded wife with a romantic gift: he had ordered a park to be built, which he named after her.

I had never heard of the Zofia Gardens and was fittingly surprised to discover such a spectacular landscaped park deep in the Ukrainian provinces. My amazement did not go unnoticed. Galina led me proudly through the sprawling grounds, past a succession of artificial waterfalls, swan lakes, cliffs, and caves that had once served the Potockis as a backdrop for their love play.

As a nod towards Zofia's origins, the park was designed around motifs from Greek mythology. At every Orpheus rock, Diana grotto, Eros bust, and Venus statue, Galina would recite to me in a voice choked with pathos relevant verses from Russian literature: Karamzin's "Ode to the Dead Orpheus", Marina Tsvetaeva's Eurydice monologue, and, time and again, Pushkin, Pushkin, Pushkin.

Her delivery was particularly insistent when she declaimed verses about the park's namesake. I realised only after the second Zofia poem that Galina had written the verses herself. They were sentimental poems inspired by Russian classics, that praised Zofia's beauty, her femininity and grace, her gift for love, and her effect on men.

By the time I had heard the third and fourth Zofia poem, it was clear to me that Galina had appropriated the story of her heroine for herself. She was Zofia. The park was hers. It was the lover who admired her, the audience that applauded her, the mirror reflecting the beauty of her soul.

The park also caused the impertinences of the present to vanish into thin air. In Galina's eyes, basically nothing had changed here since the nineteenth century. At that time, the park had been a love nest for Polish aristocrats, with Ukrainians only permitted to enter as gardeners or oarsmen for the gondolas. Today, it was Galina's love nest, where European antiquity combined with Russian poetry. The fact that there was now a state called Ukraine beyond the park walls was a regrettable historical misfortune, nothing more.

As we were on the way to the exit, Galina mentioned that the Zofia Gardens were counted among the five most beautiful parks in Europe.

"What are the other four?" I asked.

"Versailles. And of course Sanssouci…"

After a pause, she looked at me sheepishly. "I don't know the other two. You must excuse me, young man. I have not been fortunate enough to travel around the world."

For a while we walked side by side in silence. Then something occurred to Galina.

"Mezhyhirya! Do you know about Mezhyhirya? The park that Yanukovych built, our president?"

I had visited the ostentatious, private estate on a previous trip – it had been empty since the corrupt president had fled to Russia.

"You mean Yanukovych's palace?"

"You sound like the Kiev fascists! It is not a palace, it is a normal government residence. And the park is wonderful. I saw it! One day, Mezhyhirya will be mentioned in the same breath as the Zofia Gardens, I'm sure. It's a shame that Yanukovych had to flee. The Ukrainians wanted to hang him, just because he defended the Russians in the Donbass…"

While I was trying to get my head around why she was defending a president whose ill-gotten wealth she had seen with her own eyes, I suddenly remembered Bronislav Tutelman, the old dissident from Chernivtsi. Sometime in the course of our conversation, after the third or fourth vodka, he had talked about "Women of a Balzacian age" who avoided the sunlight because it showed up their wrinkles. "It's like Ukraine," Tutelman had said. "As long as peace prevailed, we did not see how divided our society was. It wasn't until the war that we could really see the hidden dividing lines between people."

The phrase struck me because I wondered if my impression of Galina would have been different had we met a few years earlier. I suppose I would have taken her for a mannered, but not disagreeable, elderly lady. We would have probably argued more about Pushkin than about Putin. It was possible we would have parted as friends. But the more strident Galina's litany about the Ukrainians became, the harder I found it to like her.

"You do not believe me?" she asked when we said goodbye. "See for yourself! Go and look at the monument these fascists want to build in Uman! To Zaliznyak and Honta!"

Maksym Zaliznyak and Ivan Honta were in a sense the reason why Rabbi Nachman had been buried in Uman.

In the eighteenth century, these two Ukrainian Cossacks had led a peasant uprising against the Polish nobility. In the conquered fortress of Uman, they initiated a bloodbath which killed at least two thousand people. Honta was so proud of his deeds that he boasted of more than thirty thousand victims when he was later tried in Poland. After his execution, bits of his dismembered corpse were displayed in fourteen Ukrainian cities, as a warning to imitators. Zaliznyak got off relatively lightly. He was handed over to the Tsarist authorities, who exiled him to Siberia.

Every schoolchild in Ukraine knows the gruesome details of the massacre, because they are described in the

"Haidamaks", one of the most famous poems written by Ukraine's national poet Taras Shevchenko.

The Haidamaki on Uman
Like heavy clouds converge
At midnight. Ere the night is done
The whole town is submerged
[…]
The ill, the cripples, children too,
All die, no one is spared.
Wild cries and screams. 'Mid streams of blood
Stands Gonta on the square
With Zaliznyak together
[…]
Until late at night they slaughtered the Poles;
Not one was let live. Yet Gonta still raved –
Oh monsters, come out! Crawl out from your holes
[…]
I want in the blood of the gentry to wade,
To drink it, and watch how it flows and turns black…
Oh winds, as ye blow, why waft ye not back
Some Poles for our blades?… Oh cruel's my fate!

It is not just the murder of the Poles that Shevchenko describes in detail. In an equally horrified tone his poem recounts that in their bloodlust, the Cossacks did not even stop at Ukrainians who had converted to the hated Catholicism of the Poles – among them allegedly Honta's own sons. The poet seems to have less sympathy for the Jewish victims of the tragedy, who were significantly more numerous. In the "Haidamaks" they do not even warrant a mention.

But they were the ones who motivated Rabbi Nachman to settle in Uman towards the end of his life. On his deathbed he asked to be buried in the old Jewish cemetery, among the dead who, half a century earlier, had been massacred in Uman's fortress. He wanted to give them spiritual support from his grave.

I found the pedestal of the monument a few hundred metres from Pushkin Street. It was empty. If I had walked past it unknowingly, I probably would have mistaken it for the plinth of a toppled statue of Lenin.

Beside the pedestal stood a police car. The windows were rolled down. Inside, two policemen were dozing in the late summer heat.

"Is a monument going to be put up here?" I asked.

The policeman at the wheel scratched his unshaven chin. "Heaven knows."

The other one yawned. "I lost track of what is going on with the monuments in this country. They are constantly tearing something down, or putting something up. I have no idea what they've got planned now. We're just posted here to keep a lookout."

His colleague pointed to two middle-aged men standing by the roadside a few metres away, deep in conversation. "Ask those two there. They know what the score is."

The men looked up from the planning sketch they were studying when I approached them. Oh yes, they assured me, there was indeed going to be a monument here. Zaliznyak and Honta, on horseback. The equestrian statue was already finished. In a month it would be hoisted onto the pedestal.

"Was that your idea?" I asked.

"Yes," said one.

"No," the other one said at the same time.

Puzzled, they looked at each other.

"Yes and no," the first one clarified. "It's a long story."

As it turned out, the communists had already decided to put up a monument to Zaliznyak and Honta during the Soviet era – as leaders of the oppressed Ukrainian peasantry in the class struggle against the feudal rule of the Poles. But then all of a sudden, it seemed, the party ideologists had no longer been sure whether the mass murder in Uman could really be interpreted as a heroic Marxist deed, because their resolution to erect a statue, which was made in 1968 on the bicentenary of the uprising, had never been translated into action.

My two interlocutors were now keen to complete the work. The more talkative of the pair turned out to be the captain of a local Cossack alliance, which pushed forward the building of the monument on their own initiative, without a municipal agreement, funded by private donations. Zaliznyak and Honta, the captain told me, were heroes of the Ukrainian Cossacks, so it was only fitting that there should be a statue of them.

I shot him a sceptical look. "Don't you think the Jews might see things differently?"

He smiled triumphantly, as if he had been waiting for this objection.

"Who is Napoleon to the French?" he asked. "A national hero. Who is Napoleon to the English, or the Russians? A mortal enemy. It's all a matter of opinion! Every nation has a right to have their own heroes, no matter what other nations might think of them."

"But why here?" I asked. Pushkin Street was less than half

a kilometre away, and as we talked, unsuspecting groups of Hasidic pilgrims strolled past the monument's pedestal.

"That wasn't our idea." The Cossack captain grinned an innocent grin. "The party decided on the location in 1968."

By the way, he continued, I had better not believe everything I had been told about Zaliznyak and Honta, who had merely promoted the interests of the Ukrainian people in Uman, which of course did not suit the Poles and the Jews, but for that you could hardly blame the Cossacks, could you, who by the way had not killed nearly as many people as was always claimed.

"The most famous work by our national poet is about Zaliznyak and Honta. So we should surely be allowed to put up a memorial to them!"

I stared at him incredulously. "Shevchenko didn't exactly portray the massacre as a heroic act."

He shrugged his shoulders indifferently. "So what? That's Shevchenko's business. To me, they are heroes."

As I listened with growing disconcertment, a sombre thought suddenly crossed my mind.

"Listen," I asked. "That cross above the lake, where the Hasidim pray…"

"Yes?"

"You don't happen to know who…?"

"Of course! That was us!"

His grin grew wider with each sentence, while I found it difficult to hide my irritation.

"Was that also the party's idea?" I asked. "Or were you just trying to piss off the Jews?"

"By no means! It is simply a very visible location for a cross."

Naturally, he told me, he had nothing against the Jews. "At least not as long as they behave. Now they are praying peacefully, but you should see what it looks like here when the festival is over. Then they get drunk, piss in the street, and harass our women."

But naturally, he repeated, he had nothing against the Jews. "Apart from the ten, fifteen bandits who control all of Pushkin Street – that is a Jewish Mafia!"

Otherwise, he repeated, he had nothing against the Jews. "But I do not see why everything on Pushkin Street has to be written in Hebrew. We are in Ukraine here!"

But most certainly, he insisted, he wasn't an anti-Semite. "My own daughter is married to a Jew. One from here, from Uman. That's perfectly fine. And you know what? He even made a donation to our monument!"

When we said goodbye, our handshake was halfhearted. It took me quite a while to shake off my anger at this cynic, who invoked Soviet resolutions, distorting poems and Jewish relatives at will to hold his skewed view of the world together. He was even more unpleasant than Galina, the guide in the park, although the two could hardly have been further apart in their ideologies.

The day before my departure from Uman I visited the lake again. Rosh Hashanah was over and the crowd had thinned. Only a few isolated Hasidim were praying on the banks. I sat down on a stone, took out my notebook and went through my notes.

Suddenly, I sensed that someone was looking at me. I raised my head. A short, fat Hasidic boy, ten, maybe twelve years old, was standing in front of me.

He stared at me and said something in Hebrew. First he twirled his sidelocks, then the threads of his prayer cloak between his fingers. Then he pointed at me questioningly.

Smiling, I pointed to my missing sidelocks and tallit, and shook my head.

Again he asked something in Hebrew, pointing with his index finger towards the lake. I assumed that he wanted to know if I came from Ukraine, and to avoid an unnecessarily complicated answer, I nodded.

He spat at my feet.

Before I could say anything, he ran away. After fifty metres, he turned and stared at me from a safe distance. He shouted something in Hebrew and tapped his forehead to indicate what he thought of me. I was too stunned to react.

It wasn't until I noticed the cross behind him that I realised he hadn't just been pointing generally at his surroundings when he'd spoken to me, but at the figure of Christ above the lake. He'd wanted to know if I was one of the lunatics who considered this bleeding impostor to be the Messiah.

The next morning I went to the bus station with my backpack. To while away the remaining half-hour before leaving for Kiev, I bought a coffee, found a spot in the sun, and lit a cigarette. That was a mistake.

"Your papers!"

A young policeman flicked through the pages of my passport.

"You know that you are not allowed to smoke here?"

"No," I said honestly. Smoking passengers were a ubiquitous sight at Ukrainian bus stations.

"Follow me!"

He led me into a narrow office on the upper floor of the station building.

"Sit down!"

After he had taken a seat at the other end of the table, he looked me squarely in the eye for a few seconds.

"You're in serious trouble," he announced. "The station is monitored by video cameras. Your offence is on record. You are a foreign national. If I gave you a ticket, it could lead to your deportation from Ukraine."

His grim expression reflected the seriousness of the situation. I had to bite my lip to keep from laughing.

Again, he riffled through my passport.

"First name and patronymic... *Dzhents Petter.*"

What he thought was my patronymic was, in fact, his Ukrainian pronunciation of my middle name, Peter. He placed a virgin charge sheet on the table, pulled out a pen and wrote down the details from my passport in spidery Latin letters.

"Address!"

I told him.

"Apartment number!"

"We do not have apartment numbers in Germany, only house numbers."

He looked up suspiciously from his charge sheet. "What does that mean, no apartment numbers? How does the postman find your apartment?"

"My name is on the door."

Silently he looked into my eyes, as if trying to put himself in a German postman's shoes.

Then he brusquely pushed the incomplete form aside.

"Dzhents Petter!" His fingertips drummed on the tabletop. "Tell me what I should do with you, Dzhents Petter!"

I shrugged helplessly. "I don't know. You're the policeman."

As he leaned over the table toward me, something like a smile appeared for the first time on his face.

"I am a policeman, but I am also a human being," he said. "We can settle this in a human kind of way."

I have never understood why the term "in a human kind of way", of all things, is used as code when demanding a bribe in the post-Soviet region.

Regretfully, I shook my head. "I'm a foreigner, I cannot do something like that."

"What do you mean?" The smile vanished from his face abruptly and his voice hardened. "What do you mean, 'something like that'? What are you implying? That all Ukrainian police are corrupt?"

"No," I said soothingly. Not all, I wanted to add, but I held my tongue.

Feigning helplessness, he shook his head.

"What am I going to do with you, Dzhents Petter? Should I issue you with a fine now or not?"

"If I have a choice, then I'd prefer it if you didn't."

"Do you regret your action?"

"I sincerely regret it."

"Are you going to do it again?"

"Never."

One minute after this face-saving finale, I was sitting on the bus to Kiev.

10

Philip and the Thief

Kiev

BY THE TIME I ARRIVED in Kiev, chestnut season had begun. They clattered down onto car roofs. Cheering children played soccer with them. They rolled down the sloping sidewalks and were kicked again, until the rolling took on a life of its own and they danced down the Kiev hills in arching leaps and bounds. Finally they came to rest in the valleys, smooth and brown and shiny, like a thousand sad eyes mourning after summer.

It was a strange autumn. September was drawing to a close, but during the days the temperature in Kiev still climbed to almost thirty degrees. Every evening, when the air noticeably cooled, a collective sigh seemed to pass through the city, as if each and every one of its inhabitants was secretly bidding farewell to the summer, which could not possibly go on any longer. But the next morning it returned. And the next. It just would not end.

I stayed in Kiev for ten days, and often the sun was just beginning to set when I went for a walk with Ksyusha and Philip. Ksyusha was an old friend I usually stayed with when I visited Kiev. Philip was her three-year-old son. Every evening before bedtime they both took a playground stroll between the neighbourhood's concrete blocks, and if I was at home, I tagged along.

Philip was the happiest three-year-old I knew. But in the course of each evening walk, sometimes just before, sometimes shortly after sunset, sometimes on the way to the playground, sometimes on the way back, he suddenly uttered the same worried sentence.

"Mama, can we go back to Kiev now?"

"But Philipushka, we're in Kiev."

"Let's go to Kiev, Mama. I want to go back to Kiev."

Neither I nor Ksyusha could get Philip to say what it was that suddenly made him feel like he was no longer in Kiev. Was it the nightfall? The sight of unknown people? A dog barking, the rustling of the trees, a strange shadow, the flight path of a pigeon? Some atmospheric shift seemed to take place every night between the prefabricated buildings that the adults could not perceive.

Ksyusha was Russian. We knew each other from Moscow, where she had grown up. She had moved to Kiev a few years ago, after she had met Roman, a Ukrainian pilot. A little later, Philip had been born.

Roman worked for a Ukrainian airline. In the morning he left the house in his captain's uniform, and when he came back in the evening, he told us about the landing conditions in Yerevan, Paris, or Minsk. He could talk about aircraft for hours. During the previous year, he had regularly flown over the Eastern Ukrainian war zone, until that day in July when an airliner with three hundred passengers on board was shot down in the Donbass. Since then, the airspace over Eastern Ukraine was closed.

On the other hand, the war had also thrown the

advantages of Roman's profession into sharper relief. Some of his Kiev acquaintances had been called up for national service in recent months, and they dreaded being sent to the front. Civilian pilots, on the other hand, were the last on the army's conscription list.

Ksyusha, Roman, and Philip spoke Russian at home, which was not unusual for Kievan families. Unfortunately, Ksyusha said, many of their acquaintances in Russia did not believe that.

"They are convinced that we will be murdered if we speak Russian here. I can explain it to them a thousand times, but they still prefer to believe what they are told on television."

Roman was fluently bilingual, like almost everyone in Kiev. Russian came more naturally to him, because he spoke it more frequently, but his Ukrainian was just as good. Unlike other Ukrainians, however, I never heard him switch casually back and forth between the two languages. Roman always paused for a moment if he wanted to switch, as if he had to consciously make the transition before he spoke. When I asked him about it once, he laughed.

"I have to readjust my thinking. So the languages don't get mixed up."

Philip understood Ukrainian, but so far spoke only the Russian of a three-year-old. He had not been speaking for very long, but he spoke all the more.

"Come, Uncle Jens, let's go to my room and get on the subway and fly into the cosmos, but with fur hats on, otherwise you'll freeze to death, and this is my pirate puzzle, and this is my zoo puzzle, and that's my plane puzzle, but Papa flies larger planes, and that's my train, it goes all the way to Moscow, Mama comes from Moscow and Papa is from

Kiev and I'm from Kiev and you're from Kiev and Uncle Sasha's from Kiev..."

After all the Russian–Ukrainian quarrels that had been a constant theme on my journey, it was good to share in the everyday life of a mixed family. The conflicts that were fought over here were not about languages or historical blame, but about nothing more serious than what time a three-year-old should go to bed.

The Maidan was a shrine. Eighteen months had now passed since the bloodbath on Independence Square. Its victims had become national martyrs in the Ukrainian collective psyche. They were referred to as "Heaven's Hundred". Around Independence Square, portraits of those who had been cut down lined the streets where the violence had escalated in February 2014. It was already dark when I walked past the memorial plaques, candles, and heaps of tribute flowers on one of my first evenings in Kiev.

A squawking voice echoed across the square. Beneath the Independence Monument, I saw a white-bearded man speaking into a megaphone. He did not have many listeners; a group of fewer than ten people stood around him. Curious, I walked towards them.

What had sounded from afar like a political speech turned out, on closer listening, to be something else entirely. The man's cadence immediately sounded familiar to me. It was the pathos-laden sing-song tone that Ukrainians and Russians automatically adopt when they are reciting poetry. At first I thought the man was spicing up his speech with a literary quotation – why else would someone recite verse through a megaphone? But after five minutes the squawked Ukrainian still sounded rhymed and rhythmical. There actually seemed to be something like a poetry reading going on here.

The man was reciting his verses off the cuff. Now and then his megaphone voice faltered, and I noticed that a second man would prompt him from the audience. Immediately, the squawking began again, as impassioned as before.

When I pulled my notebook out of my pocket to write down the few verses that I had understood in spite of the distorted sound, someone stepped toward me out of the circle of listeners. It was the prompter.

"Good evening," he said. "You're interested in our reading?"

He was about fifty and wore a beige linen sweater that was trimmed around the collar with Ukrainian folkloric patterns.

"Oleksandr," he introduced himself. "We do this every night."

I nodded in acknowledgement. "And what are you reciting here?"

His smile gave way to a look of dismay. "But... That's... You don't recognise it? Taras Shevchenko, of course!"

For precisely four hundred and twenty-three days, Oleksandr told me, he and his allies had come together at the Maidan every evening at six o'clock to recite the national poet's verses.

"Shevchenko is the only thing that unites Ukrainians," he said. "We have many churches, but only one Shevchenko."

A few other listeners joined in our conversation.

"Shevchenko is the father of the nation," a younger woman said.

"The *prophet* of the nation," clarified a man with a Cossack moustache.

"The *spirit* of the nation," Oleksandr added.

They were all veterans of the Maidan protests. They had camped out on the square for weeks during the cold revolution winter to get rid of their corrupt government.

An elderly man fished a rubber bullet out of his pocket.

"Here. This broke my collarbone."

He held the baton round up close to my face. His grin revealed a solitary incisor in an otherwise entirely toothless mouth.

Their reading, Oleksandr explained, was the continuation of the revolution.

"We are protesting against the destruction of Ukraine. There is a genocide under way, they want to wipe us out! Food is becoming more and more expensive; nobody has work; we don't know how we can pay our gas bills. The new government is even worse than the old one. They have betrayed the revolution, that's why we are here. The politicians are afraid of new protests, they want to chase us away from the Maidan. But Shevchenko is on our side!"

Meanwhile, the white-bearded man had handed the megaphone to an older woman in a floral dress.

"*Mountains beyond mountains, shrouded in clouds,*" she began. Her megaphone voice sounded just as monotonous and tinny as the previous speaker's. "*Seeded by grief and showered with blood...*"

Oleksandr looked at me. "The Caucasus!"

I nodded. It was one of the few Shevchenko poems I knew.

While the woman was declaiming, a drunk staggered up

to our group. Mumbling, he sought a partner for conversation. Since no one wanted to talk to him, he parked himself in front of the woman with the megaphone. She tried to shoo him away without interrupting her presentation. A bizarre duel developed – squawking versus slurring.

"*You came to spill your good pure blood not for Ukraine, but...*"

"Listen...! Listen to me...!"

"*... for her executioner.* You're drunk, go away! *You had a drink of Moscow's poison from the cup of Moscow. O my good, good friend...*"

"Just listen to me, will you..."

"*... My unforgettable dear friend!* Get lost, you're disturbing me! *May your living spirit soar above Ukraine...*"

"Liiiiiiiiiiiiiisten!"

"*... Fly with Cossacks over the shores!* Stop it, or I'll call the police! *Guard the dug-up mounds that stand amid the steppe...*"

In the end, two poetry lovers managed to persuade the drunk to leave. I was still struggling to hold back my laughter when Oleksandr resumed our conversation.

"This is our Hyde Park, our People's Parliament, our church of the national idea! We are calling on Shevchenko, only his spirit can save the country. People are grateful to us for this. Many stay to listen, they ask us to keep the revolution alive."

As I let my eyes wander over the small circle of listeners, Oleksandr read my thoughts.

"A priest prays, whether there are people in the church or not," he said. "We pray to Shevchenko, no matter how many listeners we have."

Then suddenly he had a brainwave. "Perhaps you could recite a bit of Goethe for us?" he asked.

Regretfully, I shook my head. "I'm afraid I wouldn't get very far from memory."

Oleksandr's disappointment knew no bounds. "Are you serious? You don't know a single Goethe poem by heart? But that is not possible! I can recite seven hours' worth of Shevchenko – at a single stretch!"

Minutes later he was still shaking his head in disbelief. "Which of us here is the European, you or I?"

I stood there for over an hour listening to this act of worship for Shevchenko. I had never been a big fan of the national poet, though in the present company I opted to keep this to myself. I knew that Shevchenko had almost single-handedly invented the literary language of Ukraine, that he had shaped the national consciousness of his compatriots like no other, that he had made great sacrifices for his beliefs. Nevertheless, I had only warmed to a few of his poems. Shevchenko's nationalism was as sentimental as it was belligerent, and neither were my cup of tea.

But his biography was unique. Born in 1814 as a serf to an ethnic German landowner named Vasily Engelhardt, Shevchenko had spent his childhood as a shepherd boy in a village southwest of Kiev. Early on, he was considered an unusual boy who decorated garden fences with chalk drawings, hung pictures in trees, and got lost in the wilderness "looking for the iron columns that support the sky", as he explained when they found him again.

Lieutenant Engelhardt did not fail to notice the talents of his young serf, and when his regiment was transferred to St. Petersburg in 1830, he took the now sixteen-year-old

Taras with him to the capital of the Russian Empire. Shevchenko's diverse gifts were also soon noticed there. He came into contact with renowned Russian artists like Karl Bryullov, who encouraged his aptitude for painting. Lieutenant Engelhardt was proud of his charge. He was less enthusiastic, however, when Shevchenko's patron suggested that he give the young Ukrainian his freedom. In the end, Bryullov hit upon an unorthodox solution: he sold one of his more valuable paintings to buy Shevchenko out of bondage for two and a half thousand roubles.

Around this time, in his mid-twenties, Shevchenko started to write alongside his painting – in Ukrainian, which, in the nineteenth century, was by no means an obvious choice. His verses could hardly have triggered more contradictory reactions. The Ukrainians and the more liberal sections of the Russian intelligentsia celebrated them. The majority of reviewers, however, puzzled over why so obviously gifted a writer should prefer to express himself in a "peasant dialect", in a "dead", an "artificial", a "joke language", rather than "enriching the universal Slavic literary canon" in Russian.

Shevchenko's early verses conjured up the rural idyll of a Ukraine where blind minstrels wander through the flowering steppe to praise with the sound of their bandura the heroic deeds of the Cossacks, that Ukrainian warrior caste who, in distant centuries, had reigned freely over their black earth, united in the Orthodox faith, until the Tsars destroyed the Cossack state. The snobbish criticism of his early work may have added to Shevchenko's growing contempt for all the actual and presumed oppressors of the Ukrainian people. For obvious historical reasons, the hatred in his later verses was directed chiefly at Russians and Poles, but also, less understandably, at Ukrainian Catholics and Jews.

He was arrested in 1847 for being a member of a secret society of nationalistically minded Kiev intellectuals. The Tsarist police classified Shevchenko as a dangerous troublemaker. His verses, the order exiling him states, romanticised the "allegedly happy Cossack era" and were in danger of giving his countrymen foolish ideas, not least of all the notion "that Ukraine could exist as an independent state." Tsar Nicholas I personally added his own note to the verdict: "Strictest security; writing and painting forbidden."

For ten years Shevchenko was kept in the southern Urals and on the shores of the Caspian Sea. Thanks to his charm, he managed to partially circumvent the Tsar's prohibitions. In the Russian province he befriended bored landowners and army officers, who smuggled his letters to the capital and hid his journals for him. Shevchenko maintained contact with his old artist friends, and when his banishment was repealed after Nicholas's death, his return to St. Petersburg was triumphal.

Even so, he was still kept under surveillance, censored, and banned from travelling. Only once, during a brief, secret visit, would he see his Ukrainian homeland again before dying of a heart attack in St. Petersburg in 1861, at the age of only forty-seven. Two months later, his remains were solemnly carried to Ukraine and buried in a small village south of Kiev on the banks of the Dnieper River.

The squawking fell silent shortly before nine o'clock. The only non-participant listeners who had held out until the very end were me and an Asian tourist who listened to the readings with a look of friendly interest on his face, though probably without understanding a great deal. To conclude proceedings, Oleksandr took the megaphone. He recited the poem that had ended each of the Maidan recitals for four hundred and twenty-three days: Shevchenko's "Testament".

When I am dead, then bury me
In my beloved Ukraine,
My tomb upon a grave mound high
Amid the spreading plain,
So that the fields, the boundless steppes,
The Dnieper's plunging shore
My eyes could see, my ears could hear
The mighty river roar.
When from Ukraine the Dnieper bears
Into the deep blue sea
The blood of foes... then will I leave
These hills and fertile fields –
I'll leave them all and fly away
To the abode of God,
And then I'll pray... But till that day
I nothing know of God.
Oh bury me, then rise ye up
And break your heavy chains
And water with the tyrants' blood
The freedom you have gained.

The district of concrete blocks where Ksyusha and Roman lived was located on the eastern bank of the Dnieper. I crossed the river on the subway every morning on the way to the city centre. The journey is a long one because the

Dnieper is wide – almost two kilometres separate its banks in Kiev. Every morning I would see the silver-grey waters flowing sluggishly southward, towards the Black Sea.

During my first extended stay in Kiev, five years before my current trip, I had lived on the eastern bank of the Dnieper too, and I had had occasion to cross the river countless times. But now I suddenly saw it in a different light. Back then I had considered it the most important river in Russian history. Now, I wasn't so sure which country's history had really played out on its banks.

On the city-centre side, in the wooded hills that line the western riverbank, a monument towers over the chestnuts. Prince Vladimir of Kiev looks across the Dnieper, a raised bronze cross in his hand. A little more than a thousand years ago, the real, living Vladimir had stood on this spot, his princely gaze surveying the river, and his hand clutching a cross that must have felt strange to him.

Vladimir was more familiar with the wooden statues of the ancient Slavic gods to whom he had sacrificed offerings of food since early childhood at the side of his father Svyatoslav. The old sovereign had personally expelled from Kiev the first Christian missionaries who had appeared in the pagan kingdom of Rus, and when his son came to the throne in 978, he distributed even more wooden gods around the realm. In other respects too, Vladimir adhered to the pagan way of life pursued by his forefathers. The virginal blood of seven wives and a hundred times as many courtesans is said to have soaked his princely sheets.

How Vladimir found God is disputed. According to legend, about fifteen years after taking office, he sent out scouts who were charged with finding out how the surrounding realms practised their faith. When they returned, they reported one by one. The messenger who had visited the Muslim Volga Bulgars got no further than the word "teetotal" before the prince cut him off: "Drinking is the joy of the Rus," Vladimir declared. "Without it, we cannot exist!"

The next report concerned the Jewish Khazars. At the word "circumcision" the prince's face grew dark, but it was the story of the expulsion from Jerusalem that really tipped the scales. What was one supposed to make of a God who turned his chosen people into nomads?

The messengers who had been detailed to report on Catholicism threw in the towel of their own accord. The German churches were not worth mentioning, they explained, since they had encountered "no glory" there.

That left Orthodox Byzantium. Vladimir noted with satisfaction that the Greeks drank and did not engage in any nonsense with their foreskins. Nor had their God sent them out into the desert, but instead had given them Constantinople, a city that Vladimir's scouts described as a paradise: "We knew not whether we were in Heaven or on Earth, for on Earth there is no such splendour or such beauty, and we are at a loss how to describe it. We know only that God dwells there among men, and their service is fairer than the ceremonies of other nations."

Then let us be Orthodox, announced the prince.

The legend about choosing the faith was likely invented by a monk who wrote Vladimir's hagiography when the Kiev Orthodoxy later canonised its founding father. In truth, the decisive factor for Vladimir's decision was probably a woman: Anna Porphyrogenita, the daughter of the Byzantine emperor. The ruler of Constantinople had nothing in principle against a dynastic alliance with the ruler of Kiev, but he could hardly marry his daughter to a heathen. Vladimir had to be baptised, and specifically into the Orthodox Christian faith.

And so it came to pass that in 988 CE, the prince held in his hand a cross with an Orthodox double crossbeam when he oversaw the baptism of his kingdom from the bank of the Dnieper. Vladimir himself had just undergone the ritual himself in Crimea, and now it was his subjects' turn. Priests who had come from Byzantium murmured Greek baptismal prayers that nobody understood while the people of the Rus threw off their clothes and sprang in the river rejoicing – at least that was how the mass baptism was later depicted on icons. In the background, the ancient Slavic wooden gods floated by, as Vladimir had summarily had them cast into the Dnieper. The river washed them to the south, and one or two Greeks probably took fright when the grinning idols later washed up on the shores of the Black Sea.

On top of all the ambiguities and legends that sprang up around Vladimir's life story, a key question arose surprisingly late in the day: was the prince Russian, or Ukrainian, or both at the same time, or neither? Which people could call him a blood relative, which country had the right to regard itself as the successor to his empire, and which church should consider him their founder?

Kievan Rus covered both the central part of present-day Ukraine and the westernmost part of today's Russia. In Vladimir's time it was one of the most powerful empires of Europe, but its short heyday ended less than two and a half centuries later with the Mongol invasion. When the Golden Horde withdrew again, Kiev had become almost an irrelevance. Instead Moscow rose to be the new centre of power in Eastern Europe.

Because the history books were henceforth written in the Kremlin, the Russian view of Kievan Rus is the dominant one today. Under Vladimir, according to the Muscovite version, the people of the Eastern Slav principalities were united. Only the Mongol yoke divided the old empire. While its residents still remained one people, they now split into three dialect groups: the Great Russian, the Belarusian and the "Little Russian" Eastern Slavs – this latter term being the Muscovite name for the Ukrainians. Moscow was therefore the new Kiev, Vladimir the founder of the Russian Orthodox Church, the Kremlin the seat of the Patriarch, and the Tsar the ruler of all Eastern Slavs.

For a long time, the Tsar's Ukrainian subjects saw no reason to doubt this interpretation. After all, this was what they had been taught for centuries by Russian historians. Russian teachers dinned it into them, in Russian, in Russian schools, using Russian textbooks. Russian painters had illustrated the history of Kievan Rus, Russian musicians set it to music, and Russian sculptors created its monuments. The statue of Vladimir on the banks of the Dnieper River, for example, had been erected at the initiative of Tsar Nicholas I, shortly after he sent Taras Shevchenko, the Ukrainian national poet, into exile.

Around the same time as Shevchenko, a first generation of Ukrainian historians began to question the Russian version of their national history. They argued that even in Vladimir's time the Rus had not been a unified area; that its central, Ukrainian part had been connected only very loosely with the northern, later Russian, borderlands. In addition, they contended, the linguistic differences between the two regions did not first originate during the Mongol occupation, and the Old Slavic that was in use in Vladimir's time was much more akin to modern Ukrainian than to Russian. Furthermore, the name Rus had always been a Ukrainian self-denomination, long before the Muscovites appropriated it and demeaned their neighbours as "Little Russians". And the foundations of Russian Orthodox theology had verifiably been laid in Kiev before the church had been exported to Moscow.

In the end the more radical among the historians scarcely wanted to acknowledge any connection whatsoever between Russian and Ukrainian history. The Muscovites, they argued, had kidnapped Kievan Rus. In an attempt to give their young empire a glorious past, they had stolen Ukraine's name and history. Naturally, the Ukrainian historians felt that their interpretation was only corroborated when the Tsarist regime responded to their attempts at reinterpretation with censorship and publication bans.

To this day the dispute is unresolved, and will probably remain so forever. Every now and then it flares up again. During my travels I heard about a backbencher in the Ukrainian Parliament who made headlines with a bizarre legislative proposal: he wanted to prohibit the Russians from calling themselves Russians, because the name belonged to the Ukrainians.

During the Soviet era, the conflict over the origin myth of the Eastern Slavs was put on hold. Issues of national descent were no longer supposed to play a role in Lenin's state: the peoples of the Soviet Union were meant to look confidently to the future, not broodingly back at the past. National dividing lines were an outmoded delusion of the old world, and they had to be overcome like class boundaries. The Tsars had suppressed the Ukrainian and Russian people alike, and in the long line of despots Vladimir was just one of the first. What did it matter who the Kievan Rus belonged to, when the Bolsheviks brotherly joined hands with their Ukrainian class allies?

"Hand in hand with the great Russian people and the other peoples of the Soviet Union, the freedom-loving and talented Ukrainian people are at the forefront of the progressive peoples of the world," I read in the preface to my Soviet edition of Taras Shevchenko's poetry, which was published in Moscow in 1951. "Across the vast Ukraine the joyful songs of the people ring out, extolling their creative labour, the freedom they have won for their culture, and the geniuses of the socialist revolution, Lenin and Stalin." If only the poet had been able to read this gross misrepresentation of his work, he would have risen from the grave and ripped the book into pieces.

The Christianisation of the Rus, the mass baptism in the Dnieper that Prince Vladimir had once observed from the shore, was, in retrospect, regarded by the Bolsheviks as just the beginning of a centuries-long aberration. After Lenin's revolution, they triumphantly tore the old icons out of the churches and threw them into the Dnieper, as Vladimir had done with the Slavs' idols nearly a thousand years before. Desecrated paintings floated down the river, past the monument of the prince who had once brought the sacred Byzantine images to Kiev.

I had witnessed the next twilight of the gods in Kiev myself. Eighteen months before my current trip, in December 2013, I had flown to Ukraine as a journalist to cover the Maidan protests. One night, while I was sitting in my hotel room writing my report, the noise of the demonstrations suddenly swelled up outside the window. The constant fear of missing anything important in the turmoil of the revolutionary events immediately drove me downstairs into the street. The uproar appeared to be coming from the Bessarabian Market, in the direction of the Lenin monument. By the time I reached it, the plinth was empty.

The crowd was so dense that I could barely make any headway. When I'd finally battled my way through, I saw Lenin lying prone on the flagstones next to the pedestal. Two men with sledgehammers were standing on his knees and chest, clobbering the huge granite figure over and over again, spurred on by the deafening cheering of the crowd. I looked on, stunned. I don't recall how long it took for the steady stream of new arrivals at the scene to squeeze me out of the inner circle of spectators.

The next morning, the first snow fell. On the way to the airport I walked past the statue again. Lenin's mutilated body was covered with a thin, white dusting of snow. Overnight, his head had disappeared.

Two old women were standing next to the monument, undecided on which side of the beheaded granite body they should place their memorial candles. In the end they put them in front of the empty pedestal, weeping.

A year and a half on from that December night, the pedestal, seven metres high, was still in the same position it had occupied since 1946. Also still in place was the Ukrainian quotation from Lenin that adorned the base: "Through united action by the working people of Ukraine and Russia, a free Ukraine is possible; without such unity, there can be no question of it."

Only Lenin was missing. The residual plinth looked like a monument to a vanished monument. The people of Kiev seemed to have grown accustomed to the sight. Pedestrians walked by without stopping or even turning their heads. It had been a matter of pure chance that I had witnessed the toppling of the monument. But it hadn't felt like that, because a long history connected me with this statue.

A few years before the Maidan protests I had been sitting in a courtroom in the Kiev Shevchenkivskyi District Court, following a truly bizarre trial that centred on Lenin's nose. That year had witnessed the first act of vandalism against the statue. On a June night in 2009 five men had propped a long ladder against Lenin's chest. One of them had shinned up it and smashed off the revolutionary's nose with a hammer. He also succeeded in damaging Lenin's chin and left hand before two policemen dragged him down.

During the offender's subsequent prosecution and trial, the Kiev communists had the monument restored with party funds. After the ceremonial reinauguration they erected a tent next to the pedestal, where volunteer guards camped around the clock. For nearly two years the communists had held out there, to protect their Lenin from further attacks. At that time they did not yet have any inkling of the forthcoming Maidan revolution.

I had met two people back then whose entire thinking revolved around Lenin, although for completely different reasons. One was named Mykola Kokhanivskiy, the man who had knocked off Lenin's nose. The other one was Vera Yefimovna, one of the old communists who had kept guard next to the monument.

On that December night during the Maidan protests, as I had watched, paralysed, while the statue was being destroyed, I was wondering how my two acquaintances would react to the news of Lenin's final fall. In the hectic days of the revolution, I had not been able to contact them. Now I was determined to finally catch up with them.

I reached the communist first. We met in the foyer of an old Soviet hotel on the eastern bank of the Dnieper. No sooner had we settled into a quiet niche with sofas than Vera Yefimovna banged her hand down, in a chopping motion on the tabletop three times in quick succession.

"Feudalism – capitalism – socialism."

She fixed me with a stare. "That's the chronological sequence. Marx predicted it."

Vera Yefimovna was close to eighty, and she had aged visibly in the five years that had passed since our last meeting. Her once jet-black hair had turned grey, and around the circumference of her pupils there were milky rings. Nevertheless, her eyes were still as fierce as I had remembered them.

Again she banged her hand down on the tabletop.

"And once socialism has evolved: Com-mu-nism!"

Instinctively, I had expected to find her dispirited. Lenin's fall, the Maidan revolt, Ukraine's new western course, all that could not have been remotely to her liking. But Vera Yefimovna looked anything but resigned, and after I had listened to her for a while, I understood why. The decisive point in her life had been the collapse of the Soviet Union. Everything that had happened since then only confirmed her view that the world was falling apart.

"NATO and the EU Parliament have decided to revive fascism in Ukraine, to boost the defence industry. The bourgeoisie needs wars!"

But none of these aberrations, Vera Yefimovna knew, was of a lasting nature. One last time the bourgeoisie had risen up. In its death throes it had brought Marx's historical progress to a halt, and capitalism had temporarily returned. But in the end it would fail, and Lenin would prevail. The bourgeoisie could destroy his monuments, but not his spirit.

"These fascists knocked off all his limbs!"

Vera Yefimovna had also seen the fallen statue that December, a few days after me.

"Only the torso was left. The police were there. They wouldn't let anyone approach the monument. The whole place was cordoned off. We will raise Lenin again, that's for sure!"

I wasn't so sure about that, but I held my tongue.

"Did you notice the rings?"

Vera Yefimovna pointed to her cataract-shrouded pupils. I nodded.

"I will fight them with willpower. Just like I did my ulcers."

She made no further comment about her ailments. She was convinced she could overcome them through self-healing. I suspected that she couldn't afford the operations.

"I'm resilient. Like everyone who worked in Chernobyl."

In the Soviet era Vera Yefimovna had been a camera-woman. At our last meeting, she had told me about the documentary that she had filmed in the restricted and abandoned reactor zone, and about the heroic achievements of the Soviet clean-up workers.

"I'm not interested in the films that are made today. There are no subject matters in capitalism. Who sleeps with whom – that's all the bourgeoisie thinks about."

She pointed at my notebook. "Write that down, it's important! All the great directors had social themes. Who was the first person to bring the common man to the screen?"

"Charlie Chaplin," I said.

Vera Yefimovna raised her eyebrows in surprise. "Correct. And which country should we thank for the first films about the proletariat?"

"The Soviet Union."

"Which directors?"

"Eisenstein, Pudovkin, Dovzhenko."

She was visibly impressed. It seemed she had forgotten that she had told me to jot down these very same sentences in my notebook five years ago. I owed my entire knowledge of social revolutionary film history to Vera Yefimovna.

She told me about her former workplace, the Kiev Dovzhenko film studio, which was named after one of the Soviet cinema pioneers, the Ukrainian Oleksandr Dovzhenko. When I asked if films were still being made there, Vera Yefimovna grimaced in disgust.

"Only bad ones. Dovzhenko would turn in his grave. Do you want to see the studio?"

I nodded. "Can I get in there just like that?"

Vera Yefimovna laughed. "With me, of course!"

We arranged an excursion. Before we parted company, I asked Vera Yefimovna to recommend a film by Dovzhenko in preparation.

She thought for a moment.

"*Earth*," she said. "The best film ever made in Kiev."

Mykola Kokhanivskiy, the man who knocked off Lenin's nose, had responded to my attempts to make contact with a text message.

"Meeting only possible tomorrow – on my way to the front."

Early the next morning I travelled to the terminus of the southern metro line and entered the shopping centre to which Kokhanivskiy had directed me. I could see him sitting in a café from a distance. He wore a mottled green camouflage suit.

"Glory to Ukraine!"

"Good morning, Mykola."

He looked exactly as I remembered him – a stocky, bald man in his mid-forties with a doughy, completely expressionless face. Even at our first encounter, in conversation with him I had caught myself thinking that his shapeless skull looked strangely unfinished, as if God had been too busy to see the work through. Now again, when I looked at him, I literally felt the desire to reach out and knead Kokhanivskiy's features into shape.

We had met during the trial over Lenin's nose, which had ended with a three-year suspended sentence for Kokhanivskiy. It had since expired, and in the light of the Maidan revolution, it seemed absurd. In the past year and a half, statues of Lenin monuments had been toppled throughout the country, without anyone being convicted or even charged. The fight against "Symbols of Communism" had become government policy. Also, the countless Ukrainian streets, squares, and cities that bore the names of Lenin and other Soviet heroes were to be renamed.

"Lenin's nose was the beginning," Kokhanivskiy said. "I was the first person who declared war on the monuments. You can see for yourself what has become of it. The revolution has triumphed."

But Kokhanivskiy's fight was not over. Just like Vera Yefimovna, he knew that Lenin's nose was easier to destroy than Lenin's ideas. For him, the monuments were symbols of the Russian policy of repression that had neither begun with Lenin nor ended with his fall. Russia did not want to relinquish Ukraine. Through military intervention, Moscow had annexed Crimea and infiltrated the Donbass, and Kokhanivskiy was now fighting against enemies who were not made of granite, but of flesh and blood. He had rallied a volunteer battalion around him and gone to war.

The first hundred, he told me, had joined up during the barricade battles on the Maidan. With wooden beams, crowbars and Molotov cocktails, Kokhanivskiy's men had fought against police detachments. "We also got hold of the first firearms at that time," he said. "Though we didn't use them at the Maidan."

I was uncertain whether the last part was true. In the final phase of the street battles, individual demonstrators had opened fire on the police. Kokhanivskiy had not struck me as a pacifist during our first meeting, and the events of recent years had certainly not turned him into one.

After the revolution, Kokhanivskiy kept referring to

himself by the battle name "Hurricane", which he had adopted on the barricades. He recruited more volunteers to his battalion, while at the same time expanding his arsenal. His fighters acquired old pistols and rifles from Soviet army stocks, and eventually they made their way to the Eastern Front, in uniforms cobbled together out of bits and pieces, to wage war against the separatists. There were now about three hundred volunteers under Kokhanivskiy's command, half of whom were permanently stationed in Pisky, a small town near Donetsk.

Kokhanivskiy had given his battalion the name "OUN" – an abbreviation for the old Ukrainian nationalist movement.

"We are Bandera's successors," he said. "We're carrying on the twentieth-century struggle for independence. We will complete the national revolution of Ukraine."

I immediately thought of Ivan Mamchur, the old OUN veteran I had met in Lviv. Was he aware, I wondered, that a volunteer battalion was fighting at the Eastern Front under the name of the nationalist movement?

"Ukraine has three enemies," Kokhanivskiy continued. "Russia first and foremost. Secondly, the enemy occupiers within…"

"The what?"

"The oligarchs. Power's in the hands of thieves who do not represent the Ukrainian nation, neither ideologically nor by blood, and it must be made clear to these people…"

"What do you mean, by blood?" I interrupted him.

He looked at me searchingly, as if trying to work out whether I really did not understand what he was talking about.

"The two hundred most powerful people in Ukraine are

Jews," he went on. "The president – a Jew. The Prime Minister – a Jew..."

He continued to count on his fingers – half of the cabinet of ministers, the party leaders, all the captains of industry. Only a few of the names he mentioned sounded even remotely Jewish.

"Listen," I interrupted him. "I understand that you think the influence of the oligarchs stinks. But what difference does it make to you whether they are Jews or not?"

He looked at me as if he doubted the sincerity of my question.

"I see," he said. "You think that it's a coincidence?"

I had to laugh. "No – a rumour."

Kokhanivskiy shook his head firmly. "I am not an anti-Semite, but I'm not blind either. Our country is being robbed. It must be made clear to these people that they have only two options: they can leave Ukraine alive – or in a coffin."

He let his words sink in for a few seconds before continuing.

"Ukraine needs a dictatorship. Of course I know that sounds unacceptable to a European. But there is no alternative. We must be cruel, otherwise our enemies will prevail. Only then can we go the way Western democracies have gone – but not before."

I took a moment to digest what he was saying. Kokhanivskiy, I knew, was a marginal figure – his battalion was small, his political influence zero, his opinion unable to command a majority. But his logic of war seemed to be telling him that the country was in his debt. He had shed blood for Ukraine. He had killed, and he had seen his comrades die.

Kokhanivskiy had felt the power of bloodshed, and he would find it difficult leaving it behind with a light heart once the war was over.

"The war," he said, "won't be over until we have recaptured the Donbass and Crimea and our enemies are defeated."

I asked him who was the third enemy he had mentioned.

Kokhanivskiy sighed. "The Europeans. They accept Russia's aggression and spit on the rights of the Ukrainian nation."

I sighed as well. In the west, in the east, even inside the country's government, nothing but enemies all around.

"Who are your friends then, Mykola?"

He crossed himself.

"We only have God. At the Maidan nobody helped us. All the same, we won. Because God was on our side."

There was another pause in the conversation. I looked Kokhanivskiy intently in the eyes. His expressionless face was hard to read, but I had no doubt that he meant it seriously.

Shortly before we went our separate ways, I realised that something had changed in him. There was still the same anger there that I had seen five years ago, but back then, when I had observed Kokhanivskiy on trial, his anger had seemed blunt and depressive, like a suppressed childish rage that could find no proper outlet. Now his hatred had a goal, and Kokhanivskiy exuded an enthusiasm he had completely lacked five years ago.

"You look happy, Mykola."

The ghost of a smile flitted across his doughy cheeks. "How would I not be happy?" he said. "Maybe I'll be struck by a bullet tomorrow, but that doesn't matter. God lets me experience a great moment – the fate of Ukraine is fulfilling! Warriors and revolutionaries are needed now, not merchants and lawyers. I am the right man in the right place. How could I not be happy?"

One Saturday I went on a trip with my host family. Roman's parents, who lived in a village near Kiev, had invited us to a shashlik barbecue.

On the way there, Ksyusha told me about an old woman from the neighbourhood.

"Everyone in the village calls her Baba Dunya. I have no idea what her real name is. She's ancient, but she's still got all her marbles. She has a lot to tell. Maybe you would like to talk to her?"

Roman's parents had lived in the village of Semypolky for several years. The little house that they had bought as a retirement home was newly renovated. It still smelt of fresh paint. Out on the terrace Roman's father slid pieces of marinated chicken onto long skewers. He was a pilot like his son, and the two soon plunged into a technical discussion about wind conditions. Philip played in the garden with a little girl from the neighbourhood. Giggling, the two of them jumped through the spray of a lawn sprinkler.

Ksyusha asked her mother-in-law how things were going with Baba Dunya.

"She is old," was the answer.

"She has been quite old for a long time," Ksyusha said, laughing.

"Lately she seems tired, though. As if she's had enough of life. I think it must be all these reports from the Donbass. She does not want to live through another war."

When Ksyusha and I visited Baba Dunya after our meal, we found her sitting on a garden bench behind her little house. She was sitting in the sun in a flower-patterned, sleeveless dress, her grey hair pulled back into a loose peasant braid, her face serious, almost combative. She was not in a good mood.

"Baba Dunya!" Ksyusha cried in horror. "What has happened to your arms?"

Deep, barely healed wounds disfigured her suntanned skin.

Baba Dunya sighed. "The cow."

The cow had broken loose during milking and Baba Dunya, who wasn't able to jump aside quickly enough, had ended up under the animal's hooves.

"Here," said the old woman, pointing first to her arms, then to her belly. "And here."

Her full name was Evdokiya Fyodorovna, but no one had called her by that name in decades. In the small village where she had lived her entire life, she was Grandma Dunya. She had turned eighty-seven this year.

She had been born just as the Bolsheviks were convincing the villagers of the benefits of collective farming. The Bolsheviks had good arguments, powerful arguments, arguments that it was better not to resist. Anyone who still refused to give up their privately owned farms must be kulaks, rich peasants, the reasoning went. The Bolsheviks expected such resistance; actually they were happy when the class enemy made it so easy for them to recognise him. In villages where the kulaks were less simple to spot, the Bolsheviks simply imprisoned the next best peasants who looked a little more affluent than the rest.

Baba Dunya recounted that her parents had owned a few cows when she was born. In the eyes of the Bolsheviks that was enough to make them kulaks – one could become a kulak very quickly in the years of collectivisation. Baba Dunya did not say exactly what had happened to her parents. The memory seemed to depress her.

We talked to her for half an hour, but she sighed more than she spoke. The terror had been followed by hunger, hunger by war, and now there was war again, and she was tired, and her wounds would not heal.

Ksyusha later told me that she'd never seen Baba Dunya so despondent. She remains etched on my memory as a woman who never in her life had much luck with cows.

I thought of Baba Dunya a few days later, when I watched the film by Oleksandr Dovzhenko that Vera Yefimovna had recommended to me in preparation for our visit to the studio.

Earth was filmed in 1930, while the "destruction of the kulaks as a class" proclaimed by Stalin was in full swing. The silent film is set in a Ukrainian village whose inhabitants are divided in their reaction to the Bolshevik collective farm campaign. You can easily guess who the good guys and who the bad guys are. A beaming, clean-shaven, confident young communist recruits villagers for the collective farm. His opponents are the kulaks: bullheaded old farmers, bearded and beetle-browed, who stubbornly refuse to see why they should give up their fields to the village community. Nor do they understand why they should suddenly stop ploughing their land in the same way that their fathers and their fathers' fathers had always done: with iron ploughs drawn by oxen. The oxen and the kulaks look strikingly similar in Dovzhenko's film.

The Soviet hero has only a weary smile left for the obstinate old farmers. He knows that a future has long since dawned in which there will be no room for kulaks anymore – or even oxen. In a long, spectacularly cut scene the hero turns his gaze to the horizon. Something is approaching the village; you do not know what. Presently, the other villagers also start craning their necks to see. All looks expectantly follow our hero's; people shield their eyes to peer into the distance. Even the animals are restless: first the horses, then the oxen nervously turn their heads to the horizon, until our hero suddenly opens his mouth and cheers. On-screen letters spell out his silent cry which half the village joins in.

"It's coming! It's coming!"

Finally it appears – the plough of the future! The ox of socialism! While the orchestral music swells to a triumphant crescendo, there appears on the horizon… crescendo, crescendo, crescendo… a tractor.

I had to laugh.

The tractor briefly becomes the central character of the film. It ploughs and ploughs and ploughs. Flashing, the steel ploughshare slices into the black earth. Tirelessly it breaks up the clods; furrow by furrow it makes order of the fields. The oxen drowse, unemployed, in the stables. The kulaks curse. The future has begun.

In an exuberance of ploughing, the hero finally flattens the boundary markers separating the collective farm from the land belonging to the kulaks. Shortly thereafter, a vindictive class enemy shoots him down. The hero dies, but his funeral only heralds the triumphant onward march of socialism. The people expel the village priest from the cemetery. In his place, a fiery communist funeral orator expounds the moral of the film.

"The enemy is in his death throes, and in his hatred of the impoverished he has taken Vasyl from us! With the Bolsheviks' Steel Horse, Vasyl ploughed up the thousand-year-old boundary furrows, with his hot blood he has signed the death warrant of the class enemy! The fame of our Vasyl will travel across the world like..." – here the speaker raises his hand above the heads of the assembled crowd – "... like that Bolshevik aircraft up there in the sky!"

Today, the film may seem like naive propaganda, but I could imagine that in 1930 it must have been hard to resist the rousing power of its images. Perhaps I would not have been sure myself at the end whether the Bolsheviks, with their righteous pathos, had somehow been on the right side of history – had I not known, that is, that hardly anything in Dovzhenko's movie corresponded to reality.

Stalin's collectivisation campaign probably killed more people than the number who perished on all sides of the front during the First World War.

It was hardly surprising that many farmers refused to join the collective farms. In concrete terms, taking that step meant giving up all of one's own land, livestock, and tools and working as a Soviet serf for a party-run enterprise. When Stalin sensed that the farmers weren't voluntarily heeding his appeals, he resorted to repression. Party members marched through the villages in search of class enemies. If they did not find any, they invented them. It was enough for a person to own a cow, a grain store, a house with a cellar or a metal roof; it was enough to be able to read and write to find oneself being singled out as a kulak. Family by family, the farmers were deported from their villages. Many were never heard from again.

At the same time, the forced transformation from private to collective farm ownership began. Peasants' huts were searched to track down saboteurs who were hiding grain supplies from the party or slaughtering their cattle to eat them before they fell into the hands of the collective farm. Soldiers dug through piles of manure, dismantled stoves, and stuck their bayonets into the walls of houses looking for hidden food. Whatever they found, they took. Fields and vegetable plots were placed under guard – whoever misappropriated state-owned property was an enemy of the people, even if he had cultivated the state-owned property himself. Scores of people were sentenced to prison or executed because they had dug up a handful of onions from their confiscated gardens or cut a few ears of corn from their fields.

In the end, no one was hiding any more food. There wasn't any left. The harvested grain was requisitioned and transported to the cities. The rural population starved. By 1932, the farmers were eating whatever they could find – grass, leaves, bark, ants, snails, worms. Some ate their dogs, others their shoes; quite a few ate the neighbours who had died of starvation. Whole villages died out, one family after another. Silence fell across rural Ukraine.

How many people fell victim to this madness is still unknown. No word of the disaster appeared in the Soviet press. Instead, one success story followed another: village X one hundred percent collectivised; village Y free of kulaks; village Z cleared of saboteurs. As Stalin's successor, Nikita Khrushchev, later explained, no one had counted the dead.

Stalin himself merely declared that you can't make an omelette without breaking eggs. Beyond that, the dictator refused to concern himself over slanderous rumours spread abroad by Western agents about an alleged Soviet famine. When the first Union-wide census to be conducted after the disaster revealed a terrifying slump in the Soviet population, Stalin promptly had the statisticians shot. Their successors hastened to provide more acceptable figures.

In his study on the Soviet programme of forced collectivisation, the British historian Robert Conquest works from the assumption that some six and a half million fell victim to the persecution of the kulaks, and that seven million more died as a result of the famine, of which five million were in Ukraine, and the remainder in the rest of the Soviet Union. Some contend that even those figures are too low. If they are correct, one-fifth of the Ukrainian rural population was killed in the early 1930s.

The black soil of Ukraine is among the most fertile farmlands on the planet.

Which makes the Holodomor one of the most senseless disasters in history.

Dovzhenko's *Earth* must be either the most naïve or the most misleading film ever made – I'm really not sure which.

Vera Yefimovna's monologue on the merits of the communist world order picked up where she had left off a few days earlier. We sat side by side in the subway as we headed towards the film studio. The train carriage grew fuller and fuller. Vera Yefimovna praised Lenin and Stalin without restraint. She did not seem to notice the irritated glances of the passengers standing around us. I, on the other hand, felt uncomfortable.

Five years earlier, during my public discussions with her, my impression had been that random listeners were not paying much attention to us. Now, however, her remarks sounded decidedly shrill. Vera Yefimovna had remained the same, but the city in which she lived had changed.

In the central recording studio of the Dovzhenko Film Studios there was an almost life-size replica of the Moscow Lenin Mausoleum. It looked like the original, but with one difference. Above the entrance there was not one, but two names prominently displayed: "Lenin" and "Stalin".

A film about the Khrushchev era had just been completed, a stagehand told us. Vera Yefimovna paused for a long time in front of the cardboard mausoleum. It had looked just like this when she had gone to Moscow in 1953, to weep over the newly laid out body of the great Stalin.

The huge studio lot was used only partially for making films today. Many of the buildings had been sublet to other companies. Vera Yefimovna, who had not been here for a few years too, undauntedly flung wide open one door after the other. Whoever stood in her way was pushed brusquely aside. She wanted to know what capitalism had done to her studio. I stood discreetly in the background while she argued with clerks and janitors. "Bourgeoisie," she muttered after each door that she furiously slammed shut again during her inspection rounds. "Bourgeoisie…"

We roamed through the old wardrobe storage rooms, with their endless rows of Second World War uniforms, Boyar coats, cosmonaut suits, and ballerina dresses. We carried on through the scenery workshops until we reached the camera corridor, Vera Yefimovna's former workplace. In the adjacent spotlight store we ran into an old lighting technician whom Vera Yefimovna knew from the old days. The two greeted each other warmly, like two long-lost friends.

"How's life?" the lighting technician asked.

"How do you think it is?" Vera Yefimovna replied. "The bourgeoisie are in power. There's nothing holding me back here. I'll probably emigrate."

The electrician nodded thoughtfully. "To Israel?"

"No, what nonsense! Why would I go to Israel? To Moscow, of course!"

"To Moscow?" The lighting technician looked at her in surprise. "What do you want with Putin?"

"Have you got something against Putin?"

"Do I have something against Putin? He stole Crimea from us!"

"Stole? That was a democratic vote."

The lighting technician said nothing. Taken aback, he just shook his head.

"Vera," he continued presently, "I always thought I could talk to you sensibly."

He let the steel door of the spotlight store slam thunderously behind him. When the sound had died away, it was eerily quiet in the camera corridor.

Vera Yefimovna snorted. "Come on," she said. "Let's go."

How quickly, I thought, friendships end in wartime.

The sunlight dazzled us when we stepped outside of the darkness of the studio building.

"Vera Yefimovna," I said. "Did I hear this right? You like Putin? But he's not a communist at all."

She ignored my objection. Something else had distracted her.

"Wasn't there a pool here?" I heard her mutter.

She shaded her eyes with the palm of her hand and scanned the premises. Having failed to find what she was looking for, she shrugged her shoulders indifferently.

"Oh well," she said. "The bourgeoisie don't need a pool."

On the way to the exit, we walked through the orchard that Oleksandr Dovzhenko himself had planted when the studio had opened in the 1920s.

"Forgive us, Dovzhenko," Vera Yefimovna murmured as she scooped up a few apples from the grass and pressed them into my hands without a word. I dropped them discreetly. Not so much because they were half-rotten, but out of a sudden superstitious fear. I was afraid to eat from the tree of communist knowledge.

As we neared the exit, a question that had been bothering me for days suddenly occurred to me.

"Vera Yefimovna," I said. "The statue of Lenin…"

"Yes?"

"What happened to the smashed remains? Where are they?"

She thought for a moment.

"I don't know," she replied. "But they'd certainly know at the *Raicom.*"

The Raion Committee of the Communist Party was a few bus stops away. In the lobby, Vera Yefimovna waved her membership card and pushed me forcefully through a metal turnstile. Behind us, I heard a security guard protesting, but before he could stop us, we had already disappeared into the stairwell.

On the second floor, Vera Yefimovna made straight for a plywood door. A young party functionary blocked her way.

"I need to see Anton Pavlovich!"

"Anton Pavlovich is in a meeting."

"Then let me see San Sanych!"

"San Sanych is in a meeting too."

I watched them arguing for a while. The functionary looked annoyed. They seemed to know Vera Yefimovna of old here.

As the quarrel grew more animated, I stepped in. I introduced myself and explained in a conciliatory tone what had brought us here. The functionary looked at me suspiciously.

"East Germany or West Germany?"

"Berlin," I said.

"East Berlin or West Berlin?"

"The poor chap grew up in the West," Vera Yefimovna said. "But he's interested in Lenin."

"So what?" the functionary snapped. "Even if I knew where the remains of the statue are, I wouldn't tell anyone. The next day, the nationalists would smash it into pieces."

It took me a while to gain his confidence. I told him about my trip to Ukraine, about the court case over Lenin's nose, about my acquaintance with Vera Yefimovna. The functionary in turn told me that during his studies in Warsaw he had once met a like-minded German comrade, a woman whom he apparently remembered with great warmth, despite the fact that she had grown up in the West. Slowly his face lit up.

In the end, he told us that Lenin's remains were under communist protection. The party had put the desecrated monument in a safe place, with an eye to restoring it as soon as the situation calmed down.

"At some point," the functionary said, "people will realise

that it is not Lenin who is to blame for their problems – but capitalism."

Vera Yefimovna and I parted ways when we left the Raicom building. She took the bus, and I the subway. We shook hands with a conspiratorial smile. There was a great deal that we did not see eye to eye on, but through our concerted efforts we had discovered that in some cellar or other in this great city, a stone Lenin was waiting for his resurrection.

On a Sunday, one of my last days in Kiev, my host family invited me on a trip to Mezhyhirya. We packed the car with toys and food, sat Philip on the backseat, and drove north along the shore of the Dnieper until we reached the former palace of the dethroned president.

I had seen the abandoned property for the first time shortly after Viktor Yanukovych had fled from Ukraine, but since then a lot seemed to have changed at Mezhyhirya. The fantasy castle had become a tourist attraction. We were by no means the only visitors. Tour buses and private cars were parked in endless rows in front of the entrance to the premises. People came from all over Ukraine to see what their president had done with the ill-gotten wealth which had in the end proved his undoing. The park was full of day trippers whose faces radiated astonishment.

Mezhyhirya looked like the playroom of an insatiable little boy. As we walked through the park, I remembered how Philip had presented me with his complete collection of toys on the first day of my visit, one after another, full of a glowing, childlike pride of ownership, even though, as Ksyusha revealed with a smile, he had not played with most of the things in a long time. Mezhyhirya made a similar impression. Yanukovych could not possibly have got round to using even a fraction of the pointless junk he had crammed into his childlike Versailles.

The 137-hectare grounds descended in gentle waves down to the bank of the Dnieper River. It included an eighteen-hole golf course, a marina, a replica of a Spanish galleon, an underground gym complete with boxing ring, a sauna bath including a salt grotto, an aviary housing ostriches, cranes and pheasants, a horse stable, a dog menagerie, a heliport, a fleet of seventy vintage Soviet cars, greenhouses, fish ponds, waterfalls, fountains, artificial streams and rockeries and a forest with a private hunting ground.

In the midst of all this stood Yanukovych's residence, a hunting lodge kind of a structure made of Levantine pine. One corner of the building was, for whatever reason, adorned with a mocked-up ruin of an ancient columned portal. Broken amphorae and the head of a horse statue lay scattered in picturesque disorder between the columns. Ksyusha stood for a long time in front of the bizarre ensemble, shaking her head in disbelief.

Inside, the master of the house had paced across inlaid wooden floors, massaged his tired shoulders in vibrating cinema chairs, fallen asleep to the sound of historic music boxes, and flushed his excrement down gilded sewage pipes. Stuffed lions, brightly polished suits of armour and heavy chandeliers graced the corridors. There was an indoor tennis court, a library with rare first editions, a beauty salon which included oxygen loungers, a cold room and a solarium, and a white grand piano, signed by John Lennon. Every square metre of the house was cluttered with expensive, arbitrary, useless stuff.

I wondered whether, in moments of weakness, Yanukovych had the creeping feeling that all these possessions would never fill his inner emptiness, no matter how many of them he amassed. Perhaps in such moments he was drawn to the gold-panelled icon wall of the private Orthodox chapel which he'd had installed on the third floor near his bedroom.

Hundreds of millions of dollars had flowed into the estate. As the first journalists clambered over the fences the morning after Yanukovych's escape, they found traces of a hasty departure: cabinets ransacked, wide-open drawers, empty vaults. Ring binders and loose sheets of paper were floating in the marina – at the last minute the guards had tried to get rid of any incriminating material. The journalists fished the documents out of the water. There were many curiosities among them, including a note in which Yanukovych instructs his gardener to please keep the deer inside the hunting grounds and away from the golf course. The majority of the files, however, documented corrupt presidential deals.

Ostensibly, Yanukovych had escaped punishment, but at root had not really done so. He had fled to Russia rather than face trial. But he left behind a palace that was one large charge-sheet. The entire country could see the sad, childish inner life of the president. He had been transformed from the most powerful man in Ukraine into the most ridiculous.

We had a picnic on the golf course and watched the passers-by. Bridal couples were especially fond of the park. You saw them everywhere, posing in front of fountains, flower beds, and duck ponds. There was no better place in Kiev to take romantic wedding photos.

Ksyusha, Roman, and I swapped notes. At some point Philip grew impatient because he did not understand what we were saying about corruption – he wanted to be a part of the discussion.

"Mama," he said. "What is this park?"

We looked at each other, at a loss for a response. It was hard to explain.

"Well, Philip, the fact is," I began. "A thief used to live here."

Ksyusha laughed. "Exactly. And the thief was also the president. As strange as that may sound."

Philip glanced around suspiciously. "Is the thief still here?"

"No, Philipushka," Roman said. "The thief ran away. The thief is now in Russia."

"Why?"

"In Russia, thieves are allowed to roam about free," Ksyusha said, still laughing.

Philip looked at his mother quizzically. His eyes were so wide, I could almost see the synapses working behind them. Ksyusha's homeland appeared to undergo a sudden transformation in his head, and it was evidently not a change for the better. His confusion broke my heart. But what else could we tell him?

"Mama," Philip said. "Let's go back to Kiev. I want to go to Kiev, Mama."

11

A German Village

Odessa–Dobroolexandrivka

ONE MORNING IN EARLY OCTOBER, I boarded an express train in Kiev which travelled directly south. I saw the sun rise and soon fall again before it was replaced by an almost full moon. The sky was cloudless, and the bright moonlight was reflected in a thousand silvery ponds. The marshes of Central Ukraine rolled past the windows, dark and sad and deserted. With an eerie clearness, the moon illuminated certain details: black pools, waving reeds, the V-shaped wake of a solitary swimming duck.

Further south the swamps disappeared, along with the trees, the hills, and everything else. All that remained was flat, black farmland that had once been covered with grass before the ploughs and tractors came, grass and more grass and nothing else. I had reached the first foothills of the Eurasian steppe, the ancient vegetation belt that had once stretched almost unbroken from Mongolia to the northern coast of the Black Sea.

It was after midnight when I arrived in Odessa. A taxi driver took me to a small hotel on the beach in his decrepit Lada. Far out, I saw moored container ships. High above the Black Sea was the moon; a glittering silver trail divided the waves. I listened to the sound of the surf for quite some time as I drifted into a dreamless sleep.

There are two versions of how Odessa was founded.

Russians tell one version. Catherine the Great, they say, wrested the northern Black Sea coast from the Turks in the late eighteenth century. To defend her newly conquered territories, the Czarina had warships stationed on the coast and established a port city on the steppe soil. To expedite matters, she hired urban planners and architects from Western Europe, who gave Odessa its characteristic style, an imaginative mixture of Mediterranean elements and Russian imperial flair. Once the job had been completed, many of these foreign experts settled down in Catherine's new metropolis, which filled up at the same time with recruited settlers and stranded sailors from around the world: Moldovans, Greeks, Albanians, Germans, Armenians, Bulgarians, Italians, Azerbaijanis, Turks, Crimean Tatars, Poles, Russians, and Jews. Less than a century after its foundation, the city had become the fourth largest in the Russian Empire after Moscow, St. Petersburg, and Warsaw, and every writer who visited Odessa, from Pushkin to Mark Twain, hailed the unique international atmosphere of the Black Sea metropolis. Its largest streets and squares are still named after French governors, Italian architects, and Spanish admirals, and although most of the city's once so colourful population has not survived the ravages of the twentieth century, Odessa is still considered by many former Soviet citizens to be the most cosmopolitan place in the Russian-speaking world.

Tariel told me the second version.

"Hadji Bey," he said. "That is what the city was called before the Russians came. It's a long story."

He snapped his gold-ringed fingers. As if from nowhere his wife appeared and placed two steaming bowls of soup on the restaurant table where we sat. Tariel, a bald, stocky man in his mid-fifties, was the owner of this Georgian restaurant. He had, like all Georgians, a penchant for long stories.

"The Russians say Odessa is two hundred years old. Nonsense! Hadji Bey will be six hundred this year!"

Long before Catherine had conquered the Black Sea coast, there had been a Turkish fortress here, he continued, constructed by Moldovan builders who settled in Hadji Bey once the job was done. Their small settlement later became the Moldavanka quarter, which now contained Tariel's restaurant. "The Russians did not found Odessa," he said. "They just expanded Hadji Bey."

Like most Georgians, Tariel did not exactly have a soft spot for Russia.

I had pitched up at his restaurant quite by chance. Shortly before my departure from Berlin, a German friend had asked me to take photos of his grandfather's former home in Odessa. His grandfather had been an ethnic German manufacturer who had managed a canning factory on the Black Sea before the First World War. His house was in the Moldavanka quarter. It was a typical Odessite residential building, with two-storey wings built around a long, narrow courtyard, which was surrounded with vine-covered galleries and old wooden windows, on whose wide transoms cats lay dozing in the sun.

Tariel's restaurant was on the street side, on the ground floor. I was just about to photograph the entrance sign with the Russian inscription "Old Barrel Organ Café" when the owner stepped out of the door. No sooner had I explained to him what had brought me there than Tariel invited me in with an effusive gesture. Like all Georgians, he attached great importance to hospitality.

Needless to say, I was not allowed to pay for the beef soup which he had served me. It was delicious. When I told Tariel that, he fell into a long monologue about the cultural wealth of Georgia.

"Have you seen Mtskheta, our ancient royal city?"

I nodded.

"The castles! The monasteries! The churches! So beautiful, they chopped off the architects' hands so they could not build anything else like it!"

The monologue ended with a few Georgian verses by the national poet, Shota Rustaveli.

"Rustaveli wrote that almost a thousand years ago! The Russians could not even read then, let alone write!"

Like all Georgians, Tariel was very proud of his country's long history.

He was also proud of the fact that Odessa was now governed by a fellow countryman. Mikheil Saakashvili, the former Georgian president, had been elected as the new governor of the region after the Maidan revolution.

"Ukraine and Georgia!" Tariel solemnly clasped his hands together to affirm the friendship between his adopted country and his country of birth. "United against Russia!"

But Tariel's greatest pride was the old barrel organ that the restaurant was named after. The instrument stood on the counter. It came from an Odessa organ workshop and had been made just before the First World War, around the same time my German friend's grandfather had been living in the Moldavanka quarter. The manufacturer's name was painted on the front of the decorative inlaid wooden case, in Cyrillic letters entwined with floral Art Nouveau motifs from which the silhouettes of two bare-breasted dancers emerged. At the foot of the left female figure Tariel had wedged a small Orthodox Mother of God icon in the wooden frame, perhaps as a counterweight to the frivolous paintings. The barrel organ was a real gem.

Tariel had found it in an antique shop in Tbilisi, the capital of his home country, where the instrument had fetched up after being used as a prop in a Georgian film from the Soviet era. An inscription added later in the curved letters of the Georgian alphabet testified to its film appearance – the two words, Tariel explained, meant something like "Good health".

He had discovered the barrel organ during a visit home, shortly after he had emigrated to Odessa to seek his fortune as a restaurateur on the far side of the Black Sea. The barrel organ had crossed the sea twice – first without Tariel, and on the way back with him.

Among the eight tunes the box could play was a Georgian dance song. Tariel played it for me. When he turned the crank, he did not keep exact time. The barrel organ droned, and the pipes were a bit out of tune. Nevertheless, the unfamiliar Caucasian melody almost brought tears to my eyes. It sounded like an oblique ode to the immigrant and emigrant town of Odessa.

When the first European architects arrived on the Black Sea coast in the late eighteenth century, they encountered a problem. Catherine the Great had instructed them to build a city in the steppe. But the Czarina had omitted to mention that the treeless, clayless grasslands contained virtually no building materials.

In the end, the Europeans decided to excavate what they needed. Under the black soil of the steppe they found extensive layers of limestone that they had mined and brought to the surface. As the housing above ground expanded, so the tunnels beneath expanded as well. The branched corridors of the catacomb system, which still exist beneath the city today, have a total length of two and a half thousand kilometres.

I descended into the darkness with a Ukrainian tour group. As we made our way through the yellowish limestone tunnels with hard hats and flashlights, our two Odessa guides told thrilling stories. After the builders had departed, the bandits had arrived. Smugglers and thieves had waged epic battles with the police in the catacombs. Soon other groups who shied away from the daylight took refuge in the tunnels. Persecuted religious communities celebrated underground masses here; lovers escaped the supervision of their parents; political groups forged plans for a coup. With the outbreak of the Second World War, Soviet partisans hid in the catacombs and fought Germans and Romanians from here. Still later, during the Cold War, the tunnels were expanded into bomb shelters, where the entire urban population could have taken refuge in the event of a nuclear war.

Along the way, I struck up a conversation with one of the two guides. Yaroslav was actually an actor. He used the guided tours as a means to fund his first directorial venture: he was filming a TV movie about the partisan war.

"The next scene will take place in the catacombs," he told me. "We are filming this mind-blowing gun battle, using genuine old war weapons. In the end, the partisans wipe out all the Romanians. There is also a Nazi officer, who naturally dies the bloodiest death of all."

All of a sudden he thought of something.

"Say, are you free next Sunday? The actor who was supposed to play the Nazi bailed on us."

The other guide joined in our conversation.

"You mean Andrey? He was miscast anyway. Doesn't look like a Nazi at all."

"You, on the other hand..." Yaroslav let his gaze wander over my body, from the top of my German head to the soles of my German feet. "Perfect!"

We exchanged numbers. I left Odessa a few days later, but in the course of my journey I repeatedly phoned Yaroslav to reassure him that I was still in Ukraine and could return to the Black Sea coast for the shooting date. I literally burned to let my inner Nazi die in the catacombs of Odessa. Unfortunately, the date for filming kept being put back. The cameraman was in Moscow; the lead actor in Kiev; the lighting technician was sick; the financial backers had pulled out. When it became apparent shortly before my return to Berlin that nothing would come of my Odessa film career for the time being, I was quite disappointed.

The next morning I caught a bus from the central market that headed in a southwesterly direction out through the outskirts of Odessa and reached the open steppe surprisingly quickly. I was looking for the old German settlement of Alexanderhilf, the birthplace of Dr. Karl Stumpp, the itinerant ethnographer.

In a prewar atlas I had purchased at a Berlin flea market years ago, I had come across a map of the German Black Sea villages. About fifteen kilometres southwest of Odessa, a dozen of these colonial settlements had once lined the banks of a small river called the Baraboy. Their names sounded as if they came from a German fairytale: Kleinliebental, Großliebental, Neuburg, Mariental, Josefstal, Peterstal, Freudental, Georgiental, Manheim, and Franzfeld.

Nowadays they bore Ukrainian names, of which only some betrayed their old German roots: Malodolynske, Velykodolynske, Novohradkivka, Maryanivka, Yosypivka, Petrodolynske, Myrne, Sekretarivka, Kamianka, and Nadlymanske.

Alexanderhilf had become Dobroolexandrivka. The bus dropped me off at a bend in the road. From the bus stop I could see the narrow river which had once connected the German settlements. A concrete bridge led to the centre of the village.

Dobroolexandrivka consisted of low wooden and stone houses, surrounded by vegetable gardens. In the middle of the village, which had about fifteen hundred inhabitants, there was an old church which had obviously not been built as an Orthodox church, although there was an Orthodox cross on its German gable. The door was locked.

An elderly man I spoke to in front of the church directed me to the kindergarten when I asked about the ethnic German population.

The kindergarten teacher was named Vera. She was in her late fifties and spoke very quietly.

"The little mice have just fallen asleep," she whispered. We stood in the courtyard of the kindergarten building. "I don't have much time. When they wake up, I have to go back inside."

Vera had grown up in Tajikistan, the child of an ethnic German father who had been deported from the Volga region to Central Asia during the war, and had met his Russian wife there. In the early nineties, when war erupted in Dushanbe, Vera had fled to Ukraine with her Tajik husband.

None of the German families who had originally lived in Dobroolexandrivka were left, Vera whispered. The Lutheran church had been used as a clubhouse in the Soviet era; now it belonged to the Orthodox Church. There were a few other ethnic Germans in town, but they had all come to Ukraine from Central Asia in the nineties, like herself. Together, they had founded a German cultural association. Vera was its director.

"What does the cultural association do?" I asked.

She looked at me uncertainly. "We sing German songs."

"What kind?"

Vera's voice shifted to a monotone German. "*Alle Vöglein sind schon da oh Tannenbaum liebe Schwester tanz mit mir beide Hände reich ich dir...*"

She rattled off the song titles nervously, as if she was uncomfortable demonstrating her inexperienced German language in the presence of a German. I felt like a teacher who has backed a student into a corner without meaning to. I quickly changed the subject.

"Does the name Karl Stumpp mean anything to you?"

She had never heard of him. The ethnographer had been

so thoroughly forgotten in his birthplace that not even the head of the German cultural association knew anything about him. In a certainly unjust way, that seemed only just to me.

From inside, we could hear a child grizzling.

"Excuse me," Vera said, still in a whisper. "I have to go."

Before she disappeared into the building, she turned around again.

"*Auf Wiedersehen*," she said.

I searched the village cemetery in vain for German graves. All the gravestones I passed by were from the Soviet era. I had scoured about half the weed-infested cemetery when an old woman approached me.

"Are you looking for something?"

"Old graves," I said. "From the German period."

She pointed to an overgrown patch of waste ground on the far side of the cemetery.

"They were buried over there. But that was a long time ago."

I walked through the waist-high undergrowth. In a few places, I stumbled over old gravestones, but they were crumbling and weathered; the rain had made their inscriptions illegible.

The old woman had stopped at the edge of the wasteland and stood watching me.

"You won't find anything here!" She called out to me suddenly. "You won't find anything good in the entire village! It's all gone down the drain! Better for you to move on!"

Then she turned and carried on her way.

I followed her advice and wandered north along the

reedy riverbank. After a few kilometres I reached the next village: Novohradkivka, the former Neuburg.

The Church of Novohradkivka was at least twice as large as the one in Dobroolexandrivka. It likewise appeared to date from the German period, and also seemed to have been used as a clubhouse in the Soviet era: "*Dom Kultury*" was written on the gable in large letters, House of Culture. But while the church of the neighbouring village was being used again as a church now, the church at Novohradkivka was in ruins. The roof had collapsed, cracks ran down the side walls, and the crumbling plaster exposed wobbly bricks. The old building towered out of the grassy sea of the steppe like a hideous shipwreck.

Of all the villages I had seen in Ukraine, Novohradkivka was the bleakest. A grey veil seemed to hover over the place, even though the sky was cloudless and the sun was shining. Rotten wooden houses and crooked stone houses lined the main street; there was scrap metal in the vegetable gardens. The bus stop at the village entrance, a small concrete cabin, reeked of urine. Under the bench there was a drunk with twisted limbs and an open mouth, sleeping off his stupor. His right hand was bleeding. No one took any notice of him.

At the grocery store I bought a pack of raisin buns and an apple.

"Germans?" The shop assistant shook her head. "There aren't any Germans here anymore."

She had to be in her sixties, I guessed. Again she shook her head. "Not for a long time. There were a few in my class at school, but that was ages ago. We called them 'fascists'."

She laughed.

"They didn't think that was funny. 'We aren't Germans,' they always said. 'We're from here!' But as soon as they were able to emigrate, they were German again. They all cleared out, in the nineties, to Germany."

"Is there a German cemetery here?" I asked.

Again she shook her head. "There used to be one. As a child, I used to clamber around in there. But the old gravestones are gone. Other people are buried there now."

I nodded silently. As I was about to leave, the shop assistant suddenly had an idea.

"Or are you looking for the German settlement?"

"The what?"

"The new houses on the outskirts. But you won't find any Germans there. There are only Kazakhs, Uzbeks, Tajiks, and Russians. They arrived in the nineties. They supposedly have German ancestors, but anyone can say that. If they're German, I'm French."

The German settlement consisted of a few dozen houses made of white, unplastered cinder blocks. The only person I met on the dusty footpaths there was an old man with a wheelbarrow full of walnuts.

"It's a good business," he said when I asked him about the walnuts. "I make a decent living. But soon the harvest will run out, and then I'll have to think of something else."

He laughed. The forefinger of his left hand was missing.

I asked him if he was German.

He shook his head. "Not me. But my wife is."

The settlement, he said, had been built in the nineties, for ethnic German evacuees from Siberia and Central Asia. The Ukrainian government had provided the land, while the funding came from Germany.

"To try and stop the migrants from moving to Germany," he said, laughing. "The whole lot of them only speak Russian. What would Germany do with them?"

"Isn't there anyone left here who speaks German?" I asked.

He thought for a moment before setting down his wheelbarrow. "Sure. Come with me. I'll take you there."

We made for one of the white cinder-block houses. The old man knocked loudly on the front door. It took a while before a second old man opened the door from inside. He looked sleepy.

"Sasha!" the walnut man exclaimed. "Look, I have brought you a German! Say something in German!"

The man looked first at me, then his neighbour, and then back at me. He seemed daunted. Again, I felt like a teacher who has put a student in an awkward position. I was just about to launch into an explanation when the man cleared his throat.

"*Es freit mich sehr, einen Landsmann kennenzulernen*", he said. "I am very pleased to meet a fellow countryman. My name is Michel. Alexander Michel."

His German was clear and melodious, and his accent did not sound like a regional flavour, but rather like the kind of High German that is spoken in very old movies.

"Alright," the walnut man said. "Then I'll leave the two of you to it."

I introduced myself in German and told Alexander what had brought me here. He listened, smiling. His face was furrowed and careworn, but his eyes had a boyish curiosity about them.

From inside, I suddenly heard a Russian woman's voice.

"Why are you standing out there on the doorstep? Come in!"

Alexander's wife was named Svetlana. She only understood a little German, so we switched to Russian as the three of us took a seat at the kitchen table. But every now and then Alexander sprinkled German words and phrases into his stories, his antiquated accent sounding more and more endearing to me with each repetition.

Although the Michels had lived in Novohradkivka for nearly twenty years, their house looked like they had just moved in. The furniture was sparse, the walls bare. After listening to the two of them for a while, I realised that they had only settled here temporarily. They wanted to move to Germany. Their application was pending with the authorities; Alexander Michel hoped to be admitted to the land of his ancestors.

He had been born in a North Kazakh steppe village named Makeyevka in 1949. Michel's parents and grandparents were not from Ukraine, but from the German settlements on the Volga, which like the Black Sea colonies had been established under Catherine the Great. After Lenin's revolution, the same drama had taken place there as in Ukraine. At first, the Bolsheviks promoted the national autonomy of ethnic Germans. Their settlements were upgraded in the 1920s to the "Autonomous Socialist Soviet Republic of the Volga Germans". When Hitler and Stalin signed their friendship treaty in 1939, the Führer even planned a visit to the Volga region, and in preparation the local Soviet authorities had distributed flags with swastikas in the German villages. Before it happened, though, the Fascist–Soviet friendship fell apart, and Stalin took his anger out on the Russian Germans. The deportation order of August 28, 1941 reads like the internal monologue of a paranoiac.

> According to credible information which has come into the possession of the military authorities, thousands and tens of thousands of saboteurs and spies are among the German population of the Volga Raions, who plan to carry out bomb attacks when given a signal from Germany. None of the Germans living in the Volga Raions have reported the presence of such a large number of saboteurs and spies to the Soviet authorities. Consequently, the German population hides in its midst enemies of the Soviet people and the Soviet power.

The insinuation that the ethnic Germans were in cahoots with the Nazis was seemingly corroborated during their deportation, when the eviction squads stumbled upon swastika flags in the houses of individual settlers. Although their owners protested that they had been given the flags by the Soviet authorities just a few months earlier, they were summarily shot. The rest, nearly half a million people, were banished from the Volga, and the autonomous Soviet Republic was dissolved. Nearly as many ethnic Germans were deported in the following war year from all other parts of the Soviet Union. The Russian Germans ended up in Siberia, in the Urals, and in the steppes of Central Asia.

Eight years later, Alexander Michel was born. As a child, he had witnessed the ghetto-like conditions under which his parents and grandparents had lived in Kazakhstan. The ethnic Germans were isolated from the rest of the population. Like prisoners, they were used as forced labourers. They had to report to the military authorities regularly to ensure that they did not leave their place of exile. These conditions were not abolished until 1956, a few years after Stalin's death. But still the displaced were not allowed to return to their former places of residence, even after their official rehabilitation in 1964, when the deportation was declared unjustified.

Three generations of German Michels had lived in the family home in Makeyevka.

"My grandfather's name was Christian, and his patronymic was Christianovich," Michel said. "My father's name was Alexander Christianovich. I am Alexander Alexandrovich."

Michel could not immediately recall his grandmother's name. He had always just called her Grandma.

"Pärwel... or Wärwel..."

"Bärbel?"

"Yes!"

Christian Christianovich Michel was a pastor. The grandfather had been in charge of a Lutheran parish on the Volga before being deported. He had smuggled a few Christian books to Kazakhstan during the expulsion, from which he read to his grandson at night, in German, so that Alexander would learn the language.

"He always said to me: Outside you can speak Kazakh or Russian or Chinese, but at home we speak German."

His grandmother did not speak a word of Russian. Until the day she died she expressed herself in the dialect of her Bavarian forebears. "It wasn't *Hochdeutsch*," Michel said. "Only my grandfather spoke standard German."

Alexander Christianovich Michel was a pitman. The father had not chosen this line of work; they had sent him down a mine after his arrival in Kazakhstan. He fell in love with a waitress in the canteen there, Michel's mother, who was also from the Volga. She, too, had not voluntarily opted for her job as a waitress.

Sometimes, Michel told me, the parents had sung German songs with their five children. He fell silent for a moment, as if he was searching through his memories.

"*Da das neie Jahr gekommen...*"

His singing voice was hesitant and untutored.

"*... hab' ich mir es vorgenommen...*"

After the first two lines he faltered.

"It was a long time ago. I was still a boy."

He couldn't remember the name of the song. Later, when I tried searching for the two lines he had sung, I found a similar-sounding poem by Goethe, but no corresponding song.

Alexander had lived in Kazakhstan until 1968, when he was drafted into the military. Around the same time his parents moved to Dagestan for medical reasons. His father had ruined his lungs in the Kazakh mines; the mild Caucasian climate was supposed to prolong his retirement years. Nonetheless, he died before Michel's grandparents, who spent their final years in Kazakhstan without ever setting eyes on the Volga again.

Alexander stayed in the military for fifteen years. "I was a *Fähnrich*," he said, in German. "A sergeant. In the Air Force."

For a while, he served in the vicinity of Leningrad, and later in the Uzbek capital Tashkent, where he met Svetlana, whose Russian parents came from the Urals. After the wedding, Alexander was posted to the GDR. For six years he and Svetlana lived on a Soviet military base at Rangsdorf, fifteen kilometres south of Berlin. The smattering of German that Svetlana spoke she had acquired during these years, although, as Soviet military personnel, the Michels had little contact with the East German population. They lived largely isolated in their barracks. Only occasionally were they able to visit the family of a Rangsdorf resident with whom Alexander had become friends back then.

"His name was Ulrich Höppner. Unfortunately, we have lost touch. Who knows, maybe he will read your book and remember me."

After Alexander's demobilisation, the Michels went back to Tashkent, to Svetlana's parents. Alexander found work as a car mechanic, or *Autoschlosser*, as he called it in his antiquated German. When the Soviet Union disintegrated into its constituent parts, life became tough in Uzbekistan. There was fear of a civil war, and the Michels, who now had two children, looked for ways to get out. Back then, in a cultural association for the Russian-German minority, Alexander heard that new settlements were being built for ethnic Germans in Ukraine. Officially, it was said that the Ukrainian and German governments had agreed to jointly right the wrongs that had been inflicted on the Germans in Russia during the war. Unofficially, Germany was trying to keep out at least a portion of the nearly two million repatriates who over the course of the 1990s were to flood into the Federal Republic. The young Ukraine, in turn, was delighted to have German money flowing into the new settlements.

The Michels left Uzbekistan in 1992. For three years

they lived in a temporary camp before settling in Novo-hradkivka, along with a few dozen other ethnic German families whose forebears had come mostly from the Volga region. Similar relocations were taking place at the same time in the neighbouring settlements. It was a strange kind of return. The old villages on the Baraboy River filled up again with Germans, though they were not the descendants of the Black Sea Germans who had disappeared from them during the war.

"Ukraine is a good country," Alexander said. "But it just can't get out of the hole it's in. When we arrived, we still had hope. But year by year, things have become more difficult."

The Michels lived off their meagre pensions. The previous winter they had cut back on the heating. This year, gas prices had increased many times over. The couple anticipated Ukraine's second winter of war with a sense of dread.

A few years ago Alexander had applied for the right to settle in Germany with his son, hoping later to be able to bring Svetlana over too, who did not have German roots. The outcome of the process was still undecided, and the television images of recent months had given the Michels little hope.

"All those war refugees in Germany," Svetlana sighed. "Now, they will certainly not let us into the country."

I assured them that the one thing had nothing to do with the other, but they would not believe me. A war had driven Alexander's ancestors from the Volga. The Michels had fled Uzbekistan out of fear of war. Then war had started in Ukraine, and now the escape route to Germany seemed to be blocked by a war again, this time the one in Syria.

"Whatever we do, we cannot escape war," Svetlana said.

Just before we parted, Alexander told me that there was another man in the settlement who spoke German.

"His name is Schäfer. But he speaks Swabian, not High German."

Whenever the two men ran into one another in the village, they always talked to each other in German for a few minutes, Schäfer in his Swabian dialect, Michel in *Hochdeutsch*, the only ones in Novohradkivka who still spoke the language of their forefathers.

In order not to forget it, Alexander would always keep his eyes open for a few minutes after he had gone to bed, just before falling asleep. He would stare into the darkness and then concentrate hard and think in German. Night after night he would listen to the sound of his own thoughts until his eyes closed and he fell asleep, and sometimes, not often, but every now and then, the German words would continue to reverberate in his dreams.

12

Revenge of the Scythians

Simferopol–Sevastopol–Bakhchisaray

THERE WERE TWO WAYS of getting from Odessa to Crimea. One of them was quite straightforward, but was also an indictable offence. The other one was legal and above board, but a bureaucratic nightmare.

The simple option would have been to fly to Simferopol via Moscow on a Russian tourist visa. But for the Ukrainian authorities, Crimea remains Ukrainian territory, even if, to quote the official formulation, it is "temporarily occupied". Accordingly, anyone flying to the peninsula from Russia is entering Ukraine illegally, since by this route travellers bypass the Ukrainian border controls. The only legal route is to travel there overland.

Although, in practice, the Ukrainians have no means whatsoever of monitoring border crossings by air, I had decided to play things by the book – partly out of sympathy for Kiev's position, but mainly out of curiosity. I wanted to know what the border crossing between the mainland and the peninsula looked like, which the Russians saw as their state border since their annexation of Crimea, while for the Ukrainians it had become the front line.

As a foreigner, it had taken me weeks to apply for the

necessary documents. I needed a special permit from the Ukrainian migration authorities, plus, as a journalist, I required credentials from the Kiev Ministry of Information. Additionally, I had to obtain a Russian press visa and an accreditation card from the Moscow Foreign Ministry, because a tourist visa would have prompted too many questions at the controversial border.

With this sheaf of official papers in my luggage, I boarded a long-distance bus that left Odessa heading east and made its way down the coast as the sun was sinking into the Black Sea.

We reached the border long after midnight. In the middle of the steppe the bus disgorged its passengers and headed back to Odessa. The night was starry. To the left and right of the road there were trenches; behind them, the coastal wind swept through knee-high grass as far as the eye could see in the darkness. A handful of Ukrainian soldiers with shouldered assault rifles were guarding a lonely concrete bunker.

The Ukrainian border checkpoint consisted of a few makeshift Portakabins. One by one, the bus passengers dragged their luggage past the weary border guards. I was surprised when one of the officers put an exit stamp in my passport.

"Am I leaving Ukraine?" I asked.

"No," he replied, as if by rote. "You are entering the temporarily occupied territory of the Autonomous Republic of Crimea."

Beyond the cabins, the no man's land began. Trundling their trolley cases and carrying their backpacks and travel bags, the passengers walked on through the night.

Presently, the column of pedestrians progressed beyond the spotlights illuminating the Ukrainian border installations; it was pitch black. No one spoke. Only the sound of the windswept steppe grass could be heard in the night, along with the rumble of rolling luggage.

After walking for about one kilometre, we reached the Russian border, which looked just as provisional as the Ukrainian one. I entered a container construction where two Russian officials sat behind raised counters. The guard on the right looked young and inexperienced. The one on the left appeared older and more alert. I went and stood in the right-hand queue.

"What is your purpose in travelling to Crimea?" the young border guard asked when my turn came.

"I'm a journalist."

"What are you planning to report on?"

"I am interested in the historical heritage of Crimea."

The officer nodded vacantly. Something had distracted him. He was looking over at his older colleague's counter, where a drama was beginning to unfold.

"Have you ever had any problems with this document?" the older customs officer was asking the man standing in front of him. The officer was waving a blue Ukrainian passport.

The Ukrainian shook his head silently.

"Well, you do now," the customs officer said coolly.

There was a pause. The Ukrainian looked at the border guard with surprise. Every head in the room turned to look at the left counter, all conversations in the queues fell silent.

"According to this document," the customs officer continued, "You celebrated your twenty-fifth birthday last April."

The Ukrainian did not look twenty-five. He looked more like forty-five. He gazed anxiously at the Russian official.

"Have you ever been a terrorist suspect?" the border guard asked.

"No!" the man replied, horrified.

"Are you preparing acts of provocation on the territory of the Russian Federation? Do you belong to a terrorist organisation? Are you smuggling weapons?"

The Ukrainian grew paler by the second. As he was being bombarded with questions, the young customs officer in front of me stared as if spellbound at his older colleague. Without giving me another look, he put a Russian entry stamp in my passport and gave me back the document. I left the container before he could change his mind, which is why, unfortunately, I was not able to observe how the drama at the other counter ended.

On the other side of the border, a second bus was waiting for the passengers. In the early hours of the morning it arrived in Simferopol, the capital of Crimea.

I slept soundly in an old concrete Soviet hotel before journeying into the city centre. Brand new signs guided my way – the Ukrainian street names had been replaced with Russian ones. Most of the differences were minimal. Vulytsya Lenina had become Ulitsa Lenina; Vulytsya Bilshovytska had become Ulitsa Bolshevistskaya. It was a paradox: whereas in mainland Ukraine everything Soviet was being expunged from the street signs, here there were new signs being erected with familiar names. All the Soviet heroes were still in place – I saw Kirov Streets, Kalinin Streets, Zhukov, Lunacharsky, and Mayakovsky Streets. Only Marx had not survived the Russification. Vulytsya Karla Marxa had reverted to its pre-revolutionary name; it was now called Ulitsa Yekaterininskaya again, after the Tsarina whom Russia had to thank for Crimea. In April 1783, after her war against the Turks, Catherine the Great had declared the peninsula Russian property, "henceforth and for all time."

The slogan beneath the ubiquitous posters of Putin sounded like an echo of the Tsarina's vow. Larger than life, Russia's ruler beamed down at his new subjects. Along with his face, just three words adorned the posters: "Crimea. Russia. Forever."

I saw the figure of a third Russian ruler as I was exiting one of the pedestrian underpasses that run beneath the wide Soviet-era avenues in the city centre. I was gradually ascending towards a blue piece of sky when suddenly the head of a statue appeared, followed by the shoulders, the chest, a raised arm – I paused on the stairs. The tunnel exit framed the upper body of a man whom, so far on my journey, I had encountered only as a phantom statue: Lenin.

Although I was well acquainted with the sight from my past trips to Ukraine and Russia, I stared at the monument as if I was looking at Lenin for the first time. I left the tunnel, crossed the square, and stood at the foot of the statue which, including the pedestal, must have been ten metres tall. Lenin's left hand rested on a lectern. In his right hand he held notes for a speech which he was not looking at. His eyes were fixed in the distance; he was reciting his revolutionary poetry in free form.

It did not surprise me that no one on the plaza was looking his way. For years, I had noticed that Russians and

Ukrainians basically treated the omnipresent statues of Lenin like trees or lampposts – people tried not to walk into them, but apart from that no one paid the slightest attention to them. Until not very long ago, Lenin's presence had simply been taken for granted. But now that it was no longer a common sight outside of Crimea, the monument in front of me suddenly seemed to exude a renewed urgency – it looked revitalised, rejuvenated, confidently anachronistic. Lenin, the silent orator, had found his tongue again.

Next to the cash register at the Central Museum of Tauris there was a small, transparent donation box. It was half-full of freshly printed rouble notes. Money was being collected to help restore the former Catherine the Great monument in Simferopol, which the Bolsheviks had blown up after the revolution. There was also a small model of the statue at the cash register. Its proportions seemed a bit wide of the mark: the empress looked very corpulent. It did not seem to bother the museum visitors, however. Note by note they filled the donation box. The rouble had returned to Crimea, and now Catherine would also return.

On the first floor of the historical museum there was a hastily scheduled exhibition: "Crimea in the History of Russia". Catherine was everywhere, and Ukraine nowhere to be seen. It was as if the last two and a half decades had never happened, as if the Ukrainian period was all a bad dream from which Crimea had finally awakened. Only fleeting mention was made of Nikita Khrushchev's momentous decision in 1954 to transfer the peninsula from the administrative area of the Russian Soviet Republic to the Ukrainian Soviet Republic. The predominantly Russian residents of Crimea had not felt the impact of this change until 1991, when suddenly their peninsula belonged to the newly independent Ukraine.

But now that this aberration was over, visitors to the museum could indulge in earlier, happier memories. The Moscow Communist Party bosses had taken their holidays on the forever-Russian coastline of Crimea, and long before them, the Emperors from St. Petersburg. A series of photographs documented the collected Black Sea trips by the last Romanov family, a few years before they were murdered by the Bolsheviks. Tsar Nicholas II playing tennis. The Tsar on the summit of Ai-Petri, with his wife Alexandra. The Tsar in a striped swimsuit, with Alexei, the childlike heir to the throne, in his arms. Princess Tatiana on the beach at Yevpatoria, reclining in a somewhat wanton pose, but modestly dressed.

A member of the museum staff laughed when I asked her whether the change of administration from Ukrainian to Russian had had much impact on the museum's operations.

"Even before that, we had little contact with Kiev," she said. "We worked more closely with the museums in Russia. The history of Crimea simply has nothing to do with the history of Ukraine."

I looked at her in surprise. Not five minutes before, she had been talking about the migration routes of the ancient nomadic horsemen who had populated not only Crimea, but also the steppes in the southeast of Ukraine. When I tried to unpick the contradiction, she just smiled sarcastically. Her expression left me in no doubt that she considered all of southeastern Ukraine to be Russian territory.

The reality was more complex. The "Wild Field", as the

steppes had once been called, had had little to do with Russia either in the centuries and millennia before Catherine's conquests. Indeed, the Central Museum of Tauris was the ideal place to corroborate this fact for yourself. The permanent exhibition was full of legacies of ancient nomadic peoples who had ruled the steppe long before the emergence of the Slavs. I saw Sarmatian harnesses, the helmets and spears of Polovtsians, Huns, Goths, and Tatars, even some Scythian hashish pipes.

There were a number of notable absences from the showcases in the antiquities room. They were the reason I was here. Missing were a sheep-shaped drinking vessel, the bronze figure of a winged griffin, a horse's bit and about fifteen more pieces dating from the Scythian era. Small slips of paper took their place in the cases, printed with the brief explanation: "Exhibit currently located in Amsterdam."

In the heart of Amsterdam, on the banks of the Rokin Canal, is the Allard Pierson Museum. This small gallery, which is steeped in tradition, actually specialises in the ancient treasures and artefacts of Rome, Greece and Egypt. Crimea was new territory for the curators of the museum when they opened an exhibition of art treasures from the Black Sea in February 2014. There were nearly six hundred objects on display from five Ukrainian museums.

One month after the exhibition opened, Russia annexed Crimea. In the short term, the news brought the Allard Pierson Museum an unexpected number of visitors – many Amsterdam residents were suddenly eager to see the Scythian gold from the Black Sea, because they associated it with the television images from Crimea.

The exhibition organisers were delighted until they realised that they had a tricky problem on their hands. The exhibition was due to run until May that year, after which time the works on loan were supposed to be returned, as had been agreed. But who should they be returned to now? Four of the five participating museums were located in Crimea. At the time of the loans, the collections had been Ukrainian state property. Now, de facto, the museums were located within Russian territory.

Soon there were demands for their return from both sides. The Crimean museums wanted to have their exhibits back. The Kiev Ministry of Culture, on the other hand, argued that the loaned objects were still Ukrainian property; they belonged to Kiev. In Amsterdam, the museum curators grew nervous. The exhibits in question were worth almost one and a half million euros. They could not risk returning the art treasures to one side and face being sued for damages by the other. In the end, the Amsterdam museum management placed the matter in the hands of a Dutch court, requesting it to weigh up legally the merits of the respective claims for restitution.

The outcome of the trial had not been decided when I visited the Allard Pierson Museum in Amsterdam a few months before my trip to Ukraine. A terrified press officer made strenuous efforts to avoid answering any of my questions. What position was the museum taking in the dispute? "No comment." Had there been any attempts to reach an out-of-court settlement with the Crimean museums and the Ukrainian Ministry of Culture? "I cannot comment on that, either." Where were the art treasures at the moment? "In a safe place." Were they still in the museum? "I cannot say anything about that." Could I quickly use the bathroom? "I'm afraid I really cannot... Yes, of course."

It all began, Valentina Mordvintseva said, with four Chinese caskets.

We were sitting in the study of the small house in Simferopol that Valentina shared with her elderly mother and a shaggy tomcat. Overflowing bookshelves lined the walls. As we chatted, Valentina took out one illustrated volume after another, in order to explain the details of the complicated story to me, which had begun with four Chinese caskets and had ended with an international dispute.

She was a wonderful woman. In the emails that we had exchanged to arrange our meeting, I had already had cause to note her intelligence, her warmth, her openness, and her humour. Now, as she sat there opposite me, a charismatic fifty-year-old woman in a blue striped sailor jersey, I hung on her every word. Even the most complex interrelations in her chosen field of research were compelling, tangible, and instantly illuminating when Valentina explained them.

She was an archaeologist. Her area was the Scythians. Valentina had curated the Crimean exhibition that was now stranded in Amsterdam.

She smoked hand-rolled cigarettes, which she stuck into a long mouthpiece. As she spoke, she pointed to a world map with the smoking end of the cigarette holder.

"The caskets came from here. And here..." – the mouthpiece wandered over the map – "... is where they were found."

A trail of smoke stretched from China to Crimea.

Valentina smiled. "Not bad, eh?"

The black and red lacquer caskets had been found in a Scythian tomb on the west coast of the peninsula. They were thought to have come to Crimea more than two thousand years ago, by some route or another. The Japanese specialists to whom Valentina had entrusted the objects for restoration could hardly believe their eyes. They had never seen anything like it; nowhere in all of Asia were there caskets of this type; the four specimens found in Crimea were the sole surviving examples.

"The Japanese had tears in their eyes when I came to pick up the caskets," Valentina said. "They begged me to ensure that they would be kept in a climate-controlled display case."

In the Bakhchisaray Museum, where the caskets fetched up after restoration, there were no climate-controlled display cases. The objects were placed in the next best storage cabinet. It made Valentina's heart bleed.

"So I came up with the idea of the exhibition," she said.

Valentina devised a plan. The dilapidated Crimean museums were home to unique treasures that the world knew little about. It was not only the lacquered Chinese caskets that had landed up on the peninsula in ancient times, but also cultural artefacts from very different parts of the world. From the east, the belt of the Eurasian Steppe led to Crimea, while from the west, it was linked by sea routes to the Mediterranean. Asian horsemen had encountered traders and colonists from Byzantium, Rome, Venice, and Genoa on the Black Sea, and their interactions were meticulously documented – the treasures of the Crimean museums told this story, and Valentina knew that little of it was known beyond the peninsula.

She decided to kill two birds with one stone. A high-profile exhibition was needed, with international participation, to demonstrate the value of the archaeological Crimean treasures not only to the world, but also to raise awareness on the peninsula itself. The Chinese caskets would have to be shown in the climate-controlled display cases of Western exhibition spaces – after that, Valentina hoped, no Ukrainian museum director would ever again dare to tuck them away in the next best cabinet.

It did not take long for Valentina, who was well-connected in archaeological circles in Western Europe, to enthuse two museums with her plan, one in Germany and one in the Netherlands. Implementing the idea in reality proved a more difficult proposition. As an archaeologist, Valentina had never been involved in exhibitions. She had no idea what to expect.

The project had barely got underway when Valentina got a call from a cultural official in Kiev. The man asked whether, in all seriousness, she really wanted to organise the exhibition without participation from the capital city. It had indeed not occurred to Valentina to call in her Kiev colleagues; after all, she was planning an exhibition about Crimea. To avoid any bad feeling, she offered to bring on board a museum in the Ukrainian capital that had incorporated individual finds from Crimea into its collection over the past decades.

The underlying reason for the call only became apparent when transport of the exhibits was being organised. A Ukrainian art haulage company offered to carry the Crimean treasures to Western Europe for four hundred thousand euros. A Dutch competitor had placed a tender for only half that amount. The cultural officials in Kiev wanted to hire the Ukrainian company. Valentina immediately understood why. The shamelessly inflated price had been stitched up in advance. Only some of the fee would go to the transportation company; the officials would split the rest among themselves. It was the usual corrupt Ukrainian scam.

Valentina informed her museum partners in Bonn and Amsterdam about what was going on. Together, they eventually managed to prevail against Kiev. The contract was awarded to the Dutch company. In July 2013, the Crimean treasures arrived safely at the Bonn State Museum.

"You cannot imagine how drunk we got after the opening," Valentina said. "The corrupt officials had lost, good had triumphed, and my Crimean plan had worked."

In January of the following year, as the protests at Kiev's Maidan were coming to a head, the exhibition was relocated as planned to Amsterdam. After that, events unfolded very rapidly.

At the end of February, armed soldiers appeared in Crimea, in unmarked uniforms. The regional parliament of the peninsula was occupied, and the government replaced by a Moscow puppet regime. Around the clock, Russian television bombarded Crimea with horror reports of the coup in Kiev – I remembered well how, during that time, I had sat incredulously in a hotel room in Simferopol following the hair-raising propaganda. I had also seen the soldiers of supposedly obscure origin when I visited a barracks of the Ukrainian military on the outskirts of Simferopol. Men with masked faces and assault rifles were blocking the gate in order to prevent the Ukrainian troops inside from turning out. They were stubbornly silent when I tried to speak to them. A Ukrainian officer who found himself trapped in the barracks told me that the unmarked soldiers were Russian troops. Later, Putin admitted as much, even though he had previously issued repeated denials that Russia was responsible for the military assault on Crimea.

Less than three weeks after the arrival of the soldiers a referendum was held, which delivered the expected results: according to the election returns, nearly ninety-seven percent of the participants voted to join Russia. Just two days later, on March 18, 2014, Vladimir Putin addressed the two chambers of the Russian parliament. Russia and Crimea, the President declared, were reunited.

Shortly thereafter, Valentina got a call from Kiev.

Valechka – a familiar official's voice said – do you understand that you will not see the Scythian treasures again? They belong to Ukraine, and we intend to take them.

Initially, Valentina told me, the museum directors in Bonn and Amsterdam had advanced similar arguments – Crimea had been annexed, and the exhibits must not fall into the hands of Russia. It had taken a while for her to explain to her colleagues that the situation was more complicated than that.

It was most complicated for Valentina herself, who was neither from Crimea nor from Ukraine. She had ended up on the peninsula because of her profession. For fifteen years she had worked as an archaeologist in Simferopol. Crimea had become her adopted home, and life on the peninsula had changed Valentina.

With her smouldering cigarette holder, she pointed again to the world map.

"The Soviet Union," she said, "was an empire. And empires do not disappear from people's minds just because they disappear from the map."

The cigarette holder pointed at Moscow.

"This was the centre. Moscow was by a long way at the pinnacle of the imperial hierarchy during the Soviet era. The capitals of all the other Soviet republics were of only secondary importance."

The cigarette holder travelled southwest, to the Black Sea coast.

"Crimea was always an exception, though. It was in direct contact with the centre because the party leadership took vacations here. The imperial status of the peninsula was higher than that of Kiev. Also the standard of living was better than it was on the Ukrainian mainland; by Soviet standards, Crimeans lived in paradise."

When the empire collapsed, she continued, something happened that the Crimean people had never been able to come to terms with. Suddenly, they were no longer on par with Moscow, but dependent upon Kiev. The rules of the game were now set by Ukraine, which in their view had always been subordinate. In addition, their standard of living plummeted below the Ukrainian average. Everything fell apart, there was no work, the buses no longer ran regularly.

"People just couldn't believe it," Valentina said. "I couldn't believe it myself when I arrived here with my Russian mindset fifteen years ago."

She took a drag on her cigarette.

"But over the years," she continued, "my relationship with Ukraine has changed. I realised that I would much rather live in a small country where there is freedom, than in a large one without freedom."

So it was that, after the annexation of Crimea, Valentina found herself caught between all fronts. Although she was Russian, she was among the few residents of the peninsula who were unhappy about the Russian annexation. Nonetheless, she continued to uphold the position of the Crimean museums in the dispute over the Scythian art treasures. She wanted the exhibits returned to the peninsula.

"They come from here. They were found here. They were cared for here by people who live and work here. Why should they be anywhere else? They should not be taken hostage, as Kiev has attempted. That would be like some marital feud, where the wife says to her husband: 'If you don't come back to me, you'll never see the children again.'"

Valentina sighed.

"There are still a few people here in Crimea who support Ukraine. But Kiev makes it very hard for them."

A few days earlier, Ukrainian nationalists and Crimean Tatar activists had begun to block food shipments to Crimea. On my journey here, I had seen them standing by the roadside with their banners reading: "Crimea is Ukrainian", "No food for the enemy." It was another wedge forced between the peninsula and the mainland. Long ago the Ukrainian banks had suspended payment transactions from and to Crimea, there were no more flights to Kiev, no trains, not even direct bus connections.

"Unfortunately, Kiev has only really become interested in the peninsula since it was annexed," Valentina said. "But if it is to return, Ukraine needs to project a self-image that has some room for Crimea."

She drew thoughtfully on her cigarette.

"I've no idea what this self-image might look like. It cannot be nationalist; Ukraine is too diverse for that."

She was silent for a moment.

"Maybe freedom. That could be what holds Ukraine together. The freedom that's lacking in Russia."

For the past few minutes we'd been hearing the tomcat meowing from the basement. Valentina got up to feed him. While she was gone, my eyes alighted upon a photo of the Chinese caskets that the story had begun with.

"Valentina," I said when she returned. "Your plan... I mean the idea behind the exhibition..."

"Yes?"

"Would you say it was a success?"

She laughed. "Judge for yourself. The caskets are now in a climate-controlled display case."

"But the display case is in Amsterdam."

She nodded regretfully. "That is the painful part of the story."

Then it dawned on her what I was driving at. "You are asking whether people in Crimea have become more aware of these art treasures? Definitely. Everyone here knows the story about the exhibition. When I go shopping, strangers ask me about it. If the exhibits return, people will receive them here triumphantly."

She laughed again. "On the other hand, if they don't return..."

She did not finish the sentence, but even so I understood what she meant. The Archaeological Institute she worked for in Simferopol had been part of the Ukrainian Academy of Sciences until the annexation of Crimea.

Since the ties to Kiev had been severed, no one knew what would become of the research facility. Valentina was not a cautious woman. She made no secret of her political viewpoint among her colleagues. Her daughter, a journalist who was critical of Russia, had already left the peninsula and moved to Kiev. Valentina was protected for the time being, because she was campaigning for the return of the Amsterdam exhibits. But if the Dutch court did not rule in her favour, things could get uncomfortable in Crimea for her as well.

"All the best, Valentina," I said, as we said our goodbyes after two hours.

She laughed at my serious tone. "Don't worry about me. My work will continue, in one way or another. Everything else is secondary."

I took a deep breath, started my run-up, and jumped into the harbour in Sevastopol.

Abruptly, the noise of the city fell silent and was replaced by the sound of my own blood pumping in my head. Shimmering sunlight filtered through the warm, greenish water, which was clear right to the bottom. Some distance below me, I could see the pieces of metal and concrete blocks that littered the harbour floor. A lonely bass was poking around in the scrap metal. As I approached, it disappeared with a short, effortless twitch of its tail.

I bobbed up to the surface. My eyes took in the dove-grey warships of the Russian Black Sea fleet, which were anchored at the far end of the bay. To their left lay the narrow passage to the open sea; to the right, the harbour promenade with its white, neoclassical façades. I swam a few laps before hauling myself back onto the small harbour pontoon, which must be one of the most spectacular urban bathing spots in the world.

Sevastopol is situated at the southwestern tip of Crimea. After three days inland, I found myself longing for the sea and had journeyed from Simferopol to the coast.

An old man in blue swimming trunks addressed me while I was drying myself off. He was sitting on the sunlit concrete steps of the floating platform, and he looked as if he had been there his entire life. His skin was the bronze of a Lenin statue.

"Young man!" he called. "Are you two metres tall?"

"Almost."

"A wonderful size. But you're just a bit thin. You should eat more meat!"

I laughed. "Thanks for the advice."

We struck up a conversation. Viktor was a retired physicist. He had spent his whole life in Sevastopol.

"But it seems to me like it's been more than one life! All the excitement last year was like a second life!"

The past few days in Crimea had taught me to steer clear of political conversations. I tried to change the topic but Viktor was unstoppable. We sat in our trunks, side by side in the sun, trying to be polite while the gap between our positions grew ever wider. The fact that we were half naked did not make things any easier.

Had I heard, Viktor asked, that the fascist junta in Kiev had called for all the Russians in Crimea to be put up against a wall and shot? Was I aware that America had planted spies and saboteurs on the peninsula, to destroy the Black Sea fleet? What did I think about the fact that the

European Union wanted to transform all Russian Christians into homosexuals? Did I know that more than five thousand violent Islamists were hiding among the Crimean Tatars, trained in Arab terror camps and raring to massacre the Slavic population? And, could I explain to him why the Western media was keeping all this secret?

Because none of it is true, I wanted to reply, but Viktor was not to be jolted from his paranoid fantasies. By now, I'd lost count of the discussions I'd had over the past few days in which I'd been confronted with the same propaganda lies, and the more often I heard them, the less I could tolerate them. Viktor was intelligent – why couldn't he see that he was being taken in by a cynical panic campaign? No less intelligent were the Russian journalists who ran the campaign – why did they let themselves be roped in to spreading fear among the populace?

"In spite of everything, it was good talking to you, young man," Viktor said when we parted after an agonisingly long half-hour. "As long as we can still find a common language, there's hope."

If he was right, the future looked bleak. We had not found a common language.

By the fourth day in Crimea, my money was running out. When making my travel arrangements, I had remembered to get all the necessary documents, but not any reserves of cash. The ATMs on the peninsula spat my German card back out again immediately – as a result of the economic sanctions, the international banks had discontinued money transfers with Crimea. After my arrival, I had exchanged all the euros and Ukrainian hryvnias I had on me for roubles.

Although I'd stayed in the cheapest hotels and – contrary to Viktor's advice – had rarely eaten meat, by now there was hardly anything left.

I had no choice: I had to return to the mainland to withdraw money. In Sevastopol, I bought a bus ticket to return to the Crimean border, and paid for one final night's hotel accommodation. With what remained of my cash, I took a day trip to Bakhchisaray, the old capital of the Crimean Tatars.

As the bus left the coast behind and headed towards the mountainous interior, I tried calling a Crimean Tatar whom a mutual acquaintance in Kiev had put me in touch with. The man was so old that he could still remember the tragedy of his people, who like the ethnic Germans had been deported to Central Asia in the Second World War, because Stalin thought the Tatars were Nazi collaborators. Only after the end of the Soviet era had they been able to return to Crimea.

It was not the first time that I had called the old man. We had talked on the phone several times since my arrival on the peninsula, to make an appointment to meet in Bakhchisaray, but each time he had put me off to the following day. "I can't talk now," he had said, or "The situation is difficult," or "There are problems." He had not been any more specific, but I registered the fear in his voice. And now, when I dialled his number again, he did not pick up.

In Bakhchisaray I toured the Garden Palace, one of the few remnants of the old Khanate that had ruled over Crimea before the Russians. The Turkish-speaking Tatars had reached the Black Sea in the thirteenth century in the wake of the Mongol hordes, and when the Mongols withdrew again, they stayed behind. For five hundred years Crimea had belonged to them, until Russia annexed the peninsula for the first time. To emphasise who was master of Crimea "henceforth and for all time", the historical legacy of the Crimean Khanate had been virtually obliterated under Catherine the Great: mosques, palaces, caravanserais, madrasas, hammams, and graveyards were all razed to the ground.

It was rumoured that the Garden Palace only escaped the same fate because Pushkin had once praised it in a poem. A bust of the national Russian poet still stands next to the "Fountain of Bakhchisaray", to which the eponymous poem is dedicated.

The palace was now a museum. Arabic inscriptions adorned the gravestones in the old Khan's Cemetery. Minarets towered above the palace wings; inside there were ornamented harem chambers, a small Crimean Tatar museum, and a severely depleted collection of Scythian Art treasures – the majority of the exhibits that were stranded in Amsterdam had come from here, including the Chinese caskets Valentina had told me about.

When I left the Khan's Palace, I called the old Crimean Tatar again. His phone had been switched off.

Sighing inwardly, I considered my options. I did not know anyone in Bakhchisaray. The political representation body for the Crimean Tatars, the Mejlis, no longer had an office in the city, the new Russian authorities having practically forced the organisation underground after annexation. Even so, I did not want to leave Crimea without having spoken to its oldest inhabitants. If anyone had historic rights to the peninsula, it was them.

It occurred to me that I had passed a mosque on the way to the Khan's Palace. I set off towards it without any firm plan.

"Brother! Got a smoke?"

Two old men were squatting on the sidewalk in front of the mosque. I dug a pack of cigarettes out of my pocket and held it out to them.

"Thanks, brother!"

I asked them if they had been to the mosque.

One of them laughed drily. "I'm Russian."

The other shook his head. "We're here with a friend. He's inside, praying."

The Russian had watery blue eyes and milky, pale skin. The other was darker, and I fancied I could discern something Oriental in his angular facial features. When I asked him if he was Tatar, he nodded.

"Isam," he introduced himself.

I squatted down on the sidewalk and explained to them what had brought me to Crimea.

Isam was in his mid-seventies. He had vague memories of the deportations he had witnessed at the age of four. He and his family had been shipped to Uzbekistan in railway cattle trucks.

"I remember the stench of dead bodies," he said. "Many people died along the way. They could not be buried; their relatives had to throw them off the moving train."

His family ended up in Tashkent. What Isam told me about their life reminded me of the stories I had heard from Alexander Michel less than a week before. Just like the ethnic Germans, the Tatars in Uzbekistan had been placed under military supervision. As a child, even Isam had been required to sign in and out of school every day. Hatred crept into his voice when he recalled it.

"Nowadays, though, you hardly dare mention it out loud," he said. "Under the Ukrainians, we could talk, but since the Russians are back in power, they'd have us believe that all these stories never happened."

His Russian friend gazed fixedly ahead, saying nothing.

I asked Isam if he was a Muslim.

He nodded. "But I only go to the mosque when I'm sober. Not when I smell of liquor."

He reeked of booze. Only now did I notice how shabbily dressed he was. His trousers were stained, his canvas cap had turned a grimy yellow at the forehead. Untrimmed three-week-old hairs stuck out of his three-day-old beard, and running from the left corner of his mouth to just below his eye there was a wide, dark scar. Isam's battered face was recognisably that of a drinker, but his gaze was clear and concentrated, and when he spoke, you could tell he had a kind of intelligence which seemed to have more to do with life experience than with education.

His Russian friend cleared his throat. "It's about time we found something to eat."

Together, we stood up. In a nearby grocery store the two of them gazed at the goods on offer.

"Too expensive," Isam said. "Let's go to the shop at the train station."

I offered to take them to a café. They looked at me uncertainly for a moment. Then, Isam shrugged. "Why not?"

We walked down the street and made for the nearest café. It was a few doors down from the grocery store. The Cyrillic lettering on the sign above the entrance was decorated in an oriental style. Inside, low divans were grouped around small wooden tables. It was a Tatar café.

I ordered three servings of *manti* and three glasses of *koumiss* – dumplings and mare's milk.

"And vodka," Isam added.

The Tatar waiter shook his head apologetically. "We don't have any vodka."

"Beer, then."

The waiter nodded.

When he was gone, Isam cast a gloomy gaze over the café.

"A lot has changed here," he said. "It looked different back then."

I looked at him enquiringly.

He nodded in the direction of the front door. "Over there," he said. "In the corner. I killed someone there."

I was sure that I must have misunderstood him. But as he continued, I realised that I had heard him correctly.

"One shot to the heart, and one to the head. He died instantly."

I didn't know how to react. Speechless, I looked him in the eyes. Isam anticipated my next question.

"He'd raped my daughter. A friend told me. I ran straight here and shot him, without thinking."

He glanced at the spot where it had happened.

"A miracle, really. Sometimes you fire ten times and you don't hit a thing, but here... two shots, two bullseyes."

He'd been locked up for ten years. Isam had not been out long, and this was the first time he had seen the site of the murder again. I couldn't believe it. Completely by chance, I had led him to the café, of all places, where he had taken a human life.

"And your daughter?"

"Hanged herself. While I was in gaol. Couldn't live with it. She was seventeen."

In my head I counted backwards. He must have become a father very late in life.

"I did a lot of things in my life at the wrong time," Isam said when I asked him about it. "Or maybe just in time. Who knows?"

For a moment he seemed to lose himself in his memories, his glazed-over eyes turned inward.

"If only I hadn't been such a good shot," he said, shaking his head.

"You regret it?"

"Of course. He had a mother, he had brothers and sisters. He was a human being."

"How did you get hold of the gun?"

Isam looked straight at me. "I always carry it with me."

He reached into the right pocket of his stained trousers. I raised my hands defensively. "Don't bother, I believe you."

He pulled the gun out of his pocket just far enough for me to see it. It was small and silver, and I remember clearly that I was surprised at how shiny it was. The gun was the cleanest thing this man had on him.

"There are lots of idiots in this city," Isam said. "I don't want to be unprepared if I happen to run into someone stupid."

The Russian sat beside us silently. He seemed to know the entire story already.

The weapon was a souvenir from Afghanistan, just like the scar on Isam's face. He had been part of the Soviet forces that fought against the Mujahideen in the eighties. Like

Alexander Michel, he had joined the army after his exile in Central Asia. Isam had only moved to Bakhchisaray, the home of his ancestors, after he was demobbed.

I asked him if his parents had talked to him about Crimea in Uzbekistan.

"Day and night," Isam said. "From morning till evening, I heard about nothing else. Crimea, Crimea, Crimea..."

His parents, he continued, had taken different views about the deportation. For his mother, it was Stalin's revenge, because some of the Tatars had fought against the Communists in the post-revolutionary civil war. His father, on the other hand, a Communist, told Isam a different story. He believed that his banishment was a tragic error for which not Stalin but incompetent party officials were to blame. Both parents had died long before their people were officially rehabilitated. They had never seen their homeland again.

"Even on their deathbeds, they talked about Crimea," Isam said. He shook his head. "I'll tell you something: Crimea is not a good place. Perhaps it once was. But not anymore."

He talked about the poverty of the Tatar village where he lived, not far from Bakhchisaray. When he mentioned the name of the place, I pricked up my ears – it was the home village of the old man I had been trying in vain to get hold of. I asked Isam if he knew him.

"You won't be able to speak to him," he said. "The Russians arrested his son. He was active in politics. The old man is terrified."

Towards the end of our conversation Isam grew restless. At first I thought that his memories of the murder were unsettling him, but when we left the café, I realised that something completely different was bothering him.

"Brother," he said. "Thank you very much for the food. Now, spare me a bit of change if you will. You know why."

He showed me his hands. They were trembling.

I shook my head.

"Brother," he repeated. "I'm not kidding you. I've got to have a drink."

His Russian friend looked away sheepishly.

I shook my head again. "Isam, I can't do that."

"Yes, you can."

"Maybe you can just go without for today."

Even as I uttered this sentence, I realised how naïve it was.

Isam shook his head firmly. "Give me some money, brother. I beg you."

He stared fixedly into my eyes without blinking. For a few seconds, none of us said a word.

In the end, I gave him the few rouble notes I had left. I wasn't sure if it was enough for a bottle of vodka, but it was my last money.

Isam headed for the grocery store without saying goodbye. Before following him, the Russian spread out his arms apologetically. "Don't be offended," he said. "When someone's in his condition…"

I nodded.

After they had gone, I realised that my hands were shaking. I didn't know why. Was it the sight of the weapon? Isam's withdrawal symptoms? The murder story, the depressing situation of the Crimean Tatars, or the accumulated tension of the last few days?

As I walked back to the bus stop I couldn't shake off my sudden sense of nervosity. I had the feeling that there were eyes following me. Twice I crossed from one side of the street to the other, so as to dodge groups of men who struck me as threatening. For the first time on my entire journey, I felt unsafe, without being able to put my finger on exactly why.

A T-shirt proved the final straw. It was worn by a fat, bald man who was approaching me on the pavement. The T-shirt was black, with two stylised male figures on the front. One figure, shown on the ground on all fours, was coloured in the American Stars and Stripes. Behind him, in the pose of a rapist, stood a second male figure, sporting the tricolour of the Russian flag. A slogan complemented the image: I FUCK YOUR SANCTIONS.

The next morning I boarded the bus heading for the mainland with an ambivalent feeling that veered between relief and depression. I was glad to be leaving Crimea. But the fact that I was happy made me sad.

13

A Handful of Acorns

Kherson–Zaporizhia

BY THE TIME I reached the Ukrainian mainland, summer was finally at an end. At the Crimean border, a cool breeze was sweeping across the steppe, and in Kherson, where my bus journey ended, I saw the first hats, gloves, and scarves being worn on the streets.

After the seemingly endless Indian summer, this sudden cold snap found me unprepared. I shivered as I walked along the banks of the Dnieper, which divided at Kherson before flowing into the Black Sea. Astonished, I watched an elderly woman swimming. After a few turns back and forth she stepped ashore and rubbed the water from her white hair with a towel.

"Cold?" I asked.

She laughed. "I grew up in the north. That makes you tough."

Vlada's family came from Western Ukraine. Her parents had registered as volunteers on an OUN list during the war. Although in the end they had never fought for the nationalist movement, they were put in a labour camp when the list was discovered after the war. They ended up in the Russian Urals, in Vorkuta, above the Arctic Circle.

Their two-year-old daughter stayed behind with her grand-mother in Ukraine until her parents were released from the camp into forced exile and had the child brought to them. Vlada had spent fifty years of her life in the Russian north; only then did she return to Ukraine.

I expected the usual tale of woe. But Vlada, a beautiful woman with intense green eyes, was uncomplaining about her misfortunes.

"Don't believe everything they tell you about the camps," she said. "The people had it good there. They were given clothes, food, medicine. They were warm. Everyone was equal. My mother is still alive and in the best of health, at eighty-six! The camp made her strong."

"But your parents did not live in that camp of their own free will," I said, aghast. "They were locked up innocent."

"What else could Stalin do?" she answered. "He had to wipe out the Ukrainian fascists. That wasn't feasible without making a few sacrifices. Today, the fascists are crawling back out of their holes. Stalin would not have allowed that!"

The entire Soviet Union, I thought as I listened to Vlada, had been one large labour camp. Its occupants had been warm and cared for, and they had all been equal. At some point, most of them must have stopped noticing that they were inmates.

I would have liked to take a boat trip upstream from Kherson, but the ramshackle ferry terminal looked like it was about to collapse at any moment.

"Are there any passenger vessels?" The passer-by whom I asked this question laughed out loud. "You're thirty years too late, young man!"

I talked to a couple of skippers at the industrial port, but all of them were travelling south, downstream to the Black Sea coast. In the end, I took a night train to Zaporizhia.

I shared my sleeping compartment with an elderly lady from Lviv, who was visiting relatives in eastern Ukraine. She was a classicist and had written a weighty tome on "Taras Shevchenko and the Ancient World". She wanted to give me the copy that she was carrying with her. I requested with a smile that she keep the Ukrainian-language book for someone who could read it more fluently than I could.

During our conversation, it suddenly struck me that I was hearing someone speak Ukrainian for the first time in a long while. Everyone in Odessa and Crimea, and almost everyone in Kiev, had spoken Russian to me. The part of the country that lay before me would scarcely present me with an opportunity to deepen my knowledge of Ukrainian either. Grateful for the chance encounter, I listened intently to my train companion.

At some point, she leaned toward me confidentially to ask me a question that seemed to have been bothering her for some time.

"Is it true that women in Germany can be priests?"

I nodded. "Among the Protestants, yes."

"Just in theory, or does that really happen?"

"Oh yes, it's quite usual," I said, laughing.

"Really? But how is that possible? How can a woman say mass when she... when she is bleeding? I can't imagine..."

I ventured an explanation, but I didn't quite get what was troubling her about the idea, so we were talking at cross-purposes.

Later, after we had retired to our bunks, I could still hear my travelling companion muttering to herself.

"I can't imagine..."

The characteristic features of the old Cossack city of Zaporizhia were three parallel lines. The first of these was Lenin Prospekt, eleven kilometres long, allegedly the longest urban street in Europe. The second was the Dnieper, and the third was Khortytsia, a long, thin island stretched out over twelve kilometres in the middle of the river.

Khortytsia had once been the centre of the Ukrainian Cossack Hetmanate, a semi-state entity that began to form in the fifteenth century on the border between two vegetation zones, the forest and the steppe. It was founded by rough-and-ready buccaneers and runaway serfs who despised the sedentary life in the Russian and Polish-dominated north. The Cossacks adopted the practice of horse-riding from the Tatars in the south, and when their wild cavalry units reached the height of their power in the eighteenth century, they were equally feared by the Tsars in Moscow, the kings in Warsaw, and the Khans in Bakhchisaray.

Apart from the principality of Kiev, the Cossack Hetmanate is the only serious predecessor state that the Ukrainians can invoke as a historical antecedent. Its role in Ukraine's national self-image is so central that I had encountered the Cossack myth at every corner of my journey. The stylised, clichéd cossacks always looked the same: I had seen their belligerent, blazing eyes, their thick moustaches, and their shaven heads with a single long shock of hair at the forehead in the menus of folksy restaurants, in the promotional material for political parties, on boxes of chocolates, biker jackets, vodka bottles, and record covers.

So I found it all the more surprising that in Zaporizhia, there was nothing left of the real Cossacks. Under Catherine the Great, who had crushed the Hetmanate at the end of the eighteenth century, all trace of them had been eradicated. All there was to see on the island was a Cossack museum, which was closed for restoration, and a reconstructed Cossack fortress, where costumed warriors bustled about with sabres and whips.

A young historian I came across in the office section of the closed museum smiled wearily when I asked him about the reborn Cossack movement.

"At some point I compiled a list of all the self-proclaimed Hetmans of Zaporizhia," he said. "It was three pages long. In this city there are more Cossack commanders than horses."

The next day, a few of the Hetmans gathered under an old oak tree across the river. They had put on their best uniforms and were celebrating a Sunday Cossack festival. The centrepiece of the festival was a long drawn-out decoration ceremony. In turn, the predominantly elderly participants stepped forward and had medals of honour for their services to the Cossack movement pinned to their uniform jackets. The Hetman who distributed the medals received one too at the very end, the biggest one of all.

The oak under which the Cossack festival took place was said to be more than a thousand years old. It was rumoured that under its canopy the legendary Cossack leader Bohdan Khmelnytsky had been elected Hetman in the seventeenth century. Supposedly the Cossacks had also written their famous letter to the Turkish Sultan here. Shortly after

Khmelnytsky's death, the Ottoman ruler had instructed the Hetmanate to submit to his authority. The Cossacks were not greatly in favour of that. They sat down under their oak and penned a jolly response.

> Thou Babylonian scullion, Macedonian wheelwright, brewer of Jerusalem, goat-fucker of Alexandria, swineherd of Greater and Lesser Egypt, pig of Armenia, Podolian thief, catamite of Tartary, hangman of Kamyanets, and fool of all the world and underworld, an idiot before God, grandson of the Serpent, and the crick in our dick. Pig's snout, mare's arse, slaughterhouse cur, unchristened brow, screw thine own mother!

The oak had seen better days. It was as good as dead. Its powerful trunk split into a dozen branches just above the ground. Almost all of them were grey and bare. Only a single branch still carried leaves.

The oak was ailing because Ukraine was ailing, one of the freshly decorated Hetmans told me. The tree, he continued, had been wasting away since the 1990s. One of its branches had dropped off when Russia annexed Crimea. But as long as there was one green branch on the oak, there was hope for the country.

"During the war, the Nazis wanted to dig up our oak and take it back with them to Germany," the Hetman said.

Presently, when we parted company, he pressed some acorns into my hand, the fruit of the old tree.

"Bring Hitler's cause to an end," he joked. "Plant an oak in Berlin!"

On the way back to the city centre, I recognised an old man on the bus who I had seen in the audience at the Cossack festival.

"Are you also a Cossack?" I asked.

He smiled and shook his head. "There aren't any Cossacks anymore, young man," he said. "There are only old men who would like to be heroes."

After a brief pause, he shook his head again. "If they were real Cossacks, they'd be at the front."

And that's exactly where I was headed the following day.

14

The Love Story of Kovyl and Tipchak

Donetsk–Novoazovsk

THE LAST TOWN before the front was Artemivsk. It was a grey, provincial industrial settlement, with two small squares in the centre. Each contained an empty plinth of a statue. Lenin had disappeared from one, while the other had been home to Fyodor Sergeyev, better known by his *nom de guerre* "Artyom", one of Lenin's early revolutionary comrades. The city itself had been named after Artyom, which meant that Artemivsk was one of the many places in Ukraine that would need to be re-christened in the light of the new policy of de-Sovietisation. No one could tell me if the same rule applied to Artemivske, the popular brand of sparkling wine that was bottled here.

At my hotel, a wedding celebration was in full swing. I lay awake until the early hours of the morning. When the corridors finally stopped reverberating to the sound of the reception, I realised that my insomnia had less to do with the noise levels than with the state of my nerves. Although there had only been a handful of firefights in the area in recent days, the thought of crossing the front kept me awake. My plan was to head for Donetsk, the embattled capital of the separatist region.

Shortly before six, I left the hotel and walked to the bus station with my backpack. There was still half an hour before the departure of the first bus to the front, but there were already more than thirty passengers waiting. Almost all of them were heavily laden with waxed-canvas bags and cardboard boxes full of food. They came from the separatist region; they had crossed the front to shop and were now returning. As I eavesdropped on their quiet conversations, my anxiety disappeared. It was comforting to be part of a crowd that routinely took on what had seemed to me, as I lay awake the previous night, to be an incalculable risk.

The small buses that went to the front left on the half-hour. The first one swallowed up the front of the queue. I made it onto the second one, but standing-room only, next to the driver. The aisle was so full of luggage that I could only get my left foot down on the floor.

We had just left Artemivsk when the sun rose over the steppe. Its first slanting rays broke across the pale yellow grass covered in morning dew. The day began with an intense silvery gleam.

Autumn had come late, only to now transform the landscape all the more rapidly. The foliage of poplars and birches by the roadside looked dull and flaccid, as if it had withered in the rainless, Indian summer heat. Lacking any red hues, the colour of the leaves was more sickly than autumnal – I saw only dry yellow, dull beige, and washed-out green. It was as if the trees were adapting to the camouflage suits of the Ukrainian army, rather than the other way around.

The battle tanks and multiple rocket launchers that I had

seen roll past the windows of the train on my way to Artemivsk were nowhere to be seen in the last few kilometres
leading up to the front. They had been withdrawn behind the
agreed ceasefire lines, or perhaps, as some people alleged,
simply moved out of the eyeline of chance observers. The
soldiers at the checkpoints we passed carried assault rifles.
Occasionally, I saw the barrels of heavier machine guns
protruding from the firing slits of concrete bunkers.

I had spent an entire evening before my departure
reading the complicated provisions in the peace negotia-
tions regarding weapons of particular calibres, but failed
to make much sense of them. Military technology was a
closed book to me, and at root I was only too happy at my
inability to classify the various weapons I saw into different categories. That way, it wouldn't even enter my head to
think of certain instruments of murder as somehow less
monstrous than others.

After driving for an hour we reached the last Ukrainian
checkpoint. Ahead of us, a long queue of cars stood nose to
tail, but buses had priority and so the driver swept past the
private vehicles in the emergency lane. He dropped his passengers off right in front of the checkpoint and then headed
straight back to Artemivsk to pick up his next load.

One soldier checked our luggage, another our documents. The second man hesitated briefly when he saw my
German passport, but my military credentials were in order,
and after a few routine questions he waved me through. On
the far side of the checkpoint, minibuses from the separatist region were waiting. Most of these collective taxis were
going to Donetsk. It took less than ten minutes for the first
one to fill up and pull away.

Just a few hundred metres away was the separatists' checkpoint. The soldiers there were equipped with the same assault rifles as the Ukrainian army, at least to my untrained eye the weapons looked identical. Above the stacked sandbags of their road barrier hung the black, blue, and red flag of the "Donetsk People's Republic". The separatists waved the bus through unchecked. I let out a sigh of relief – the front was behind me.

The hilly steppe landscape that we passed through over the next one and a half hours was visibly ravaged by war. Flattened warehouses and factory façades riddled with bullet holes lined the highways. Several times the bus detoured onto smaller side tracks, presumably to avoid damaged roads or minefields. A bridge that looked intact from above turned out to be resting precariously on several buckled concrete piles. I only noticed the damage when the driver gingerly drove the bus down the riverbank to cross a makeshift pontoon bridge.

Shortly before we got to Donetsk I saw the skeleton of a completely burnt-out church through the bus windows. The gutted building stood forlornly on the steppe; only the blackened metal framework remained. Three cupolas towered above the nave. Although their exterior cladding was gone, the bare, curving struts still clearly described the ghostly outline of three onions.

As they gazed out of the windows, my fellow passengers were just as tongue-tied as I was. I would have liked to know what was going through their heads, but no one said a word, and the man on the seat next to me was staring fixedly ahead with such a gloomy expression on his face that I did not dare to speak to him.

The first passengers alighted on the outskirts of Donetsk. The gloomy fellow sitting next to me suddenly became animated.

"What's going on?" he shouted to the driver. "I thought we were going past the shopping centre! Why aren't we turning off?"

Without turning his head, the driver replied, "If you want to go to the shopping centre, you need to say so. I only go there on request."

"I have to get off there," my seatmate exclaimed. "Step on it, will you, I'm late! I need to get to a funeral!"

As the bus turned off, I sensed my chance.

"A relative?" I asked.

The man turned his face to me. He was around thirty.

"A friend," he said. "My oldest mate. We went to school together before he moved to Donetsk."

He seemed to have just been waiting to pour out his heart to someone – I had read his expression completely wrong.

"I still can't believe it," he said. "A few days ago his wife called me. She was totally beside herself. He'd suddenly vanished. An angler found his body floating in a river. They'd shot him. I don't know how his wife is going to cope. The kids... they are so small."

He shook his head in desperation.

"Do they know who did this?" I asked.

"His car was found a few kilometres away, under a bridge. He was a taxi driver. Maybe he was robbed by his passengers. Police say that three men in camouflage uniforms were seen in his car. But what good is that? There's a war going on in the Donbass. Every second person here is running around in camouflage."

A few minutes later we arrived at the shopping centre.
The man shook my hand before he got out.

"Don't stay here too long," he said.

At first glance, Donetsk looked bewilderingly normal.
I couldn't say for sure what I had been expecting to see,
what traces of war I had unconsciously conjured up in my
mind's eye. I merely registered my surprise at their notable
absence.

It was a cold, bright clear Sunday. The city was full of
pedestrians. Looking at ease, they strolled in pairs or groups
along Pushkin Boulevard, past crowded café terraces,
balloon sellers, candyfloss booths, and souvenir stalls. The
shops lining the boulevard were mostly open, and their
range of goods was clearly aimed at a more affluent clien-
tele than the junk shops in the provincial Ukrainian towns
I had travelled through in the past days and weeks.

A photo exhibition on Pushkin Boulevard illustrated
how Donetsk had acquired its wealth. On display were old
black and white photographs from the early years of the
industrial metropolis. The city had only come into being
in the late nineteenth century, when the Tsarist regime
had discovered that deep beneath the fertile black soil of
Eastern Ukraine there was something even blacker, even
more valuable: coal.

An industrialist named John Hughes who had traded
his native Wales for the Donbass built the first coal-fired
blast furnaces on behalf of the Russian Empire. He also
established a steel mill on the banks of a small river called
the Kalmius. The workers' settlement that grew up next
to it was named after Hughes, although in the Cyrillic

transcription of his surname a few letters were lost: hence-forth, the rapidly expanding industrial city was known as "Yuzovka". Less than half a century after its founding, it already boasted more than one hundred thousand inhabit-ants, and by the later Soviet era, the population soared to a million. After the revolution, the Bolsheviks had dropped the foreign, capitalist name Yuzovka and replaced it with a more familiar one: Stalino. A few years after Stalin's death, the city was again renamed, this time for the river Donets, which flows through the northern part of the coalmining region.

As I followed Pushkin Boulevard south, I suddenly real-ised there was a persistent noise bothering me. It was so quiet that I only really became fully conscious of it after I had been registering it somewhere in the back of my mind for a few minutes. A dull thundering sound filled the air. It recurred at regular intervals, and every time it was imme-diately followed by a quieter echo. I stopped walking and listened intently. When I heard the noise again, I realised that it had to be artillery fire.

Seeking help, I looked around. The boulevard was full of people, but no one except me seemed to have noticed anything.

"Can you hear that?" I asked an old man who came walking past with his dog.

He stopped and looked at me enquiringly.

"This thunder," I said, pointing uncertainly to the sky.

Together, we listened. When the sound came again, the man nodded briskly. "It's a way off," he said. Without waiting for my reaction, he moved on.

It was only at second glance that I noticed Donetsk had

become a frontline city, but once I'd spotted it, it was ever more apparent. Little stickers showing an assault rifle with a red line through it were stuck on the café doors. Many of the promenading couples on Pushkin Boulevard consisted of women in short skirts and men in mottled camouflage. Everywhere I looked there were soldiers, while policemen were nowhere to be seen. Outside of the immediate city centre every other shop was closed; on some streets there wasn't a single business left. Their owners seemed to have abandoned the embattled city along with all the other war refugees. A total of nearly two million people had fled the Donbass since the beginning of hostilities, more than half of them to Russia, the rest to Ukraine. In some houses, I saw hardly any lights on in the evening. Entire office blocks seemed to have been vacated. In many places even the streets were eerily deserted. The dwindling population no longer filled the city, Donetsk seemed to flap around them like a dress that had grown too large.

The supermarkets evidently had trouble stocking their shelves. In some there were substantial gaps, while in others, attempts had been made to conceal the shortfall with endless rows of identical canned goods. Almost all the billboards on the streets were empty or pasted over with the separatists' propaganda posters. One read, "Celebrating the first anniversary of the judicial system of the Donetsk People's Republic." Another showed two uniformed men with weapons drawn, standing guard over a prone figure, apparently a looter. "It is the state's duty to protect you and your property," the caption below read. Countless posters showed Alexander Zakharchenko, the separatist prime minister – Zakharchenko with children; Zakharchenko

with pensioners; Zakharchenko in camouflage; Zakharchenko in dress uniform.

The Donetsk Opera had shifted its entire programme to
the afternoon because of the curfew, which came into effect
at eleven o'clock in the evening. Outside the opera house
was a glazed noticeboard containing no playbills, but a large
poster of Stalin. I stopped in front of it, irritated at the familiar moustachioed face. It was a propaganda poster from the
Second World War. "Our cause is just, we will destroy the
enemy, victory is ours." ran the slogan under Stalin's likeness. I had not been surprised to see a large statue of Lenin
a few streets away, but why a poster of Stalin should be displayed in front of the opera house was harder to fathom.

"What is Comrade Stalin doing here?" I asked an elderly
passer-by.

The woman glanced at the poster and shrugged an indif-
ferent shrug. "Heaven knows."

At the southern end of Pushkin Boulevard there was a
large park. Between the flowerbeds a man in a wheelchair
spoke to me.

"Brother! Got any spare change for an invalid?"

I gave him a few roubles. He was in his fifties. His salt-
and-pepper beard framed a strikingly handsome face. His
left leg was missing.

"War wound?" I asked.

He unbuttoned his uniform jacket. Underneath I could
see white gauze bandages that covered his entire chest.

"They couldn't save the leg, but they removed two bullets
from my chest. There's still one bullet in my body, just in
front of the liver. The doctors say they can't get it out – it's
too dangerous."

He grinned a wide grin. The laughter lines at the corners of his eyes crinkled like the flexing body of an accordion. For a disabled veteran he was in remarkably good spirits.

"Igor," he introduced himself. "You want to hear how the war started?"

"Oh yes," I said. "Absolutely."

"It's simple. The freemasons are behind it! At the beginning, two of these Rockefellers ran into each other. One of them says to the other: Listen, brother, I've lost seventy billion that I need to recoup somehow – let's start a war! All right, says the other, I'll have a word with Obama. Then Obama speaks to Merkel, Merkel to Putin, Putin to Yanukovych…"

"Merkel to Putin?"

"That's right. They are all in cahoots. Anyhow, the war in Donbass wasn't enough to make up the seventy billion, so Putin spoke to Assad, and now it is continuing in Syria…"

Igor's grin grew wider as he explained world affairs to me.

At some point I interrupted him. "If you could see it all so clearly, why did you go to war?"

He shrugged. "I needed money. My mother said: Go and register as a volunteer, the pay is good."

Igor had fought against the Ukrainian army with the separatist troops until one of his legs had been shot away last summer. They had promised him a disability pension, but so far he hadn't seen a penny. He lived on the cash that people strolling in the park slipped to him.

I asked him if it was true that Russian troops were fighting in the Donbass.

"Are you kidding? Without them, we wouldn't have

lasted three weeks. Whenever the going gets tough, they come over the border and help us out. By the way, you want to hear a joke?"

"Go ahead."

He proceeded to tell me not one joke, but fifteen in a row. Each one was dirtier than the last, and Igor laughed at each one at least twice as long as his narrative had lasted. His laughter was so contagious that I had to join in, and because Igor thought I was laughing at his jokes, he laughed even more, which in turn made me laugh more too, until eventually we were both helpless with laughter, unable to stop.

"Tell me," I asked when I had partially regained my composure, "How come you're in such a good mood?"

"Quite simple," Igor said with a grin. "I'm in love! I have found the woman of my life, and I tell you, brother, that love is all that matters! I had to lose my leg in order to understand that!"

Again he began to laugh. "Isn't that insanely funny?"

We laughed so loud and so long that the strollers in the park shot irritated glances at us. Igor was the happiest man I met throughout the entire Donetsk People's Republic.

During my trip, I had got into the habit of visiting the local history museum in every Ukrainian town. Over time, these little exhibition centres, which despite their regional focus looked remarkably similar wherever you went, had grown dear to my heart. In the first hall there was almost always the skeleton of a mammoth or, if no suitable bones had been unearthed in the area, a lifelike mammoth replica, covered with shaggy fake fur. The prehistoric hall was followed by endless glass cabinets with stuffed animals and dried plants, before the natural history section gave way to the historical exhibits. This wouldn't have been complete without a war diorama, the three-dimensional reenactment of a key battle, with plastic soldiers parading in a painted alcove, accompanied by dramatic music. Depending on the size of the museum, sometimes an entire floor, but at the very least a whole room, was dedicated to the Second World War.

I expected no significant deviations from this scheme when I visited the Donetsk Museum of Local History. It was situated in the northern part of the city centre, a few hundred metres behind the football stadium. I approached the museum on foot – and froze in shock when I finally set eyes on the three-storey building. Its left wing was in ruins.

Only fragments of an external wall were left. Through its glassless windows I could see nothing but bright blue sky. At first I wondered if the building was perhaps in the process of being demolished, but as I drew nearer, I could see the bullet holes. They disfigured the entire façade of the remaining part of the museum. In the open courtyard there were a few stone sculptures from the time of the ancient steppe peoples. They, too, had been hit: parts of their arms, shoulders and faces were chipped. One was missing its head.

It wasn't news to me that residential buildings had come under fire in Donetsk. I also knew that some 2,500 civilians had lost their lives in the war. But I had only read about skirmishes on the city's outskirts. The museum was right in the centre. It must have been fired upon from a distance. I also saw the telltale signs of artillery fire on the façades of the surrounding buildings. At the next corner, there was a small kiosk whose metal cladding was riddled with holes like a colander.

The museum entrance was right next to the destroyed wing. I was surprised when I spotted an elderly woman coming out of the door – the building was so badly damaged that I had thought it was deserted.

"Is the museum open?" I asked.

The woman nodded. "But there's not much to see."

A plump, white-and-ginger coloured cat was prowling across the dark entrance hall.

"Isn't he a fine fellow?" the ticket lady asked when she noticed me looking at it. "He came to us during the war. His owners probably abandoned him when they fled. The city's full of stray animals."

I bought a ticket. When the woman noticed my foreign accent, she immediately assigned me a guide. The guide's name was Lyudmila, and she had lived in Magdeburg for several years, as the wife of a Soviet soldier. Lyudmila was very shy. When I looked into her eyes, her voice became so quiet that I could barely understand her. I tried not to look at her, which wasn't easy because otherwise there wasn't much else to see. Only three small rooms of the museum were accessible; the rest were sealed off due to the war damage. The first room was full of stuffed birds. The second had furniture from the turn of the century. In the third there were a few Scythian pottery vessels alongside Soviet flower vases. It was the saddest assortment of museum exhibits I had ever seen.

My questions about the war damage unsettled Lyudmila. She referred me anxiously to the director. All she would tell me was that the destroyed part of the building had housed the natural history collection.

"Was there a mammoth?" I asked curiously.

Lyudmila nodded. "A skeleton. Thankfully it survived."

The director, a man of about forty named Deniz Kuznet-sov, received me in his office on the first floor, together with his older deputy, Tatyana Koynash. The shattered windows of the office had been sealed with plastic wrap. Above the desk hung a large portrait of Che Guevara.

I introduced myself and explained what had brought me to Donetsk. "I am writing a book about Ukraine and I'm interested…"

"Then you've come to the wrong place," the director interrupted me coolly. "We're no longer part of Ukraine."

The conversation made a faltering start. The two of them heard me out with noticeable mistrust; they seemed to be looking for hidden signs that would unmask me as an agent of the opposing side. I did my best to focus my questions on the museum, so as not to get caught up in the mine-field of politics right from the start. It took a while before the monosyllabic responses of my interlocutors gradually became a bit more detailed.

The museum had been attacked in the summer of 2014, over three days in late August. No one was injured; the rockets landed late at night and early in the morning, when there were no employees in the building.

"We look upon it as a targeted terrorist attack," the direc-tor said. "It's barbaric to attack a museum. The Ukrainian troops are barbarians – you can write that down!"

A large portion of the animal and botanical specimens had been buried under the collapsed part of the building and were damaged irreparably. One of the rockets had crashed through the floor of the natural history wing and penetrated the basement room below, where part of the antiquities collection had been housed. Tatyana, the deputy, later showed me the centuries-old pottery whose shards their employees had picked out of the rubble and reassembled. There was so little left of some that the vessels which had been reconstructed consisted of more holes than clay.

The news about the museum's destruction had reached the director at the front, and his deputy at the beach. Deniz Kuznetsov, who had volunteered to join the separatist forces, had been fighting against the Ukrainian army north of the city, while Tatyana Koynash had been on vacation by the Azov Sea, south of Donetsk.

Both of them immediately returned to the city, to save what could be saved. It had rained during those August days. All of the windows were broken, the projectiles had left holes in the roof, and there was water everywhere. Frantically, the museum staff transferred all the intact exhibits to the undamaged parts of the building. The mammoth skeleton found a place alongside an architectural model of John Hughes' former steel mill. A diorama of the Second World War battle of Saur-Mogila ended up next to an armchair that had once belonged to the composer Sergei Prokofiev, who had grown up in a village near Donetsk. Stuffed foxes, rare steppe grasses, preserved black soil samples, Orthodox icons, Soviet propaganda posters, Cossack guns and Tatar sabres, KGB medals and SS helmets, old wooden ploughs and early tractor models, Scythian harnesses, embroidered Ukrainian blouses, Russian samovars, Bolshevik hats, items of Tsarist uniforms, execution orders, exile verdicts, and court documents – the entire history of the Donbass fetched up in one large, unsorted pile.

Now that history had to be pieced together again. Step by step the rooms of the museum had been restored, one after another they would be refilled with exhibits. Not only with old ones, but also with new ones, because while the museum staff sorted through the past of the Donbass, they were simultaneously documenting its present.

The director and his deputy told me about the new exhibits, which over the past year and a half had ended up in their collection. They had kept the first posters that the demonstrators in Donetsk had created to protest against the coup in Kiev: "America, hands off of Ukraine!" – "Stop the Bandera fascists!" – "No one forces the Donbass to its knees!" When self-appointed representatives of the people had proclaimed the Donetsk People's Republic in April 2014, a copy of their declaration of independence had ended up in museum storage. Just one month later, Kuznetsov and Koynash added the ballots that the separatists had used for their referendum about the independence of their republic. They had also obtained a copy of the official results – 89 percent in favour.

I had already seen a few of the other new exhibits. In the museum's entrance hall, fragments of the weapons that the Kiev government had deployed in response to the uprising in the Donbass were on display. Splintered rocket components, detonated mines, and exploded tank shells lined a long, accusatory sidewall. Among these were the missiles that had destroyed the museum.

Kuznetsov and Koynash had already had occasion to put their newly acquired artefacts on display elsewhere. When the Donetsk World War II Museum, which was on the other side of the football stadium, had reopened last May to mark the seventieth anniversary of the war's end, the two had curated a special exhibition on the current war there. Its title was: "The Fight against Fascism Continues".

As I listened to the director and his deputy, I wondered more and more whether, after the museum's reopening, the history of the Donbass would still look like it had before. When I asked, Kuznetsov gave me a searching look.

"I know what you're driving at," he said. "We're not planning to rewrite history."

After a brief pause, he smiled a smug smile.

"But surely the part of the exhibition dealing with the Holodomor won't be the first we reopen."

Time and again during the recent clashes in Eastern Ukraine, the issue of the artificially induced famine of the thirties had come to the fore. Several Holodomor monuments had been pulled down by the separatists during the war.

"The subject never had much significance in the Donbass," said Tatyana Koynash. "People starved in the countryside, not in the industrial areas."

"Holodomor, Holodomor," the director interrupted. "If I hear that word one more time! People starved throughout the Soviet Union, but in Ukraine they had to invent a name for it. As if it hadn't affected anyone but them!"

Kuznetsov's initial reticence had now finally dissipated entirely, and his tone grew impatient.

"Kiev forced the subject on us. The Ministry of Culture instructed us to create a room in the museum about the famine. We had absolutely nothing to display – there's virtually no archive material about the Holodomor in this area. In the end, we commissioned an artist, who set up a few coffins and wrote 'Holodomor' above them, because nothing better occurred to him."

I listened silently while the rage in Kuznetsov's voice increased. His deputy fell silent too.

"It's always the same story with the Ukrainians," he said. "They never blame themselves; it's always other people who are responsible for their misfortune. Russia, Russia, Russia – I don't know what the Ukrainians would do without Russia. Their entire self-image would collapse if they had no one else to blame. Who established Ukraine as a state in the first place? Lenin! And the Ukrainians topple his monuments! It's ridiculous!"

When Kuznetsov stopped speaking, there was an uncomfortable silence in the room.

I cleared my throat. "Neither of you two are Ukrainians, I take it?"

Kuznetsov shook his head. "God forbid."

"You won't find many full-blooded Ukrainians in the Donbass," Tatyana Koynash said. "I would call myself a Russian, but what exactly does that mean? My family has other ethnic roots too, just like all the families here. All this nationalism is nonsense. I don't understand what the Ukrainians expect to get from it."

"They want to prove to us that they're not Russians," Kuznetsov said drily.

I pointed to the portrait of Che Guevara above his desk.

"I see that Lenin isn't the only one you like?"

He smiled.

"Quite right. I'm a communist. I want a Donbass free of oligarchs. We will get it, too, I promise you that. The war has changed people here. We won't let ourselves be exploited any longer. Especially not by cowards who fled rather than fight for the Donbass."

Again his smile turned smug. "There are a lot of weapons in circulation here. All those oligarchs who are planning on returning should remember that. They'd be living rather dangerously."

These closing words of his finally prompted me to recall who Kuznetsov reminded me of. It was Mykola Kokhanivskiy, the furious battalion commander from Kiev. In their stance on Ukraine, the two might have represented opposite extremes, and maybe they had even come face to face at the front. But they were spiritual brothers in their hatred of the oligarchs, their unashamed propensity for violence, their belligerent fury.

I found out what Tatyana Koynash thought about Ukraine only later, when she showed me round the museum warehouse on her own. She, too, had been hardened by the war. Her voice was full of hatred as she told me how she had run through the streets of Donetsk clutching her grandson's hand, as artillery shells were falling all around. But unlike her superior, Tatyana seemed to have grasped that no real help could be expected from the Russian side – that Russia was only taking advantage of the Donbass as a flashpoint.

"I hope the Ukrainians come to their senses," she said. "They shouldn't send us any Nazis who just want to impose their will on us, but normal, intelligent people we can talk to."

It sounded desparate. But at the same time, it sounded like the only way to end the war.

When I said goodbye to the two museum directors, I asked for their advice. I had heard about a nature reserve on the Russian border, a steppe park where the old grasslands of Ukraine were conserved in their original form.

"You wouldn't happen to know how to get there?" I asked. Both shook their heads.

"All I've heard is that the park manager fled to Ukraine," Tatyana said. "I've no idea whether or not anyone's still working there."

"It's in a military zone," Kuznetsov added. "So many different forces have been stationed there lately that nobody knows where the mines are buried. You'd better stay away from there."

I took pot luck and boarded a rural bus heading for the Sea of Azov. According to my map, there was only a single highway leading from Donetsk to the coast through the narrow southern part of the separatist-controlled area. Running parallel to the road, a few kilometres further east, was the Russian border. The nature reserve had to lie somewhere in-between.

On some sections of the highway we encountered hardly any traffic; often, the bus was the only vehicle in sight. There were harvested fields on both sides of the road. Yellow stubble contrasted sharply with the black, rich earth of the steppe, which ran in a flat expanse towards the horizon, and was vaulted by a leaden October sky.

On several occasions we drove past separatists' checkpoints, but none of the armed men went to the trouble of stopping the bus. Just after a village called Telmanove, in whose Cyrillic transliteration I only recognised the name of Ernst Thälmann at second glance, we passed two abandoned, apparently decommissioned tanks by the roadside.

Their gun barrels were pointing at each other, but the sight was not a menacing one, on the contrary, the tanks looked like two friends reaching out to one another in their death throes.

When, after almost two hours of driving, a sign reading "Samsonove" came in sight by the roadside, I asked the driver to drop me off at the next junction. An icy steppe wind hit my face. The bus drove off and left me alone. As far as the eye could see there were no cars or people in sight, just endless, flat fields.

I turned off onto a small dirt road. The narrow poplars by the side of the road offered little protection against the biting wind. After the first few minutes, I pulled my hood up. Furious gusts whipped around my ears. Their whistling was so deafening that I would not have heard a tank, even if it had been hard on my heels.

I walked along the dirt road for about an hour before the outbuildings of an old collective farm came into view ahead of me. Behind it lay a tiny village, whose dogs barked collectively when they scented the arrival of a stranger. Two old men were chatting over a garden fence. As I approached them, their conversation ceased. The two of them regarded me with undisguised curiosity. I enquired about the steppe park. Without uttering a word, the men pointed to the far end of the dusty village street.

The last house in the village was situated on the bank of a small river crossed by a narrow footbridge. On the far side stood a man in camouflage fatigues.

"From Germany, you say?"

The uniformed man scratched his unshaven chin, perplexed. Apparently, he was the park warden.

"Germany... Not bad. In that case I should probably fetch the boss."

The boss was Alexander Mikheyev, a broad-shouldered, unceremonious man in his fifties who greeted me with a good-humoured slap on the shoulder. He had something of a cheerful bear about him, but his broken-veined, choleric face told me that the bear's mood might easily change.

Mikheyev had not been in the post long.

"My predecessor – well, it's a long story. In a nutshell, he's not here anymore."

When I looked for the name of the predecessor later, I learnt that the separatists had sent him packing. It was not the only administrative post in the Donetsk People's Republic that had been reallocated in the past year and a half.

"You came here from Germany to see the steppe?" Mikheyev asked.

I nodded.

He whistled through his teeth in appreciation before leading me into the park grounds.

"A thousand hectares," he said. "Virgin steppe. No plough has ever tilled this soil."

A small administration building abutted on a horse stable. Next to it rose a low hill, and behind its knoll the steppe park proper began. We were still talking at the bottom of the hill when from afar there suddenly came the muffled drumming sound of galloping horses' hooves. The rhythm was unmistakable – *Tapatam, tapatam, tapatam.*

Mikheyev had heard it too. We listened in silence as the drumming noise grew closer, until suddenly the figure of a horseman appeared at the top of the hill, thundering down towards us at full gallop.

It was a picture of such timelessness that I forgot for a moment where I was. A tingle ran through my body, as I experienced a millennia-old fear. No matter how fast I ran, the rider would catch up with me, and wherever I fled he would find me, there were no hiding places in the grass. That's what it must have felt like – the settled peoples' primal fear of the steppe peoples.

The rider brought his horse to an abrupt halt immediately in front of us and dismounted. The animal was dark chestnut and exuded a calmness that surprised me. It breathed steadily through its nostrils, showing no sign that it had just been ridden hard. The rider was in his twenties and looked just as calm as his mount.

"Vitya," he introduced himself. He was the park's stable manager.

Mikheyev noticed my fascinated gaze.

"Have you ever been on a horse?" he asked.

And so it was that I did not enter the steppe on foot, but on the back of a horse named Sultan. Mikheyev went back to the administration building, while Vitya trotted along on foot beside me. At first he held the reins in his hand, and later, when the horse got used to me, he handed them to me.

There wasn't a great deal to see at first glance. Rolling hills undulated to the horizon; there were no trees, and hardly a bush to interrupt the view. The steppeland grass was yellow and straw-like. It seemed lifeless, and it would stay like this until spring came. Viewed from a distance, the ground seemed to be covered with a monotonous blanket of grass. It was only up close that it revealed its diversity. Single-stemmed and knotty branched stalks bent over side by side in the wind, withered flowers trembling at the tips, some of them feathery, others umbel- or spike-shaped. Rather than a monoculture, hundreds of different grasses were growing on the steppe.

It was only on the eastern fringe of the park, about three, maybe four kilometres away, that I saw a few isolated trees, which appeared to be poplars. They formed a line. When I asked Vitya if they marked the Russian border, he nodded.

"Is there a fence?" I asked. From a distance, I could not make out any border facilities.

"Only a shallow ditch. When we take the horses into the steppe to graze, they sometimes stray over to the other side."

"What do you do then?"

"Nothing. They come back of their own accord. And the Russian border guards don't bother about horses, as long as there isn't anyone riding them."

In a few places stone sculptures poked up above the grass, roughly hewn figures that were legacies of the ancient steppe peoples. By now, I had seen so many of these old gravestones in Ukrainian history museums that I could tell the difference between them to some extent. Most of the figures in the park seemed to come from the Cuman era; they had to be about a thousand years old. A few more weathered stones looked like grave figures of the Scythians and Sarmatians, who had roamed the steppe about a millennium before the Cumans.

Vitya told me that almost all the stone sculptures came from other parts of the steppe; they had been gathered together in the park. Only one statue stood in its original location, on top of a kurgan, an ancient burial mound, which rose up in the middle of the park. The figure was missing its head, but the arms, folded beneath its belly, told me that it had to be a Cuman tombstone.

On the kurgan, Vitya pressed the reins into my hands. Sultan immediately responded to the pressure of my thighs, falling into an easy trot. As soon as we got too far away from the kurgan, Vitya whistled the horse back, and although we did not exactly pelt through the grass at a heroic gallop, I could still feel the blood pumping faster in my veins. I suddenly felt as if I was one with the steppe – I was riding through the millennia, a Scythian, a Cuman, a Cossack. I was overcome with the urge to squeeze my thighs together tightly against the horse's flanks, to charge across the Russian border and beyond, as far as Kazakhstan, and on to Siberia, to Mongolia, as far as the steppe reached.

Only after a brief moment of bliss did it occur to me that a Russian border guard would surely have shot me off the horse.

On the way back to the stables, Vitya told me that he lived in Samsonove, the village on the edge of the park.

"Are there more Russians or Ukrainians living there?" I asked.

He paused. The question seemed to confuse him.

"Well," he replied uncertainly, "In the past, when there was still the Union, we were all Russians in a way. Now, some are Ukrainians. I have no idea how many there are of each."

Vitya was too young to have consciously experienced the Soviet era. His answer put me in mind of something that Valentina Mordvintseva, the archaeologist from Simferopol, had said. Empires, she'd told me, do not vanish from people's minds just because they disappear from the map.

Mikheyev, the park director, was still busy when we got back to the administration building. While I was waiting for him, a young female colleague called Tamara showed me around a small steppe museum. The display cases were full of stuffed animals and dried grasses.

Tamara pointed to two small tufts of grass, which were labelled with little squares of cardboard, one of which read "Kovyl" and the other "Tipchak" – feather grass and sheep's fescue.

"On the steppe, these two grasses often grow side by side," Tamara informed me. "There's an old legend about it. Perhaps you have heard of it?"

As it happened, I did know about the legend, from a book. It was set in the far-off days of the Principality of Kiev, when the Slavs had been at war with the steppe peoples. One night, two opposing armies set up camp beneath a mountain, the Kievans on one slope, the Cumans on another. The Kievans charged a young warrior by the name of Kovyl with keeping watch, while the Cumans ordered a girl named Tipchak to do the same. During the night, the two guards met one another on the mountain and fell in love. They whispered declarations of love until dawn, even though they did not understand each other's language. When the warring parties awoke in the morning and saw what had happened, they decided the lovers could not be separated. They were allowed to leave together. And ever since that time, feather grass and sheep's fescue have grown together side by side on the steppe.

"No," I dissembled in reply. "I don't know the legend."

I wanted to hear my guide tell me the story in her own words.

"It happened like this," Tamara began. "Two hostile armies encamped one night on the steppe, not far from one another. The commander of one army was called Kovyl, the commander of the other, Tipchak. During the night the two fell in love and betrayed their armies. When this came to light the next morning, the lovers were killed. Since those days, feather grass and sheep's fescue have grown where the lovers' blood was spilt on the steppe."

I would have liked to stay on the steppe a bit longer, but Mikheyev had other plans for me. He wanted to show me the second park that came within his administrative domain, a bird sanctuary on the coast of the Azov Sea. We drove south in his old Lada Niva that afternoon.

The leaden sky grew darker and darker, while the fields became paler. Increasingly, the soil lost its black hue. It turned brown, then beige, until shortly before Novoazovsk it changed to sand where no steppe grass could take root. Rain-soaked reeds characterised the coastal landscape; by this time it had started to drizzle.

In the company of a young biologist from the park administration, Mikheyev and I walked along the beach. The icy wind drove the rain in our faces; here on the coast it blew even more fiercely than on the steppe. Its hiss rivalled the roar of the surf. We had to shout to make ourselves understood.

Mikheyev paused at the foot of an observation tower.

"That's not for the likes of this old man!" he bellowed. "Up you two go!"

Obediently the biologist and I climbed the wet metal steps. Up aloft, the wind blew with such violence that we had to cling to the railing in order to keep from being swept off the platform. The biologist stretched out an arm. I recognised the narrow spit of land he was pointing at, but the wind swallowed half of his bellowed explanations.

"... Seagulls... herons... cormorants... nesting area..."

After we had climbed back down, Mikheyev led us to a long, low concrete building at the water's edge. It was an old Soviet holiday home built for mine workers from the Donbass. The building now belonged to Mikheyev's nature reserve, but it had not been used for a long while. The smashed windows and doors were barred with metal grilles. Looking through them I could see bare concrete walls and the remains of splintered furniture. On the coast side of the building, the brown waters of the Azov Sea crashed thunderingly against a concrete quay wall.

I only understood why Mikheyev had brought me here when his bear's paw slapped me on the back.

"My international friend!" he cried. "I want you to find us an investor who will restore the workers' retreat!"

Incredulous, I stared into his rain-drenched face. The plan was so harebrained that it took me a few seconds to come up with a response. What investor, I thought, would put his money into a banana republic not recognised by the international community and isolated behind a frontline?

"Alexander," I yelled. "How would your investor even be able to get here?"

"We can easily figure that out!" he yelled, grinning. "We'll dig a tunnel for him! Under the Russian border!"

We spent the night in Novoazovsk. Mikheyev actually lived in Donetsk, with his family, whom he saw only at weekends since he'd been transferred from the city's environmental agency to the coast. Throughout the week, he slept in a small service apartment in the building that belonged to the park administration. There was a second bed which he offered to me.

In its tiny galley kitchen, Mikheyev fried eggs with sausage. In addition, he piled white bread, pickles, marinated aubergine, dried fish, and beer onto the table. He finished by taking a litre bottle of vodka down from the shelf.

"I hope you can take a few glasses," he growled. "I can never tell with you strange Westerners. You always want to do everything by the book."

His mood had darkened noticeably since he'd realised that I didn't think much about his plans for investors.

"You're always trying to impose your rules on us. Democracy, human rights, freedom – I can't listen to that shit anymore. Men fucking men: that is all that your freedom amounts to! You're welcome to it, your fucking freedom!"

It was a strange night. To smoke, we decamped from time to time to Mikheyev's office, which was across the hall. To drink, we went back into the kitchen. Above his office desk, Mikheyev had hung a little portrait of Alexander Zakharchenko, the separatist prime minister. No sooner had we sat down under the portrait to smoke than we began to argue. When we repaired to drink in the kitchen, we made peace again. So it went, back and forth, back and forth, until well past midnight, when the vodka started to run low.

"Gorbachev gave you Germans reunification," Mikheyev said darkly. "But we're not allowed to unite with Russia if we want to? Explain that to me!"

But before I had a chance to explain anything, he was off again.

"You can't imagine how much I admired Gorbachev when he came to power. The first Secretary General who dared to show his face, in person, to the workers! Like a real human being, without a prepared speech. It was because of him that I joined the fucking party."

Mikheyev took a drag on his cigarette.

"But then he went and messed it all up, the son of a bitch. Everything! I hate the guy. Half the world was ours, we had a good life, and then he had to go and let the Union fall to pieces."

Enraged, he pointed in the direction of the window.

"Ten kilometres from here there is now a border that separates Russians from Russians! I hope Gorbachev's happy, the motherfucker!"

Between the ring binders on Mikheyev's office shelf, I'd noticed a small icon of the Mother of God. I did not realise quite what it meant to him until, back in the kitchen once more, Mikheyev started telling me about his family. His father had been an Old Believer, one of those stubborn arch-Christians whose forebears had seceded in protest from the Orthodox Church in the seventeenth century. The father came from a small Old Believer community in Belarus. As a young man, during his term of military service, he had managed to get into trouble with his superiors – Mikheyev did not go into the details. The Soviet authorities suggested that Mikheyev's father atone for his misconduct by doing "voluntary" work in the coalmines of the Donbass, a course of action that was recommended to many back then who, in some way or another, fell foul of the law. And so the Old Believer father had become a miner.

Mikheyev had grown up in Donetsk. As a child, he

explained, he often went with his father to Belarus, to visit the village of his Old Believer ancestors. By then the Soviets had demolished the village church, but the cemetery where the Old Believers were buried still remained.

"One day," Mikheyev recounted, "we were visiting our family grave. I was very small at the time. An uncle bent down to me and said: Your great-grandfather is here, and your grandfather, and all your ancestors. One day you'll be here too. You wouldn't believe how I cried! Mama, I sobbed, I don't want to die!"

Just before we drained the last of the vodka, my thoughts returned to that sentence about empires and the way they do not disappear from people's minds. Repeatedly, Mikheyev referred to the "Russians" who had been separated by borders, but he seemed to use the word more in the sense of Soviet citizens, for he himself was not really a Russian, at least not entirely – his father hailed from Belarus.

"That's nonsense," Mikheyev said when I asked. "Half-Russian: what's that supposed to mean? My father was a Belarusian, my mother, Ukrainian. I am Russian!"

The next morning I woke up pretty hungover. If Mikheyev felt the same, he gave no sign of it. It was Friday. He wanted to get back to Donetsk after lunch and he offered me a lift. As I waited for him in his apartment, I caught occasional snatches of his thunderous voice from the office on the other side of the hall.

"Where are these fucking papers? Must I do everything around here myself? Bring me the papers, you son of a bitch!"

I did feel a bit sorry that his colleagues were having to

pay for our bender. But I liked Mikheyev after a fashion. Without even knowing me, he had allowed me to look deep into his bear's heart. I hadn't liked everything I'd seen there, but I was grateful to him all the same.

He dropped me off in Donetsk that afternoon. It was my last day in the separatist region; the next morning I planned to return to the other side of the front. I spent the evening with two English journalists who were staying in the same hotel as me. That was how I got to know Roman.

He was a friend of the two Englishmen. They had met him the year before when they were in Donetsk reporting on the fiercest fighting during the war. Roman was in his early twenties and had been a student back then. His university was not far from the Donetsk History Museum, and on that day in August when rockets hit the museum building, he had been standing right next to an open window.

"The blast was so powerful that I was blown across to the opposite wall," Roman recalled.

We talked about the destruction of the museum. Roman did not believe it was a targeted attack. The two Englishmen, who had also been in Donetsk those days, had seen missiles being fired at the Ukrainian positions on the outskirts from the direction of the football stadium. They assumed that the Ukrainians had returned the fire and hit the museum accidentally.

Roman, who was short and slight, but charismatic in his quiet way, had completed his marketing studies during the war and then worked for an advertising agency in Donetsk. Since then, his bosses had fled to Kiev, along with the company. Roman was unemployed.

"Marketing is a superfluous profession in the Donetsk

People's Republic," he said, grinning. "There's no longer a market. The separatists have switched to a planned economy."

Roman was not a friend of the separatists. The only thing keeping him in Donetsk was the sick grandmother he was taking care of. It was clear to him that he had no future in the city, and the only thing that saved him from despair was his sense of humour.

"You can only view the things that happen here with irony," he said. "Otherwise you'd go crazy."

Almost all of his friends had left the city. None of them, Roman said, supported the separatists, and none had participated in their independence referendum.

"The only ones who voted were the nostalgics who hanker after a return to the Soviet Union. People like my parents. We argue constantly."

He laughed.

"The Germans are clever. You decided that Fascism was a mistake, so now you can move on. Here, no one's sure whether Communism was good or bad. That's why Ukraine can't move forward."

Later that evening, when the conversation had turned to other themes, Roman abruptly asked me a question whose meaning I did not understand until later.

"Just imagine for a moment that we were walking from Egypt to Israel," he said. "How long would it take?"

I shrugged. "No idea."

"Think about it. How long?"

I pondered this for a moment. "Maybe two months?"

"No longer?"

"Maybe longer."

"But not forty years?"

I shook my head, without understanding what he was getting at.

"Then why does the Bible say that Moses led the Jews through the desert for forty years?"

I laughed. "That's Biblical language. Forty years just means that it was a long journey."

"Perhaps," Roman said. "But I think that it really was forty years. Moses deliberately spun out the journey. Guess why."

"Tell me."

"So that the older generation would die en route," Roman said. All of a sudden, there was a cruel note in his voice that wasn't like him.

"Moses knew the old ones wanted to return to Egypt," he said. "They wanted to go back into slavery."

15

Friendship of Peoples Street

Milove

OCTOBER WAS DRAWING TO A CLOSE when I embarked on the final leg of my journey. I had crossed the front with the two English journalists. Our paths had separated in Severodonetsk, an industrial city north of the separatist territory.

At the bus station, I set my backpack down on a wooden bench that was covered with the first frost of the year. You could see little puffs of condensed breath forming every time the waiting passengers exhaled. There was a smell of winter in the air.

The bus I was waiting for went northeast from here. Its final stop was at a border town called Milove, half of which I had heard was in Ukraine, while the other half was in Russia.

As I climbed aboard, I was in high spirits. The front was behind me, the finish line ahead of me, and less than a hundred and fifty kilometres separated me from the end of my long journey. I had no idea that it would be the most depressing one hundred and fifty kilometres of the entire country.

I had assumed that it would be a three-hour journey. In

the event, it took more than seven. The narrow country roads looked as if an angry God had smashed the tarmac; in some places the bus had to inch its way around the deep potholes at a walking pace. This state of decay continued seamlessly on the roadside. Everywhere I looked I could see abandoned industrial buildings, ramshackle collective farms, collapsed warehouses, crumbling residential buildings. The small towns we drove through seemed to have lost all reason to exist. The factories were shut down, the shops boarded up. Only the people had remained, for whatever reason. Helplessly, they watched as their living environment deteriorated; no one seemed to have the strength to oppose the omnipresent decay. The streets, the squares, even the houses were completely bleak and undecorated.

In the centre of each village stood an empty statue plinth. Although the sight was a familiar one to me by now, it suddenly depressed me. I shed no tears for Lenin and his statues, but their absence only emphasised the general desolation here. In each ruined settlement there now stood yet one more ruin – a meaningless, crumbling, ugly pedestal.

"They tear down the monuments without asking us," the old man sitting next to me said. "Nobody has seen these people here before. They're strangers. They appear, screaming 'Glory to Ukraine', then they smash Lenin to pieces and disappear again."

The farther eastwards we journeyed, the more clearly I felt that something had gone badly wrong here. Before setting off, I hadn't realised that the entire border area was part of the "anti-terrorist operations zone", as the frontline regions in Ukraine were now officially known. On the entrance and exit of each town, the Ukrainian army had set up roadblocks where armed soldiers stopped the bus. They checked identity cards, searched luggage, and asked questions. As soon as they alighted, the passengers started swearing. They complained about the delays that had for a year and a half now made every journey a nuisance; they complained about the soldiers' suspicious questions and their hostile attitude. A yawning chasm seemed to separate the army from the local population. It appeared that the armed men were as alien to many people here as the out-of-town patriots who came to destroy the statues of Lenin.

At the final checkpoint before Milove, I was ordered out of the bus.

"What are you doing here?" one of the soldiers asked. He held my German passport in front of my nose accusingly.

I explained that I was a journalist and wanted to see the frontier zone.

"See the frontier zone? Are you kidding?"

I continued to assure him that my visit had nothing to do with the war, that I was only interested in how people on both sides of the border...

"On both sides? You want to go to Russia?"

"Yes."

"Get your luggage off the bus," snarled the soldier. "You're staying here."

The bus went on without me. I was ushered into a small wooden hut, which the border troops used as their head-quarters. The soldier, who still had my passport in his hand, contacted a supervisor on the phone. While we waited for him, he asked me questions about every stamp in my passport. His expression did not turn any more friendly when he heard that I had been in Crimea and Donetsk.

The superior officer who arrived twenty minutes later was more affable. He told me that Milove was not an international border crossing, but just an interstate one. Russians and Ukrainians were allowed to cross it, but foreigners were not.

"The border here is a bit unusual," he said. "Come with me. I'll show you."

We drove to Milove in his military jeep. The officer stopped at a crossroads at the entrance to the village. On the far side, the street ended in a paved corridor. About a hundred metres away I could see a customs barrier.

"That's the border crossing," the officer said. "Stay away from it. Understand?"

I nodded.

We turned right and followed a road that cut through the village.

"That," said the officer, "is 'Friendship of Peoples Street.'"

He pointed to the houses on the right-hand side…

"Ukraine."

… Then he switched to the left side.

"Russia."

Pedantically, he repeated the two gestures.

"Ukraine – Russia."

Finally, he pointed to the electric poles that lined the Russian side of the road.

"Video cameras."

He looked into my eyes. "You are allowed on the Ukrainian side, but not on the Russian. You may not cross the street. Got it?"

I nodded again.

"Please respect these rules," he said. "Otherwise, the

Russians will arrest you and claim we are to blame because we let you into town in the first place. They relish that kind of scandal."

I gave him my promise.

He dropped me off in front of the only hotel in town and wished me a safe journey.

There wasn't much to see in Milove. The town was made up of low stone houses and vegetable gardens, with a few Soviet apartment blocks in between. In the market place there were old women selling fruit and cheap children's clothing. The small history museum was closed – it was Sunday. The Second World War Memorial consisted of crumbling concrete soldiers. The statue of Lenin was missing.

I crossed the town aimlessly three times in succession. Involuntarily, I kept ending up at Friendship of Peoples Street. It seemed to exert a magnetic pull on me, precisely because I had promised not to cross it. I felt like a child sneaking around a forbidden closet.

The officer had told me that, strictly speaking, the road did not separate one town, but instead linked two towns, the Ukrainian Milove and the Russian Chertkovo. The railway lines that ran parallel to Friendship of Peoples Street on the Russian side, where the train station was situated, formed a kind of natural border between the two. In between, sandwiched between the tracks and the road, lay a strip of land about fifty yards wide and three kilometres long, which for some reason belonged to Russia, although the railway lines separated it from Chertkovo.

The tracks could be crossed in only two places. The first was the border crossing; the second was a footbridge connecting the market square of Milove with the railway station in Chertkovo. On the Ukrainian side, at the foot of the bridge, a border guard kept watch.

The Russian strip of land along Friendship of Peoples Street was only sparsely populated. Most of the buildings looked like railway depots. In between, there were a few one-storey residential houses and a huge Soviet-era grain silo.

Yuri had the grain silo in his field of vision every day of his life. I wondered if that was why his expression was so melancholy. He was in his mid-forties, and although he looked sad – or maybe precisely because of that – he was a handsome man. With his greying beard and calm, dark eyes, he reminded me a bit of Anton Chekhov.

Yuri was the owner of a small grocery store on the Ukrainian side of the road. I had ended up here out of sheer hunger; there were no cafés in Milove. I bought a couple of waffles and some bananas, and we struck up a conversation.

The Russian silo, Yuri told me, had been out of commission for eighteen months. The reasons were complex. The silo was only accessible from the Ukrainian side. Its entrance was on Friendship of Peoples Street. The Russian peasants, who had once stored their grain there, used to simply drive their lorries across the open borders in the surrounding countryside in order to get to Milove. Then the war broke out. Because fighters from Russia started entering the Donbass clandestinely, Ukraine had closed its border – at least the section that was still under its control. Since then, Russian citizens had only been allowed to enter the country via designated border crossings by presenting their passport. For the Russian farmers, therefore, the silo had become useless. It took too much time to wait in the customs line.

The Festival of Friendship had also fallen victim to the war. Every summer, residents of Milove and Chertkovo used to gather in front of Yuri's grocery store. Folk singers and dance groups performed together, and local politicians from both sides of the border called for Russian–Ukrainian solidarity. The festival had not been held for the last two summers. There was no longer anything to celebrate on Friendship of Peoples Street.

Yuri viewed recent developments in Ukraine with scepticism.

"These new patriots are good at destroying things," he said. "But so far they haven't created very much."

The war had hit Milove hard. The town had never been prosperous, but in the last fifteen years, Yuri said, life here had become very hard for some.

While we were chatting, an old woman came into the store. She wore a flower-patterned headscarf and walked with her body severely hunched over.

"Sonny," she said. "How much is this loaf?"

Yuri told her the price.

"And the other one?"

She enquired after the cost of all types of bread, but seemed unable to decide on one. In the end, Yuri wordlessly took a loaf of white bread off the shelf and stuffed it in the old woman's coat pocket.

She crossed herself several times.

"God give you good health, sonny," she whispered before leaving the store.

Yuri watched her depart.

"That's how it is all day, every day," he said, shaking his head. "Medicine, cooking gas, firewood, everything has become so expensive that there's nothing left over from their pension for these old people. They live on bread, and sometimes their money doesn't even stretch to that."

Life was better on the other side. The neighbouring Russian village was not much larger; Milove had six thousand inhabitants, Chertkovo ten thousand. Even so, Yuri told me, he had always had the feeling of entering another world when he crossed the border. In Chertkovo, there was a train station, a cinema, cafés, and urban bus lines. The history museum was larger; the streets were lit at night; there was even a crossroads with a set of traffic lights.

Nothing of the kind existed in Milove. There wasn't even a public toilet. When the stallholders at the market needed to use one, they dashed over the footbridge to the Chertkovo train station. They went to Russia to pee.

Coincidentally, the Sunday I arrived in Milove was the day of Ukrainian regional elections. Yuri had not cast his vote. The last mayor of the town, he told me, had promised the voters that he would finally erect streetlights, supply all homes with mains water, and set up a toilet at the market. They were modest enough pledges, but he had kept none of them. His most promising successor had simply adopted the election platform of his predecessor, though he dropped the pledge about the toilet.

The far east of this country, I thought as I listened to Yuri, is just like the far west of Ukraine. People gaze wistfully across the border, where life is better.

We talked for quite a while. Eventually, Yuri offered me the little plastic chair that was standing in front of his counter. I gratefully accepted. There was nothing to do in Milove, and between Yuri and me there had immediately developed one of those spontaneous friendships that I only know from travelling. I stayed for an hour, then a second, and a third. Buyers came and went while we swapped our life stories.

Yuri had travelled the seas for ten years. He had dreamt of it as a child in Milove, where during the Soviet era his mother had run the local Palace of Culture, which was now closed. Back then, Yuri had often leafed through a Russian magazine called *Around the World* and, full of longing, had looked at pictures of distant countries. The yearning to be able to visit them one day was so strong that he enrolled at the Maritime Academy of Odessa after leaving school.

The epaulettes with the Soviet hammer-and-sickle emblem that still adorned his uniform in his first year of study were replaced in his second year by the blue and yellow of the newly independent Ukrainian Navy. When Yuri graduated, he opted for the merchant fleet. As a ship's engineer, he voyaged around the world on merchant vessels; he had seen Egypt, Cuba, Brazil, China, Nigeria, Mexico – all the exotic places from his childhood dreams. For eight, nine, ten months at a stretch he was on the move, with nothing around him but the sea and the stack of books that he kept by his bunk, which always ran out quickly, but in every port there were other Russian-speaking seafarers with whom Yuri could exchange reading material.

One day, though, he'd had enough. Light-hearted, without resentment or any parting sorrows, he turned his back on his job and returned to Milove. He had never liked cities; their noise reminded him of the din in ships' engine rooms. He felt better in his small home town, even if he wasn't keen on all the changes that Milove had undergone in his absence. Friendship of Peoples Street, which Yuri remembered undivided, had become an interstate border by the time he opened his grocery store.

He was not unhappy in Milove. His life here was quiet, but it was the life he wanted. Whenever he was seized by the old longing for the sea, which happened sometimes, Yuri just fell into a reverie. He would then leaf through his memories, the same way he had scrolled through his magazines as a boy.

Still, I wondered, when we finally shook hands and parted long after closing time, what would have become of Yuri if he had not ended up here after his maritime career, in Milove, on the war-torn border of Ukraine, across from a vacant grain silo, but somewhere else? The head of a successful retail chain, perhaps. Or an actor: he could have played Chekhov. Or – who knows – he could have become my best friend.

I stepped out into the cold, dark night. The last thing I saw on Friendship of Peoples Street before returning to my hotel was a wavering cyclist. He seemed to be drunk. Sometimes he rode on the Russian, sometimes on the Ukrainian side of the road.

Acknowledgements

MANY FRIENDS AND SUPPORTERS contributed to the genesis of this book. My special thanks go to all those who have shared their stories with me. I received invaluable help from Ksyusha Gvozdina, Roman and Philip Dmytrychenko, Olga and Moritz Gathmann, Pavel Lokshin, Thomas Hölzl and Diana Stübs.

Thanks to the Robert Bosch Stiftung and the Literarisches Colloquium Berlin for funding parts of my research trips, and to everybody at Rowohlt and Haus Publishing for their invaluable support.

Also, I would like to thank all the authors whose works I have used as source material:

Karl Anders (*Mord auf Befehl. Der Fall Staschynskij*, Tübingen 1963)

Neal Ascherson (*Black Sea: The Birthplace of Civilisation and Barbarism*, London 1995)

Aleksander Blok ("The Scythians" (1918), translated from the Russian by Kurt Dowson, in: *International Socialism*, 1st series, No. 6, Autumn 1961)

Kate Brown (*A Biography of No Place. From Ethnic Borderland to Soviet Heartland*, Cambridge, MA 2003)

Mikhail Bulgakov (*The White Guard*, translated from the Russian by Michael Glenny, London 2006)

Bundesgerichtshof (German Federal Court of Justice, verdict on Bohdan Stashynsky, dated 19 October 1962, case number 9 StE 4/62)

Paul Celan ("Death Fugue", translated from the German by John Felstiner, in: John Felstiner, *Paul Celan – Poet, Survivor, Jew*, New Haven 1995)

Robert Conquest (*The Harvest of Sorrow. Soviet Collectivization and the Terror-Famine*, Oxford 1987)

Yevhen Denisenko (ed., *Litopys Donbasu. Putivnyk po ekspozytsiyi Donetskoho oblasnoho krayeznavchoho museyu*, exhibition catalogue of the Donetsk Regional Museum, Donetsk 2005)

Oleksander Dovzhenko (*Zemlya*, silent film, Kiev 1930)

Katja Gesche (*Kultur als Instrument der Außenpolitik totalitärer Staaten. Das Deutsche Ausland-Institut 1933–1945*, Cologne 2006)

Andreas Kappeler (*Kleine Geschichte der Ukraine*, Munich 1994; *Die Kosaken. Geschichte und Legenden*, Munich 2013)

Paul Robert Magocsi (*Ukraine: An Illustrated History*, Toronto 1995)

Ivan Mamchur ("I todi proty lyudey pishly tanky. Do 60-richya Kenhirskoho povstannya", in: *Dzvin*, No. 5, 2014)

Anna Reid (*Borderland. A Journey through the History of Ukraine*, London 2015)

Gregor von Rezzori (*The Snows of Yesteryear*, translated from the German by H. F. Broch de Rotherman, London 1990)

Vasyl Rosman ("Kalynivske chudo", in: *Odyhytryya*, No. 6, 74, 2008)

Joseph Roth (*Reisen in die Ukraine und nach Russland*, Munich 2015)

Eric J. Schmaltz / Samuel D. Sinner ("The Nazi Ethnographic Research of Georg Leibbrandt and Karl Stumpp in Ukraine and its North American Legacy", in: *Holocaust and Genocide Studies*, No. 14, 1, 2000)

Taras Shevchenko (*Selected Poetry*, translated from the Ukrainian by John Weir, Kiev 1977; *The Complete Kobzar. The Poetry of Taras Shevchenko*, translated from the Ukrainian by Peter Fedynsky, London 2013)

Toon Vugts (ed., *De Krim. Goud en geheimen van de Zwarte Zee*, exhibition catalogue of the Allard Pierson Museum, Amsterdam 2014)

Andrew Wilson (*The Ukrainians. Unexpected Nation*, New Haven 2002)